Life is Meeting

LIFE IS MEETING

by

JOHN HUNT

Lord Hunt of Llanfair Waterdine

HODDER AND STOUGHTON

LONDON SYDNEY AUCKLAND TORONTO

Part of the account of the 1973 return visit to Everest which appears on pp. 124–5 first appeared in a modified form in *Climber and Rambler* in 1973. The lines from Hilaire Belloc on page 13 are quoted by permission of A. D. Peters & Co., Ltd.

British Library Cataloguing in Publication Data

Hunt, John, *Baron Hunt*, b. 1910
  Life is meeting.
   1. Hunt, John, *Baron Hunt*
   2. Mountaineers – Great Britain – Biography
  I. Title
  941'.082'092'4   GV199.92.H/
  ISBN 0 340 22963 2

The pleasure I have derived from writing this book has been in the memories it has evoked of people and events in my lifetime and experience—especially people. My enjoyment has been the greater for the opportunity it has given me, before tidying up the manuscript, to renew acquaintance with, and consult some of those with whom I have shared these experiences.

It is to all of them, in gratitude, that I dedicate this book.

Contents

Illustrations

ACKNOWLEDGMENTS

1   National Tourist Organization of Greece

2   Royal Geographical Society

Illustrations

Maps

First Beginning

From quiet homes and first beginning,
    Out to the undiscovered ends;
There's nothing worth the wear of winning
    But laughter and the love of friends.

Hilaire Belloc

FOR SOME YEARS PAST I HAVE BEEN SAYING THAT I WOULD LIKE to write another book, but without much conviction; with enough, and more, of other things to do, I kept putting off the moment of testing my own resolve. Even when, last October, I came to the point of making a start, I set about it in a mood of uncertainty, feeling that I ought to have a theme to guide my pen, but not finding one. I began to put down some recollections more or less at random, with no special regard to the times from which they were drawn; I had no idea how much writing might be involved, or whether the separate pieces could be made to fit together. It was only towards the end that the episodes, when placed approximately in a chronological sequence, seemed to form a kind of pattern. Some events from my working life, others which had filled my leisure, chanced just about to balance one another in length; which tempts me to comment defensively that this is not an accurate index how I have spent—or mis-spent—time over the years! Gradually a point emerged which was central to all the embryo chapters, so simple that I am now surprised that it had eluded me at first. It made a bridge, or synthesis, not only between the various events, but between work and leisure.

Martin Buber, the Jewish philosopher who was a refugee from Germany before the war and the centenary of whose birth has been celebrated in 1978, once wrote, 'All life is meeting'. The truth of these four words has grown on me for many years since I first read them. If life has any meaning between birth and death, as I believe it has, it is to be sought through meeting and sharing experiences with other people. In this book I have recalled a number of events in my life; anything achieved only came about because the various enterprises were shared, with whatever degree of success or failure, with other people. The memories which endure are, in the main, the friendships which these

13

experiences have given to me. Martin Buber's words ended my search for a theme, provided a title and dispelled my hesitation in putting all these memoirs into a book.

Not that I was unduly deterred from continuing to write, theme or no theme, once I had made a start. Prompted by diaries, maps, reports and photographs, I found myself launched upon a voyage of re-discovery which was rewarding and, at times, quite exciting. I have no illusions of self-importance about the minor successes and their nominal rewards, whether they were in war, on some peace-time mission or on a mountain. Leading climbers will be quick to point out that the expeditions which I have related produced only modest results, and that the mountaineering routes which I have described do not bear comparison with the great deeds of daring and stamina which are performed today. I do not deny this, nor does it dismay me. I am content with the thought that sufficient unto my days were the dis-coveries and delights which they brought to myself.

These experiences were renewed as I brought them back from the past. I was surprised to find, on unlocking each compartment, how much was still there, to pick and choose from. My enthusiasm grew as I opened one cupboard after another and pulled out by-gones for an airing. No matter whether anyone else would be interested in what I had found, I was hugely enjoying myself, indulging in another illusion: that the past can become the present.

My perspective is, therefore, a personal and selective one. The opinions I have expressed bear on one or other side of an argument and may not expose, let alone do justice to other factors or points of view. In only two chapters, however, 'Crime and Circumstance' and 'What Price Democracy?' have I ventured into problems which have more than an historical and academic interest; I admit that both these subjects deserve treatment in greater depth than is possible in a personal kind of book.

This is, therefore, mainly a story about happenings in my life, the people I have met through those events, and how we did things together. I do not see it as an autobiography, but I came to recognise it as inevitable that I should start at the beginning, if only to explain how I came to be at the point of departure for the first episode which I have recalled and which began in 1934, when I was twenty-three. In providing a brief sketch of the years before that time, I have omitted a photograph of myself in a sailor suit at the age of three.

My paternal grandfather came from a family of Bristol merchants; he made a small fortune by exporting tea from Japan and I remember him as a stout and benign old gentleman with a full white beard, who could always be relied on to produce a ju-jube from a tin box in his waistcoat pocket, to delight his grandchildren. As the eldest of a family of six, my father had demonstrated his independence by breaking away from that background of commerce to enter public service in the Indian Army. My mother, Ethel Crookshank, the youngest member and only girl in another family of six children, was born in Calcutta in much less wealthy circumstances. The Crookshanks were Scots and Irish by origin and there was also a Spanish connection from my maternal grandmother; the family included some interesting characters in its lineage: Don Aguila, the 'Great Captain' of Ferdinand and Isabella's reign, whose name is legendary in southern Spain; an apprentice boy who helped to defend the gates of Derry against the Pretender, James III; and Sir Richard Burton, soldier, explorer, linguist and ardent researcher into erotic oriental literature. My mother's immediate background, however, was steeped in military tradition which went back over several generations. Her father had founded a regiment – the 34th Sikh Pioneers – which my father eventually joined. My maternal grandfather died of wounds sustained during a campaign in Tibet when my mother was four, and the family was brought up by my grandmother in straitened circumstances on her widow's pension. I remember her in her latter years as a gentle and very good-looking old lady. She must have been a remarkable person in her prime, to bring up six children on her own, and to create such a united family as they were.

All my mother's brothers joined the Army; one of them, her favourite brother Claude, went into his father's regiment, where he became friendly with my father and introduced him to my mother. They married in 1908; six years later, when I was four, and my brother, Hugh, but a year younger, she was widowed. My father was reported missing in Northern France in November 1914, but my mother had to wait until 1921 before his death was finally established as 'killed in action' at the place where his remains were eventually found. Like her own mother before her, she was left with the responsibility for bringing up her children, my younger brother Hugh and myself, with money from my father's estate which was strictly administered by his brother, my uncle Geoffrey.

So I scarcely remember my father. I could conjure him up only from two or three mental snapshots in a child's mind: one of myself sitting in the sidecar of his motorcycle, on which he was venting his feelings after it had broken down; another when he came into the nursery in our little house at Camberley, where he was attending a course at the Staff College. He asked me if I could whistle. On another occasion he wanted to know if I could tell the time. The answer to both questions

produced tears and shakings of my head. I was only three at the time.
I think he was a rather serious and intense person; this, at any rate, is
what his photograph makes him look like. My mother worshipped him.
As little boys, we were scarcely aware of how hard those war years, and
afterwards, must have been for her, and how much she needed love
and sympathy. It was understandable that she looked especially to me
to fill her husband's place and live up to the standards which, she
constantly assured me, he had stood for: the words 'honour' and
'honesty' loomed rather large in my early life. It was a kind of condi-
tioning for eldest sons which was normal in middle-class families at the
time and I do not remember having resented it. But those high expectations certainly gave me an anxiety complex lest I should fail, and an
intensity of purpose to succeed. Hugh, I fancy, was less inhibited than I
was, in developing his sense of fun. It was fortunate for both Hugh and
myself that my mother was a woman possessed of great energy and
enterprise, as well as being artistic and having a lively sense of humour.
She enjoyed displaying it by making situations and stories rather larger
than life.

Hugh and I were sent to school at Marlborough, whose rigorous
régime I did not particularly enjoy and during which time I achieved
no special distinctions apart from modern languages, and derived little
pleasure except a liking for rugby football and a love for the solitude of
Savernake Forest. I was glad to exchange the playing fields for the
countryside where I could pursue my interest in birds and butterflies;
my brother and I used to escape into the forest on Sundays, where we
played secret games with the toys we brought from home. We longed
for the holidays, when we sometimes stayed on a farm in Devon,
sometimes went to Switzerland. Returning to school was always a
traumatic experience; I was often home-sick there.

Then came success. The whole ambiance in my mother's family
being military, avuncular pressures upon me to follow in my father's
footsteps into the Army, though well-intentioned, were inexorable,
and I duly complied. To the delight of the family I passed first of my
year into Sandhurst and, by dint of earnest effort while others, more
sensibly, were enjoying life at the College, I passed out again in the
first position as a Senior Under-Officer, with a gold medal and a
special sword to show for it. Thus far I had lived up to those high
expectations, but at the expense of much youthful fun, which I will
always regret. I can, in fact, recall only one lighter-hearted moment
during that period, when I played the part of a girl friend to David
Niven's lead in a College sketch. I knew virtually nothing about girls
and had proceeded no further in my advances than holding hands with
a nice little blonde girl called Eileen, a next-door neighbour who used

to accompany me to a Kindergarten school when we were six years old. It was apparent that David had much more experience in the matter.

My brother, Hugh, to his lasting credit and with some advantage in being the younger of us, resisted suggestions that the Navy or the Diplomatic Service would be worthy careers for him, which might bring appropriate credit to the family name, to add to those of the judges and generals in the genealogical tree. With my mother's support, deriving from her own love of music and drama, which she had acquired as a school girl in Weimar, and despite disapproval from the uncles, Hugh turned to the stage and found a distinctive identity for himself, making a distinguished career in the theatre, as director successively of the Abbey Theatre, Dublin, the Bristol Old Vic, the Old Vic in London and the Elizabethan Theatre Trust in Australia. He later became head of the first academic Drama Department to be established in this country at Manchester University. Hugh displayed an independence of mind and a kind of courage which I lack, but which has been emulated by my eldest daughter. For Sally, in her generation, decided to be an actress, revealing artistic talents which are to be found on both sides of her family.

As for me, having opted for conformity, I was launched upon a Service career, on a note of further expectations from my family. On leaving Sandhurst I was commissioned into a famous regiment, the King's Royal Rifle Corps (the 60th Foot, now the Greenjackets) and posted to the 2nd Battalion at Tidworth. After a dreary year on Salisbury Plain life promised some excitement, when I boarded a troopship at Southampton with a draft of the Dorsetshire Regiment, outward bound for India. But the beginnings of this new experience were unpropitious; there followed another dull year, with a few bright interludes, in the hot and dusty confines of Lucknow cantonment. The Battalion moved to Calcutta early in 1932.

I am a Revolutionary

1931–40

I FOUND THE LIFE OF A SUBALTERN SERVING IN A BRITISH REGI-
ment during the early 1930s a compound of boredom and frustration.
It was difficult in that far-off land and in that period of peace which
preceded the advent of Hitler, to find meaningful an existence consisting in the daily round of barrack-room inspections, orderly room
and other duties, drill and weapon training, even the occasional
tactical exercises in the countryside beyond the garrison. Nor did I
care for the social round—we called it poodle-faking—of drinks,
dances, garden parties and swimming côteries at the Gymkhana Club
in Lucknow or Tollyganj, Calcutta's equivalent of Hurlingham. I was
shy and sexually inexperienced; I shunned the pretty girls who arrived
from England every winter looking for husbands, escorted by their
hopeful mothers and unkindly known as the fishing fleet. Indeed, I was
nicknamed by some of these damsels, whether in disappointment or
dislike, the aloof blond. In fact I was a bit of a misfit, a loner and
doubtless somewhat of a prig.

Relations between officers and other ranks were friendly and informal. Among the officers our differences in rank and seniority, saving
a slight deference paid to the commanding officer, were set aside in the
Mess. Indeed, for most of the officers, educated at Eton with only a
slight leavening from Harrow and elsewhere, the bond of a common
heritage was particularly close. But I sometimes felt that the cult of
esprit de corps in those days of the peace made my brother officers
somewhat inward-looking, especially in regard to their social contacts.
There was a mild inference not only of functional, but of social,
superiority. Not for nothing had we earned the label 'the rude, rich
Rifles'.

I was impressed by the combination of informality and efficiency
which we contrived to achieve. But I tended to seek my contacts outside the circle of officers, among other units and among civilians in the
places where we were stationed. I also resisted pressure to conform by

playing polo, preferring instead to organise and play games with the other ranks, especially rugby football, for which I have retained a life-long passion and which was the only competitive sport at which I was reasonably proficient. Though I enjoyed the weekend outings with other officers into the *mofussil*, crouching beside some *jheel* in the early morning light, listening to the sounds of unseen creatures as we waited for flights of ducks at dawn, I was a deplorable hand with a shot-gun. Yet I have to thank those shooting weekends for an awakening interest in India, the country where I was born and in which my father, my maternal grandfather and my mother's brothers had served as soldiers in the Indian Army. Something of my own sense of heritage stirred within me as I glimpsed another kind of life from which we Britishers from a *gora paltan* so effectively insulated ourselves in our cosy garrisons. Here on the land I witnessed the constant struggle of a simple people subsisting in direst poverty, toiling to extract from the soil the crops of paddy and jute, corn and vegetables in their seasons, handicapped by primitive tools, debilitated by malaria and undernourishment, working in extremes of climate, overwhelmed from time to time by disasters of drought and flood. Here was a people born into privation, subject to the rigid discrimination of their caste system, exploited by money-lenders, humbling themselves before the ruling strangers from a foreign land; a people whose character and philosophy had, like the Ibos of South-Eastern Nigeria, been moulded by the great rivers which flow through their land; a people which has produced great poets. Yet precisely because of these hardships, here were human beings who, thrown upon their own meagre resources, were held together by bonds of staunch family loyalty and an abiding sense of community in their village life.

I became aware too, of something else, in striking contrast with the slow, repetitive grind of existence for villagers in Bengal and the United Provinces (now Uttar Pradesh), and the fatalistic acceptance of their lot. Something dynamic was astir even in the depths of the countryside. As in the towns, so also in these remote areas where we soldiers came to amuse ourselves by shooting duck and sandgrouse, young people in the High English schools, mostly Hindus, were dreaming of an India independent of the British Raj. Youthful idealism in Bengal, then as throughout the ages, was eager to respond to a challenge; the challenge was from political activists who were not willing to accept the campaign of passive resistance preached by the Mahatma and who were impatient to be rid of the British occupation. One autumn, while camping with my company beneath the walls of the local gaol in Midnapur District during a training exercise, I heard the unearthly sound of prisoners groaning and yowling during the execution of a terrorist. Bengal was in the grip of a wave of revolutionary fervour at that time; three successive magistrates had been murdered in that District, two attempts had been made on the lives of the Governor of the Province; a raid had taken place on an armoury, followed by a bomb attack during a cricket match in Chittagong District; several police officers had been killed.

The Government called for volunteers from the Army to be seconded to the police in Bengal. Up till that moment life in India had seemed pointless for me; I had been bored and dissatisfied. Deeply troubled though I felt by that hanging in Midnapur gaol—it is a memory which has influenced my thinking about capital punishment ever since that day in 1933—here was a job which needed to be done; here at last, was a chance for action. I had a facility for languages and, by dint of working with a *munshi* in the hot afternoons while others took their siesta, had attained the Higher Standard in Urdu and sat for the Interpretership examinations. I applied for a tour of duty with the police and was accepted.

That decision marked one turning point in my life. For the following eighteen months, first in Bankura District and later in disturbed areas of Chittagong and Noakhali, I worked as a plain-clothes officer in the District Intelligence Branches, with the rank of Additional Superintendent. Our job was to gather information about the underground movements attempting, by one means or another, to force the British Government to grant independence to India. There were two secret parties engaged in this revolutionary purpose. The Anushilan party, mostly drawn from older, well-educated Bengali Hindus, were working on long-term plans for an armed national uprising, which after patient preparation, would erupt throughout the Province; it had links with similar movements in other Provinces. Another group, the Jugantar party, preferred a campaign of active violence to break the morale of government officers, using terrorisation and murder; it was a precursor of the world-wide phenomenon so familiar today. As is the case with the official and the Provisional IRA, there was little sympathy between these hot-headed desperadoes and the more far-sighted conspirators. Because of the ever-present threat which they posed, the Intelligence Branch was mainly preoccupied with the task of exposing and destroying the terrorist movement, using special powers conferred by the central government. We were empowered to search without warrants, arrest and detain suspects indefinitely without preferring charges and bringing them to trial. Additional garrisons of troops were posted in the main areas of trouble—pre-eminently Chittagong in the east and Midnapur in West Bengal. Like the others in the small band of officers who had been selected for duty as temporary policemen, I was also charged with providing liaison with the troops.

For a young man with no experience of civil administration, scant knowledge of the law, no training in covert operations and no previous contacts with the people among whom I was to live and work, including the Indian Army, this was an exciting new world, full of surprises, pitfalls and a certain spice of danger. Bankura provided me with a quiet initiation into the organisation of the Intelligence system and the officers who manned it, in an area which had not been stricken by the atrocities in the neighbouring District of Midnapur. It was a useful introduction to the totally different situation obtaining in my next posting, to Chittagong in the south-east corner of the Province. Here roamed numerous terrorists, well organised in local groups deep in the countryside. They had brought off several notorious outrages, and we had recently created two martyrs and folk heroes by hanging a school teacher, Surjya Ranjan Sen, and a young fanatic, Tarakeswar Dastidar. The scene at their execution as these two men died with the words 'Long Live Freedom' on their lips was related to me with relish by the incumbent Military Intelligence Officer, Captain Ivor Stephenson of the 8th Gurkha Rifles. It left me with a nagging feeling that our actions were striking at symptoms rather than causes. Morale in the local Jugantar Party was high; police officers were afraid to travel in the interior to seek for secret agents, or 'sources'; our information about their activities and membership was correspondingly low.

At the time of my arrival the local authorities had just embarked on a drastic policy of counter-terrorism, whose purpose was to weaken the influence of the Party, especially in areas where its members moved freely, harboured by a cowed population among whom they also were winning eager young recruits. Under the forceful leadership of the District Magistrate Adam Hands and the MIO, Ivor Stephenson, the District was being subjected to a deliberate programme of harassment by the battalion of the Additional Garrison. Raids and searches in the villages were conducted by the troops, often acting on little or no firm information, on the theory that the terrorists, if they were not fortuitously caught in the cordon, would be driven into some other area where our intelligence had improved. Whether or not there were Party members in the area at the time, it was hoped that local people would be deterred from sheltering them in future.

Hands and Stephenson were a most effective partnership; the magistrate dour and squarely built, the soldier with a fine record from the First World War, slim and tall, fast speaking and brimming over with imaginative and ruthless schemes.

One particular terrorist leader, named Benode Behari Datta, became a legendary figure among his own followers and the forces of law alike, escaping time and again from the cordons and searches. Indeed, it became difficult to discern the truth about his exploits from the ever-growing fantasies woven about him. I have abiding memories of those operations. Beginning before dawn, the Gurkha soldiers would move silently towards a village, deploying in a wide circle as they approached, creeping closer until, in the growing light, a police officer would advance, to a chorus of barking pie dogs, calling on the villagers to come out, or stay in their houses as the case might be. Sometimes there was reliable information about a wanted man; all of us would be in a high state of tension as we were led by an informer to the suspected 'shelter'. Occasionally the tension was dispelled when shots rang out and the barking reached a crescendo, to which was added the wailing of women. More frequently it ended in anticlimax, the nest deserted.

Effective though they were, these tactics in Chittagong District were disliked by some of the senior police officers. There was doubtless an element of professional jealousy in this—an attitude delightfully portrayed by those unfortunate American police officers whose noses are so regularly put out of joint by the brilliant Mr Cannon in the BBC television series. But even some junior officers whose livelihood was intimately bound up with the Bengali people, for many of whom they were kith and kin, such crude methods of countering violence with violence were distasteful and a matter of shame.

I hated to see humble dwellings ransacked in a search—often fruit-less—for arms. It was a sentiment recently expressed anew by the President of Bangladesh, the successor State of that part of Bengal: 'Why should fifteen families suffer to find one criminal?' he asked. Suspect members of the Jugantar Party, mostly schoolboys of sixteen or seventeen, would be subjected to frightening ordeals to force them to speak. Often, after witnessing or taking part in these inquisitions which I deeply disliked, I was left with a feeling of admiration for the guts of these youngsters who refused under duress and even fear of death to betray their leaders. Yet one could hardly marvel less at the readiness of others to risk exposure and death from their Party comrades by becoming our agents. Of course there was a much needed financial reward, but some of our contacts were acting from the genuine conviction that violence was not the way when they kept their secret night-time rendezvous beneath a pipul tree or at the corner of a paddy field with one of my Bengali sub-inspectors and, occasionally, myself.

The use of troops, not only in aid of civil power, but also as the main arm for restoring law and order in precedence to the police forces, can quickly become a threat to democracy. It is vitally important that, as soon as order is restored to the point where the police can again assume control, the armed forces should hand over responsibility to the civilian police and return to barracks. But the use of troops has been shown elsewhere than in Bengal to be an inescapable, if temporary, expedient in situations where, because the local population is itself being terrorised, or where there is some local sympathy for the terrorists, the latter have gained the upper hand to the extent where the police alone are unable to glean information, or even maintain order. Strongly though I deprecate this policy as a means of dealing with situations which constitute a threat to the State, there are circumstances in which there are no alternative means for the State to defend its existence. Such a situation has arisen in Northern Ireland, as I found when I was to be involved there much later on.

In Bengal in the 1930s I believe that such ruthless measures were initially inevitable. Many villages lived in a state of terror, their inhabitants in double jeopardy. The crucial need was reliable information and there is no doubt that the operations of the troops paid dividends by enabling us to gain 'sources'. Intelligence officers whose lives had been endangered before the troops arrived when they had gone into the *mofussil* were able to move around with more confidence and do their work.

Living and working under those strange conditions during which, for weeks at a time, I had no contacts with other Europeans, I grew to admire and enjoy the company of the officers of the District Intelligence Branches who were my subordinates, but who also became my friends. They were men of courage and a high devotion to duty, whose native cunning served us well in the difficult and subtle task of engaging agents from among the revolutionary parties and working with them without exposing them. There was, for instance, the sub-inspector who assisted me during my first few months at Feni, in the eastern area of Noakhali District, Lokenath Chandra Das. Lokenath Babu was a plump and genial man with a ready chuckle, whose only concession to the uniformed discipline of the police force of which he was a plain-clothes member, was a small moustache. To my initially undiscerning eye, he was no different, apart from the .38 revolver strapped to his dhotied waist, from any of the clerks and shopkeepers whom we British army officers used to dub as indolent, devious and spineless. We were woefully ignorant of the astonishing feats of arms of the Bengal Army in the days of the East India Company a century and a half before our time.

Beneath that easy manner was a man of spirit and character. Lokenath shared with most Bengali Hindus a crafty mind which he brought to bear on the machinations of the young terrorists. We had many an

adventure together. I recall one dark night, travelling with Lokenath in
my crazy little green Austin Seven to make a rendezvous with one of
his sources, who had promised to bring Benode Datta by a ruse, so
that we could capture this elusive and legendary character. As we
rattled along, two glowing eyes could be seen watching us from the
verge of the track. 'Ah,' whispered Lokenath, 'a jackal on the left. This
time we are going to be lucky.' But he was wrong and despite his
disappointment he was able to produce his customary giggle.

   With growing information about the membership, location and
plans of the terrorists, we were in a position to arrest the leaders and
pre-empt their intentions. Indeed, towards the end of that period of
revolutionary unrest in Bengal, the ultimate in absurdity was reached;
the best 'sources' of the Intelligence Branch were in some instances
the Party leaders themselves, and the DIBs were in a position more or
less to control the Party. To a degree we were, in fact, in danger of
prolonging the very existence of the Jugantar Party, as Intelligence
officers zealously added to their lists of 'sources' and in doing so,
gained credit for themselves in the eyes of their superiors. But that
was towards the end of 1935.

   Noakhali, immediately to the north of Chittagong, spanned the
tributaries which form the Delta of the Ganges. It was a District of
poor natural resources, exceptional poverty and ill health, disregarded
by officialdom. It was to that District that I had been sent by Stephenson
when Benode Datta and other terrorists were reported to have retreated from the scourge of the military in Chittagong. It was my task
to activate the local DIB and extend the campaign in that area.
Although there were a few near misses, during one of which shots
were exchanged, I never succeeded in catching the elusive Benode
Datta. He simply vanished from the scene. Equally imperceptibly, law
and order regained the upper hand – at least for the time being – as the
policy of detention and house arrest began to grip.

   The increasing flow of information revealed the fact that many
young Jugantar Party members were being recruited from the high
schools of Bengal, and were in some cases among the most promising
pupils. As my police duties became lighter, I made a point of getting
to know the staffs and pupils of many of these institutions, and by so
doing had my first taste of working with young people which was to
bear further fruit at a much later stage in my career.

   To begin with it struck me as quite extraordinary that the rural
schools located in remote places, and some of them impossible to reach
other than on foot, should be operating a syllabus which led through
ten classes to university examination standards. Young Bengalis as they
passed through this system were progressively weaned from their homes

and background as cultivators and became orientated towards the largely imaginary prospects of university degrees and careers in the towns. Lively young minds suffered first from boredom and, later, from disillusionment and discontent. That 'Failed BA (Calcutta)' qualification, mocked in the West, was literally all that many young men could hope to offer.

On top of this unrealistically academic bias, the children's classroom studies were not, I found, balanced by any extramural activities organised by the schools themselves. As I made friends with head-masters, I urged upon them the value to discipline and morale of giving responsibilities to chosen senior pupils, and of encouraging non-academic activities and interests. Knowing some of the most active Party members by name, I suggested that they might be appointed as prefects, or captains of activities. In Noakhali District and later in other Districts in which I served, I embarked upon a constructive programme among the young people, along lines which, unbeknown to myself, some magistrates in other Districts, notably Percival Griffiths in Midnapur, had tried before. I instituted a scheme of house captains and games competitions within the school, culminating in District championships, and it was found that a politically active character could often be transformed simply by giving him responsibility. While it lasted it was, for me, a thrilling experience to watch the enthusiasm of boys being channelled into activities more appropriate to their age and circumstances than the study of seditious books, the making of bombs and the plotting of murders. I noted with satisfaction that some of the young revolutionaries accepted responsibility in their schools to the exclusion of subversive activities. But in the climate of Bengal and against a centuries-old background of different traditions, such a scheme demands constant personal encouragement and it lapsed gradually after my departure. Fortunately terrorism was on the wane at the same time.

The lure of active service which had drawn me into the arena against the revolutionary movements in Bengal also provided me with an experience much more lasting and profound in its value. Travelling throughout my Districts, whether on police duties or on those con-structive missions to the schools, I grew to know and love Bengal. Usually I would go by cycle along the rough village tracks or balancing precariously on the narrow *bunds* dividing the paddy fields. Sometimes I would go by country boat, lying on the boards beneath a matted awning while the boat glided with infinite slowness along the canals, through the floating mattresses of water hyacinth, to reach a village deep in the interior. Once or twice I rode on an elephant, less com-fortably and equally slowly. Later, to speed my journeys, I acquired

the ancient Austin Seven with faulty brakes, in which I had hunted
Benode Datta with my friend Lokenath. When the Austin finally
ended its existence—and nearly mine—against a tree, I bought an
outboard motor and attached it to a sampan—a most dangerous
combination. For comfort rather than as a disguise, I often used to
dress as a Bengali Muslim, wearing a *lunghi*. Richard Burton, a distant
ancestral connection of mine, had done much the same, with far more
talent and daring, while serving as an Intelligence Officer under Sir
Charles Napier in Sind, nearly a century previously. My overnight
stops were in dâk bungalows, or in the homes of boys whose police
antecedents were well known to me. I became accustomed to Bengali
food, I enjoyed especially the *sandesh*, *rashogollas* and other sweetmeats
in the bazaars and a drink of cool coconut juice in the sweaty heat of
the day. I loved watching the fishermen casting their circular nets
over a flooded paddy field to catch small fish and big prawns, and
children playing *ha-doo-doo* and other country games in the mud on
the village square. In that flat fenland I was especially conscious of the
vast skyscapes: the huge build-up of cumulus cloud as the monsoon
period approached; the dramatic pageant of the sunsets. Even the
brassy sun at midday, which only mad dogs and Englishmen braved,
and the torrential monsoon downpours became an acceptable part of
the pattern of existence.

Of course, there was a price to pay for this unconventional life.
Benign tertiary malaria afflicted me every few months at incon-
venient moments, leaving me a tiresome guest in some village while I
recovered from that debilitating disease. Once I was struck down by
food poisoning and remained helpless in an empty shed until my plight
was reported to the District Magistrate, Arnold Whittaker, who came
to fetch me and whose wife, Helen, nursed me with motherly care; it
was a near thing. But despite it all, I was happier in this strange
existence than I had been during all the years of military service. I
liked the Bengali people, whom we British officers were wont to
view with some contempt for their softness and lack of warrior
qualities, for their unctious manner and devious ways. Those sentiments
were dispelled as I learned to know the village folk as people—their
kindness, their humour in adversity, their passion for cleanliness, their
love of children and their staunch family loyalties. I began to understand, too, the nascent patriotism in India which inspired the young
generation to dare all in a belief, however ill-conceived, that methods
no matter how foul, pursued with courage however great, were
justified or could triumph against the British. Before leaving Noakhali
I wrote a treatise in my headquarters in the dâk bungalow at Feni;
it was entitled 'I am a Revolutionary', I sent it to the Deputy Inspector-

General in charge of the Central Intelligence Branch at Calcutta who, not surprisingly, returned it with a deprecating note. No doubt it was an emotional and poorly drafted piece, but it was an attempt to interpret the mind and motivation of the young, misguided idealists who were responding to the call for freedom. One man's terrorist is another man's freedom fighter. Even in 1935, and increasingly as my service in Bengal continued, I became aware that repression, or even the kind of constructive alternatives to subversive activities which I had attempted to introduce were no real answer to a need as deep and far-reaching as the yearning of a people to be free to steer its own destiny. I had yet to learn that people who respond to the call of political leaders to fight for the freedom of their country are apt to be sadly disillusioned when once that objective had been attained. I left Bengal in 1935 convinced that Britain was wrong not to make a bolder step when passing the Government of India Act, and grant full Dominion status, for which its leaders were ready to accept the responsibility.

Had we acted more quickly it is possible that the Indian continent would be united today. It was during the period of increasing provincial responsibility, with the British retaining ultimate control, that Mahomet Ali Jinnah's Moslim League made rapid advance towards the nationhood of Pakistan. I was especially aware of the fact that in Bengal, the eastern part of which was to become East Pakistan and, later, Bangladesh, Hindu and Muslim villagers normally lived and worked happily side by side – they were all Bengalis. Indeed, the forebears of those Muslims had been forceably converted to a new faith under the Mogul empire two centuries beforehand.

I returned to the police in Bengal in the autumn of 1937, after a further spell of military duty in Burma, to find a very different situation in the Province. Terrorism had been suppressed and abandoned. Order had been restored, the détenus released and the Additional Garrison withdrawn. Overtly, life for the representatives of the ruling power and for the people had resumed the old contrastin patterns. But for those in the know, plans were afoot to bring about social and political changes which would alter the existing order more fundamentally than the revolutionary plotters and terrorist activists in the Anushilan and Jugantar Parties had foreseen. The detention camps had provided ideal seed-beds for the Communist Party of India to plant the germs of their aims, not only to remove the ruling power, but to create an egalitarian society in a country ridden by caste and dominated by its petty princes and other owners of the land.

From the viewpoint of a junior and temporary police officer in the Intelligence Branch the situation was far more obscure than it had been two and a half years earlier. Information was much harder to come by;

in the absence of overt criminal acts there was little we could do to prove the authorship of subversion and to thwart plans to overthrow society. It was a situation which continued until I returned to England in 1940. Life in the Intelligence Branch settled into its normal pattern. Bureaucracy crept in, to detain officers in the writing and studying of reports, where we had earlier roamed in the interior and lived rough. Gone were the raids and secret midnight rendezvous with agents. I still toured in my new Districts – first in Rangpur in North Bengal and then in Midnapur, where I had first become starkly aware of terrorism and its ultimate penalty. Meeting people where they lived and worked was still at the heart of the job.

Perhaps it was as well for democracy that the plans of the CPI were frustrated by the outbreak of war, which some of the revolutionaries hoped to turn to their advantage. A few escaped to Japan, there to organise an Indian liberation force for which its sponsors provided no opportunity to return in triumph to their homeland. Liberation came in the immediate aftermath of the end of hostilities, in an appalling bloodbath of internecine strife which divided the continent. It tragically separated Bengalis who, while of different religious faiths, had for centuries lived peaceably side by side in those villages I had known so well.

When I again rejoined my regiment in 1940, I left India more than ever convinced that we British, who for 350 years had ruled India, giving so much of enduring value of which we have just cause to be proud had, not for the first or last time in our history of colonial rule, failed at the end to choose wisely the time to go.

2

Kashmir and the Karakoram

1931–35

IT SPEAKS ELOQUENTLY OF THE EASY AND PRIVILEGED LIFE OF A British Army officer in India between the wars, that I should have been granted a month's leave within two months of joining the 1st Battalion of my regiment, following my first overseas posting and after little more than one year's commissioned service. I had, of course, but a single thought: to set forth for the Himalayas. With John ('Tiger') White, a brother officer who was also a skier, I spent that month of absence from duty on a modest, two-man expedition, exploring some mountains in Kashmir which were little known at that time. My friend and I departed in a high state of glee on the long, hot dusty rail journey to Rawalpindi 'fearfully pleased' according to my diary 'to get away for a time from the boring military routine'. It was Tiger who had, in fact, written to suggest that I pack my skis in my baggage for India. The letter had reached me while ski-touring in the Western Alps just before I embarked.

In those days the Pir Panjal range, which rises above the western edge of the Vale of Kashmir, was an admirable testing ground for young explorers. Although I possessed some technical skill and experience after six alpine seasons, with a few of the great classic routes to my credit, and had been skiing since the age of ten, I was soon to discover how much remained to be learnt about travelling and subsisting in the high mountains. As early as the late 1920s Gulmarg, now a well-developed tourist area, and the high slopes of the Khilanmarg above the village, was the scene of conventional skiing activities at Christmas and Eastertide, with some good social fun and games organised by the newly formed Ski Club of India. But even at that time, when ski lifts had not been invented and you had to climb uphill in order to earn your run, the sports of skiing and mountaineering tended to bring different types of person into the mountains. Among the skiing fraternity there was little incentive to venture further afield into the vast area of untracked valleys and ridges which lay hidden by the main ridge above the Khilanmarg, whose average height was about 14,000 feet. Here was a 'blank on the map' in a massif of alpine proportions in a Himalayan setting; this was our objective.

There were certain episodes in life, undramatic and unexceptional in themselves, which stand out as fresh in memory as if they happened yesterday. Such an event was our arrival in Tangmarg, at the foot of the mountains and, at that time, the end of the motorable road; there followed the walk up to Gulmarg and the long plod up some 3,000 feet through the snow-covered forest in order to arrive at the Ski Club's mountain hut where we were to stay. It was a day when my senses were intensely alive to every sight and scent and sound: the shouting, shoving pony men competing for our custom, vying with one another to load our gear into their decrepit-looking little *tats*; the excitement of reaching the snow line near the village; the fir cones and pine needles of the tall deodars bestrewing the melting snow under the trees. 'I felt I had been transported to some Swiss scene. I could not resist seizing my skis from a coolie and strapping them on,' I wrote at the time. And as, with mounting anticipation we wended our way up to the highest slopes, there was that dramatic dénouement when we debouched on to that huge, tilted plateau beyond the forest. In the Alps, there is for me always a moment of delight when I first catch sight of the mountain hut which is to be the point of departure for tomorrow's climb; there, at the top of the slope and 800 feet higher, perched beside a great gully carved in the mountain wall, was our refuge.

Today, two-man Himalayan expeditions are becoming popular, partly in reaction against the small armies of mountaineers who have invaded the big peaks in the past twenty years. This was, in fact, how both my expeditions in the Pir Panjal were composed. I much prefer to travel and climb with small groups of friends, but I am inclined to think that there are advantages, even for a modest venture such as this, in having four people in the party rather than two; all too easily, only one man may remain fit, and unable on his own to carry on the programme. Tiger White was a friend whose company I greatly enjoyed. He was the perfect foil to my intensity and restlessness. An Irishman who was amply endowed with native charm and blarney, he was only reluctantly stirred to action. His other nick-name '*Charpoy*' fitted him more aptly than 'Tiger', for he was never happier than when discoursing—preferably in a horizontal position—about what should be done and how to put the world to rights, with no intention of doing anything about it personally. So during those following weeks I found myself exploring mostly on my own, the requisite demands on Tiger's energies having proved to be excessive. Certainly it was a very strenuous

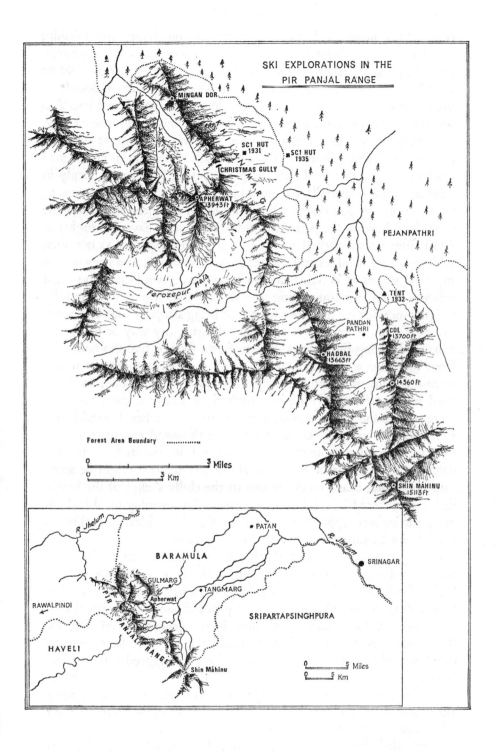

SKI EXPLORATIONS IN THE
PIR PANJAL RANGE

MINGAN DOR

SC1 HUT
1931

SC1 HUT
1935

CHRISTMAS GULLY

GULMARG

APHERWAT
13943ft

PEJANPATHRI

Ferozepur nala

TENT
1932

PANDAN
PATHRI

COL
13700ft

HADBAL
13663ft

14360ft

SHIN MÁHINU
15113ft

Forest Area Boundary ··············

0 _____ 3 Miles
0 _____ 3 Km

R. Jhelum

PATAN

BARAMULA

R. Jhelum

SRINAGAR

GULMARG

PIR PANJAL RANGE

TANGMARG

Apherwat

RAWALPINDI

SRIPARTAPSINGHPURA

HAVELI

Shin Máhinu

0 _____ 5 Miles
0 _____ 5 Km

time which, however, imposed no strain on our happy relationship;
I had no regrets about having been thrown on my own resources.
Solo climbing and skiing, especially in an area where there would be
scant hope of being found and rescued if a mishap occurred, does have
the merit of greatly sharpening your focus and your faculties. You
observe the terrain with greater attention, you navigate more exactly,
you study the condition of the snow and you concentrate on your
climbing or skiing technique. And a great advantage of this heightened
sensibility is that the total experience is engraved the more deeply in
your memory — especially the mistakes you make. Any mountaineer,
let alone the average skier, on learning that I explored that erstwhile
secret land beyond the Apherwat ridge for several days and nights in
April from a tent pitched on an exposed snow ledge at 13,000 feet,
with only two blankets and no mattress for bedding, and firewood as
my only means of cooking and melting snow, would conclude that
this was masochism amounting to a kind of madness. It was the folly
of ignorance, for we had not thought to bring sleeping bags or primus
stoves. If there were risks of accident, of losing my way or becoming
exhausted during those steep swoops down four or five thousand feet
from the ridge and back again on foot, they were forgotten in the
intense delight of skimming, hopefully master of my fate, over the
hard snow surface, only slightly melted by the sun; the conditions
were perfect for spring skiing. Later in the day, when I would turn
back to climb up those same four to five thousand feet to reach my
tent, it was a different matter; the snow had deteriorated to the con-
sistency of soggy porridge and the effort was great; it might be some
four hours later that I would return to the chilly shelter of the lonely
little tent, where I '. . . did not sleep much. The evening meal had not
been particularly appetising owing to the difficulties of making a
fire.' And after some days I had had enough of it.

Feeling very satisfied after plotting on my sketch map a number of
ski itineraries, some of them as long as the famous Parsenn runs in
Switzerland, I started back on the longest journey of all. It proved to
be a nightmare, as I plunged knee-deep in soft snow across the forest-
clad mountainside, heading hopefully in the general direction of the
Khilanmarg. Indeed, I was lucky to make it, for after four hours of
this I was about at the end of my tether. I staggered into the hut
'utterly weary and suffering acute pain in my eyes — but never had
cocoa tasted so good! And what a joy it was to speak to someone again
after those days of silence.' There followed forty-eight hours of snow
blindness, a very unpleasant affliction.

I was glad that Tiger was able to enjoy our last day, when we
climbed together to the summit of Apherwat. I will always think of

The East Face of Peak 36 from the camp on the Peak 36 glacier.

The summit party, Jimmy Waller, Rowland Brotherhood and the author, at 23,000 ft.

Crossing the Hushe nala by zak, Masherbrum at the head of the valley.

that undistinguished peak with gratitude, for it was a stepping stone to the higher mountains. The day was radiantly fine and the air crystal clear. From the top we gazed across the cultivated flatness of the Vale of Kashmir far below us, with its fields and roads fringed with poplars and the Wular Lake reflecting the sky, out to the great peaks beyond. They stretched, rank upon rank, into the northern distance. There was Nanga Parbat, notorious for the death of Alfred Mummery and his Gurkha companions, and shortly to be the scene of much greater tragedies for two German expeditions; there was Haramosh, later to witness a disaster to an Oxford University expedition. And there, further still, was K2, second highest mountain in the world, surrounded by a bristling array of Karakoram giants, clearly etched against the blue horizon, but yellowed with haze. Already my mind was out there, fathering future deeds.

We ran swiftly down 5,000 feet into the Ferozepur nala, a deep gorge which divides the range. Beyond that gorge we could see further areas of virgin snow topped by some attractive peaks; one of them Shin Máhinu (15,113 feet) was nearly the height of Mont Blanc and the highest in the range. They beckoned me to return and visit them the following springtime. But sufficient unto the day was the beauty thereof, for as we climbed back towards our hut 'Spring was definitely on its way. We came upon crocuses and primulas in the snow-free patches; the air was redolent with the scent of pine needles.' It made a marvellous end to my first expedition in the Himalayas.

I returned to the Pir Panjal in April 1932, this time with another friend. R. A. S. Thomas was an equally congenial companion and a very different character. A fast-speaking Welshman, he was employed as a taster in a family tea exporting firm in Calcutta. Ricky was a ball of energy. A bold and skilful skier who took the thousand feet of Christmas Gully straight from top to bottom with the verve of a ski champion in the 'seventies; a year later he was to pass his gold downhill running tests and take part in the famous Arlberg–Kandahar Race. Our first discovery was that the Ski Club of India hut had vanished. We eventually found it after digging down through six feet of snow; it had been smashed to matchwood by a colossal avalanche, which must have come roaring down Christmas Gully. This was a setback, and a revelation of the scale and nature of Himalayan avalanches, activated by a combination of heavier snowfall and greater heat than in our European Alps; to my alpine-trained eye, the site had seemed safe enough.

So we resorted to a tent and, after a few days on the far side of the ridge, where I introduced Ricky to some of my earlier discoveries, we

3

set out upon our main objective: to explore the southern area of mountains, in which the only names were those of summer pastures, Pejanpathri and Pandanpathri, and the highest mountain in the range, Shin Máhinu. But once again the expedition was reduced from two to one; this time it was caused indirectly by the energy, rather than the lethargy of my companion. We were travelling towards the Feroze-pur nala, traversing steep and awkward slopes in the forest, from which the snow had partly melted; I was in the lead and had reached a point where I could see no way forward. I had taken off my skis and advised Ricky to do likewise. But in his enthusiasm and confidence he ignored the advice and forged ahead. Suddenly he skidded on an icy patch of snow and in a flash was sliding on his side down a steep slope of pine needles towards the gorge which enclosed us on our right. Almost before I could grasp the consequences, he had reached the end of the little slope, where it fell away in a cliff. His skis caught on some bushes hanging out over the edge and turned him head downwards — and he fell over the brink.

There followed an awful silence, and I began to panic. Clinging insecurely to branches I made my way to a point where I could see over the edge. There he lay, stretched out motionless on his face. I shouted to him but he did not stir. Searching around I was able, some-how or other, to climb down into the gorge and reached Ricky's side about fifteen minutes later. It was with an immense sense of relief that I found him sitting up, badly concussed and complaining of pain in his back. The problem now was how and where to get help; the only chance seemed to be to continue down the gorge, for there was no question of climbing back the way I had come down. Leaving all our gear we started down, Ricky leaning heavily on my shoulder. The journey was nightmarish, for we broke continuously through the surface crust, trying not to fall into the torrent and not knowing whether, at any moment, we might be stopped by impassable cliffs. Somehow, after what seemed an eternity in time and must have been about six miles in distance, we struck the path and arrived at Tangmarg. I put Ricky to bed in the dâk bungalow and telephoned for a taxi; presently a car arrived which took us to the hospital in Srinagar.

So once again I set forth alone. This time, instead of camping at the top of the mountains, I chose a site near the tree-line where it was less cold and I was able to dig the tent into a trough lined with fir branches. Ignorance was bowing out to experience. For a week I explored that southern area until my sketch map was richly coloured with routes — and until loneliness and sheer boredom drove me down to the valley. I adopted a regular daily routine to make the most of the snow condi-tions, I would leave the tent soon after dawn and climb rapidly up three or four thousand feet (my diary records somewhat boastfully a speed of 2,400 vertical feet per hour), until, at about 10 a.m., the sun had softened the surface. Within half an hour I would be back at the tent: a meal and a wash and long hours to rest and read, and generally while away the time. A welcome visitor in those days was a lone Kashmiri who, hearing of my whereabouts, came up several times bearing delicious, pink-fleshed snow trout which he caught with a trident spear in the Ferozepur nala.

When I next visited the Pir Panjal, in 1935, it was to try out tents and sleeping bags before setting out to those Karakoram mountains I had dreamed about since first catching sight of them in 1931. At the fringe of the forest, where the track emerges onto the Khilanmarg, was a brand-new solidly built log cabin. Sited 800 feet lower than the ill-fated plank structure which had been our base in 1931, it appeared to be safe from any avalanche danger. Once again, I was to learn that the natural forces in the Himalayas are of a different order of magnitude than in the Alps. I set up my tent outside the hut. But during the night a great gale sprang up; the tent walls were soon so laden with snow that I was driven into the shelter of the building. Next morning, in a blinding snow-storm, I groped my way down to the valley. I was just in time. Two nights later the whole gigantic slope of snow lying on the *marg* began to move, inexorably pressed downward by avalanches thundering down the gullies from the main ridge above. The hut was crushed by the sheer weight of snow and in it died three Army officers — and my old friend the *Chowkidar*, or hut warden.

I would be indulging in unwarranted fancy if I were to suggest that the hopes I had entertained of reaching that far horizon of the Karakoram, as I stood on the summit of Apherwat in 1931, were transferred to the mind of Lieutenant James Waller, Royal Artillery, who in 1934 was planning a daring attempt to climb a mountain of over 25,000 feet which he had spotted, unnamed but coded as Peak 36, on the Survey of India map. More prosaically, he was looking for companions for this venture. Having persuaded two young RAF officers stationed in Quetta to join him, and realising that the party lacked mountaineering experience, Waller had made enquiries from the Himalayan Club in Calcutta; my name had been suggested. But his letter asking me to join the party did seem like the answer to those hopes of four years' standing. I was due to have a long leave in 1935 after ending my secondment with the Police and I accepted with alacrity.

At the age of twenty-three, Jimmy Waller was a remarkable young man. His knowledge of climbing was limited to some scrambling in

Kashmir and a small expedition to the peaks of Nun and Kun in the
Great Himalaya in the previous year; with such slight experience and
equally slender resources it was, to say the least of it, audacious to
presume that this party of four, only one of whom had a reasonable
record of alpine climbing, could tackle an unreconnoitred peak only
slightly lower than Kamet, the highest mountain climbed at that time.

One member of the party, Rowland Brotherhood, had no climbing
experience at all. The expedition would certainly not have passed the
stringent standards for approval of the Mount Everest Foundation
which, fortunately for us, did not exist at that time. But Jimmy was
quite undaunted; his enthusiasm was infectious and he was brim full of
imaginative ideas.

The last Westerners to visit the area in question were two Americans,
the intrepid and formidable Fanny Bullock-Workman and her long-
suffering husband, who had travelled through the mountains twenty-
three years previously and recorded their poor opinion of the local
Balti peasants who, they said, could not be relied upon to carry loads
over high and difficult terrain. So, as we would have to do most of our
own load carrying, Jimmy had designed a sledge to haul our gear over
the long, relatively gentle glaciers, which were reported to be not
unlike those in the polar regions. He had also invented a special harness
to enable the climbers to carry a double load: one pack on the back and
the other on the chest. His parents, both doctors of medicine, advised
on a high-altitude diet providing a high-calorie value for a minimal
weight of one pound twelve ounces per man-day. Skis and Canadian
racquettes were included in the baggage. The test of these imaginative
ideas lay ahead of us; they were to prove not entirely satisfactory in the
event. Meanwhile there was the more immediate need to find the
mountain and discover a feasible route up it. The Bullock-Workmans
in their book *Two Summers in the Ice World of the Karakorams*, without
experience of climbing mountains of that order of magnitude or
difficulty, had offered no views on the subject, beyond remarking that
Peak 36 had 'a commanding personality'.

Rowland Brotherhood and Dr Stewart Carslaw joined Jimmy and
me in Srinagar towards the end of April. 'Doc' Carslaw had reached
the advanced age of twenty-nine, but the rest of us were in our early
twenties and there was the immediate rapport of youthful enthusiasm.
There were also two others, very important members of the party.
Apart from providing my name, the Himalayan Club had supplied
two of their outstanding Sherpas, holders of the Club's coveted 'Tiger'
badge. Palden, a big solid and serious man, was a veteran of the famous
1924 and 1933 Everest expeditions, on which climbers had reached
points only 1,000 feet below the top on the north side. His young

compatriot Dawa Thondup, smaller and always smiling, had also been a porter on the 1933 expedition, and was one of the two survivors who had struggled back through the storm on the Silver Saddle of Nanga Parbat after the tragedy which befell Willi Merkl's German expedition in 1934. This was my first acquaintance with the splendid Sherpa people, and the first of a number of mountain experiences which Dawa Thondup and I were to share in the course of the following twenty years.

We set forth on 30th April, travelling long distances each day, eager to get to the big peaks. We crossed the Great Himalayan range on skis by the Zoji La, along which a main highway now carries goods and tourists swiftly to Leh, capital of Ladakh. We travelled down the hot, dusty, deep gorges of the Kargill and Indus valleys, through villages which stood like oases in the prevailing dryness and gay with apricot blossom, to the wide, sandy valley of the Shyok river, where we crossed its turbulent waters in a crazy old wooden barge and continued upstream on the far bank to the large village of Khapalu. Again we had to cross the river, this time by a precarious-looking raft called a zak, consisting of a number of goat-skins overlaid by a framework of poles, which kept the boatman's mate busy reinflating as we were swept violently downstream on our way across the turbulent waters. From here we were to enter the main range to the north. And yet again by zak across the Hushe river, at the head of whose valley stood one of the giants of the Karakoram, the 26,660-feet high Masherbrum.

Although Masherbrum is among the twenty-seven highest mountains in the world, my mind was attuned to alpine scales. With the eye of faith I traced a route up its icecliffs in terms of hours rather than weeks. The ever-optimistic James must have been nursing similar flights of fancy, for in 1938 he was to lead another expedition to that mountain, which nearly ended in tragedy. But that morning it looked benign and magnificent, its eastern facets shining in the sun.

Our route led us into the narrow gorge of the Saltoro valley, from both sides of which tremendous granite walls soared up seven or eight thousand feet, topped by spires as challenging as any of the Chamonix aiguilles. It was here, with the precipices hemming us in, and the sheer scale of the scenery positively overpowering, that I began to wonder how we could expect to climb, not only to the heights of those pinnacles, but a further five thousand feet or so higher still.

On 12th May we reached a large Balti village, Dansam, shaded by mulberry and apricot trees. From our inadequate maps it appeared to be a convenient centre from which to start our search for Peak 36. The villagers, in their shapeless homespun woollen tunics, baggy trousers and round flat headgear, greeted us warmly. We were the first white people who had come there for twenty-three years, yet several of the elders recalled the Bullock-Workmans as recent visitors. The time gap of a quarter-century seemed not to register with them and they insisted that it was only '*picchle sal*' (last year) that the Memsahib and, incidentally, her husband had been there; it was of course, Fanny who had made her mark upon them. Unlike the two American explorers, we were favourably impressed by some of these big, bearded and husky men, who were delighted at being asked to sign on with our caravan.

We divided into three parties to pursue our search. Jimmy Waller and Dawa went north up a side valley, the Kondus nala, into which a number of glaciers appeared to drain and which formed part of the glacial system of our peak; Brotherhood and Doc Carslaw, who had travelled two days later than Jimmy and I and had only just reached the village, were to extend Waller's reconnaissance in the same area; Palden and I continued up the main valley to climb to the Bilafond La, at the head of a long glacier of that name from which the Workmans had sighted Peak 36 in 1912.

A week later all three parties returned to Dansam exhausted, but with undimmed exuberance, for a fascinating exchange of news and views. We had only enjoyed one fine day and I, for one, had slept little. Brotherhood and Carslaw had drawn a blank; the glacier they inspected lay immediately beneath the forbidding cliffs of the South Face of Peak 36, the summit of which had remained shrouded in mists. I had gone twice up to the 18,000-feet pass with Palden and, on the second visit, had a brief but clear view of the peak and its neighbour, Peak 35. I was thrilled by the spectacle but not at all hopeful that we could reach the foot of the South-East Ridge, by which alone it seemed at that stage, that a route to the top might be forced. Jimmy, however, although he had not sighted Peak 36, had discovered an uncharted glacier which appeared to lead, in a series of sharp bends and steep icefalls, round the flanks of what he believed to be our mountain. There would be serious technical problems, for we would have to find a way through the lower of two icefalls, but it seemed to him that we might avoid the higher icefall, and short-cut the sharp bend at that point, by crossing a col at 18,000 feet to descend upon the upper reaches of the glacier; this should lead us to the foot of the South-East Ridge. All this was highly speculative; if Jimmy was mistaken, the chances were that our whole enterprise would fail. But it might be one clue to our problem: that of getting to within striking distance of our goal. It seemed a chance worth taking. We set off up the Kondus nala and arrived on the afternoon of 23rd May at the remote hamlet of Korkondus, near the upper end of the valley.

Korkondus was the terminus of human life in those parts, so far

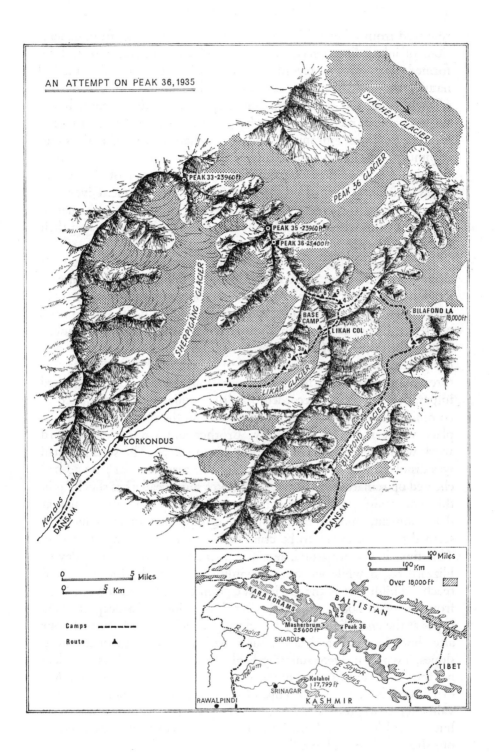

AN ATTEMPT ON PEAK 36, 1935

PEAK 33·23960 ft
PEAK 35·23960 ft
PEAK 36·25400 ft
SIACHEN GLACIER
PEAK 36 GLACIER
SHERPIGANG GLACIER
BASE CAMP
LIKAH COL
BILAFOND LA
18,000 ft
6 5
4
3a
3
1
LIKAH GLACIER
KORKONDUS
BILAFOND GLACIER
Kordus nala
DANSAM
DANSAM

0   5 Miles
0   5 Km

Camps -------
Route   ▲

0   100 Miles
0   100 Km
Over 18,000 ft

KARAKORAMS
BALTISTAN
K2
Masherbrum
25600 ft
Peak 36
R. Indus
SKARDU
R. Shyok
TIBET
R. Jhelum
Kolahoi
17,799 ft
SRINAGAR
R. Indus
RAWALPINDI
KASHMIR

removed from other habitations that the villagers were, from generations of inbreeding, nearly to a man and woman, cretinous and deformed. I am sorry to record that our sentiments were of a practical
nature; we needed porters—fifty able-bodied men—and scarcely one
of them fitted the description. But they seemed willing enough and
we were able to recruit just enough porters to make a start next morning. The start was unpropitious. No sooner had we arrived at the snout
of Jimmy's glacier, known locally as the Likah, than our men struck
for higher wages: they demanded one rupee instead of the twelve
annas which was normal on the main routes at that time. Given that
none of them had ever worked for anyone else before, whether as
porters or otherwise, I began to feel that we had underestimated their
native intelligence.

The scene next day, as I led this heterogeneous crew through the
maze of crevasses and séracs of the lower icefall, would have raised a
laugh on the movie screen. We tied everyone on to six separate ropes
at one-metre intervals: porters, three sheep, several goats and Jimmy's
red setter, Tony, with our four selves and the two Sherpas as leaders.
But on the far edge of the glacier, the porters dumped their loads and
refused to budge. It was already getting late and the weather was
threatening a storm. In this critical situation, drastic measures seemed
imperative and Jimmy recorded that 'the coolies were determined to
commit suicide by spending the night out on the snow slope and in a
place where rocks fell frequently. Brother and I put in some hard
work with our iceaxes; we were not cutting steps. The suicide squad
was dissolved and by evening everyone had reached Camp 2 and had
cheered up remarkably.' In case this strikes some readers as shocking in
this more enlightened age of half a century later, I can only say that at
that moment, and in those somewhat desperate circumstances, it
seemed to us necessary to be cruel to be kind. Worse was to come.
This time it was a natural, not a man-made crisis. For four days a
blizzard raged while we were struggling to cross the Likah col and
reach the high part of the glacier. We climbers found ourselves cut off
from the main body on the col, after descending waist-deep on fixed
ropes at the end of a terrible day, during which we had worked hour
after hour in a gale and heavy snow to lower loads down the steep
slopes. Two of us were suffering badly from snow-blindness; we had
no food and, with no primuses, could obtain no liquid either. My
diary records that we took cups of snow into our sleeping bags in a
vain attempt to produce some water. By 31st May the ordeal was over;
but we had lost several precious loads in the deep new snow; one of
our sheep had been blown from the col and another was buried somewhere on the glacier.

So shaken were we by this experience that we made a fateful decision: to change our line of communications. On that first fine day I had made a long lone reconnaissance on skis to the head of the glacier, reached the foot of the South-East Ridge of Peak 36 and, on the far side, had thought I identified a connection with the Bilafond La. I was the only member of the party who had been to both places, and on my advice, we decided to switch our communications right round by the route which I first reconnoitred. Brotherhood, revealing a cheerful disregard of himself which was typical of the man, volunteered to make the connection; he left us on 2nd June on this important mission. During the rest of the week the rest of the expedition gradually ferried our baggage to the head of the glacier and established our Base Camp there, safely sited under the foot of the ridge. In that time we also pushed our reconnaissances further round and under the eastern skirts of the mountain, very conscious of the impending icecliffs above us; the route we travelled was strewn with iceblocks. By crossing another col on the ridge dividing us from the Bilafond La we reached the foot of the South-East Ridge and, to our great excitement, found what might prove to be a promising route towards the summit. Jimmy and I also made a tentative attempt to climb to the crest of the South-East Ridge. It involved us in some steep ice climbing and we had to conclude that there would be little chance of establishing a line of camps by that route. But we also made a most unwelcome discovery. I had been mistaken in thinking that there was a connection between our Base Camp and the Bilafond La. It now looked as if Brotherhood's errand was in vain and we were even uncertain whether we would be able to make contact with him; in fact, by suffering an optical delusion I had committed a howler of enormous dimensions.

Seeking to make amends, Jimmy and I, with Palden, set off early on 8th June, descended to the Peak 36 glacier, which runs from the foot of the East Face to join the great Siachen glacier. We then moved along the foot of the ridge we had crossed, guessing at a possible gap where Brother and his men might appear; we were also making a large assumption that he would arrive at all. So the excitement was tremendous when, only a matter of minutes after we had set up our tents to provide a marker for Brother to see us, a number of figures, diminutive in the distance above, dramatically appeared at the very spot which we were keeping under observation; it seemed like a miracle. But separating us was a thousand feet of very steep snow slope, some of which was bare ice and all of it requiring numerous steps to be cut to make the connection possible. We were tired after our long and rapid journey, but such was the excitement that I started up at once with Palden. It was very hot and I was by no means fresh for the strenuous bout of ice climbing which followed. At last I reached the level of the col on which Brotherhood and his men were waiting, but a little to their right; at least we were in shouting distance. Brotherhood, who might justifiably have voiced a complaint about the appalling error which would cost him nearly a fortnight's fruitless journey, was his usual calm and cheerful self. We quickly agreed that there could be no question of opening a new line of communication down the slope by which I had climbed, the angle was 55 degrees and we lacked sufficient rope to fix a handline down the 1,000 feet; he would simply have to return and re-open our original route. Nowadays Himalayan climbers would be equipped with thousands of feet of rope which they would fix, and then slide their way up and down with jumar clamps in safety and with relatively little effort. But we had only the amount of climbing rope needed for our security while climbing. As a parting gesture, his men hurled three bundles of firewood down; we had lost a good deal of paraffin during the crisis crossing of the Likah col and were short of fuel. The final irony was to watch that precious wood being swallowed up, one bundle after the other, in the gaping jaws of the Bergschrund below. Bidding them a sad farewell Palden and I carefully retraced our steps and crawled exhausted into our tents.

Later, Palden left us to return to Base with the bad news of that day's events; Jimmy and I watched him as he crossed the Bilafond ridge at the point where it abutted against the East Face of the peak. We were well aware of the danger of our route around the mountain from Base Camp; but as is so often the case, we did not believe that it could happen to us. We were unprepared for the spectacle which we witnessed a few minutes afterwards, when a colossal avalanche broke from a long line of séracs above the col and thundered down the precipice, pounding into the surface of the Peak 36 glacier with a noise like a war-time V2 flying bomb. Countless iceblocks hurtled down on either side of the col, obliterating our tracks; a dense cloud of snow vapour rose from the wreckage for about a thousand feet, obscuring the mountain from our view for several minutes. It was a stupendous spectacle. Had Palden been later by as little as fifteen minutes in making the crossing, he would have vanished without trace. The line of march to the foot of the East Face, impossible by the Bilafond La, was in fact exceedingly dangerous by the route we had perforce to take. Recovering our wits, we moved our camp close in under the foot of a subsidiary ridge on the East Face, which ran down from a remarkable glacier platform some 2,000 feet higher; from that little plateau our hopeful eyes traced a route through some huge crevasses and up to the crest of the South-East Ridge. Then, wending our way through the labyrinth of enormous iceblocks thrown down by the mountain a few hours earlier, we made our way over the col and back to Base Camp, determined to delay no longer in making our bid for the summit. Food and fuel were running short; and I think we were feeling the effects of all the setbacks and storms, combined with those three weeks of strenuous activity at about 18,000 feet.

But hardly had we arrived, when the elements struck again. Another four-day blizzard kept us in our tents while snow piled up outside. In my diary I find frequent resort to strong adjectives to describe the conditions: '11/6: The snow has piled up outside and there is no sign of clearing tonight . . . truly terrible weather'; '12/6: a terrible day'; '13/6: This ghastly weather'. But that day it cleared and, with our telescope trained on the Likah Col, three miles down the glacier we saw Brotherhood and his party on their way back. We hastened down, myself on skis ahead of the others and there was an affectionate reunion. All was forgiven in our delight to see each other and exchange our news. As hopeful now as we had been in the doldrums the day before, we made a determined move across to the East Face and established an advanced base, ready to assault the peak by 'rush' tactics. Apart from limited food and fuel, our period of leave allowed us little time to spare.

But on the very evening of our arrival in Camp 4 on 14th June another period of heavy snowfall began: a blizzard blew for 56 hours. It was only on 18th June that we were able to force our way up to the glacier platform and establish Camp 5. '. . . had a terrible time making a track. With my ice-axe I had to clear a way by scraping one foot of new snow off the slope before I could get a foothold . . . 150 feet at an angle of 60 degrees in waist-deep snow.' I recall that we were scrupulous in taking clinometer readings to measure accurately the angles of slope. But luck seemed to be with us, for that afternoon I was able to climb 800 feet above the platform, flogging a furrow above and ahead of me in which I could lever myself up with my elbows and stamp steps in the continuing steepness. We were all set to fulfil our high expectations.

In glorious weather on the 19th Brother, Jimmy and I—Doc Carslaw had been unwell and unable to take an active part for several days—accompanied by Dawa, Palden and Rahim, a stout-hearted local man, pushed on up the face and, after great luck in finding a way across a monster crevasse, pitched our tents at what we believed to be 23,500 feet; in fact this was an overestimate which was to cost us dearly, for in our crash plan we had decided to cut out a higher camp which had featured in Jimmy's earlier calculations. The day had not been without its excitements. While in the lead I had started a windslab avalanche which knocked Brotherhood off his feet; I was at the line of cleavage of the slabs when they parted from the underlying snow, and was able to hold him. But a little later Brother and I started another windslab, a big one this time, with blocks one foot thick, which began sliding away from the board-hard underlying surface. We were carried down several yards and would have gone further had I not managed, with great good fortune, to arrest the fatal movement by a desperate thrust of my axe, aided by a slight ease-ment of the steepness just above a line of cliffs. It was a very near thing; yet, my mind dulled by the effects of altitude, I had no sense of fear at the time.

On 20th June, slowed down by lack of oxygen and taking about six breaths for each step, we climbed to the crest of the South-East Ridge at about 300 vertical feet per hour. It should have been a moment of triumph, for the difficulties were over and the summit lay only a quarter of a mile away along a broad and gently angled slope. But by over-estimating our height at Camp 6 we had already climbed 2,500 feet and, with about 1,000 feet still to climb, we found we had shot our bolt. The weather decided the issue. The wind had moved from the favourable eastern quarter to the west. Clouds were streaming vertically upwards over the ridge from the depths of the Sherpigang glacier beneath us and, knowing the signs only too well, we realised that a storm was imminent; we were beaten. Brother and I made a token effort to gain more height by continuing for a further half hour in which we climbed 200 feet and reached about 24,500 feet before acknowledging defeat; we were moving as in a dream, but probably looked the worse for drink.

Very tired now, we turned back. One big snow slope which had caused me great anxiety on our way up had already peeled off in an avalanche while we had been on the ridge. Before we reached the tents Brother became exhausted and had to be supported; all of us were badly in need of rest. But as climbing leader I was sternly insistent that we press on down. It was now snowing heavily and visibility was poor. I knew that, were we to stay, we would be marooned and afterwards would make an exceedingly rapid descent in an avalanche. On the way down I had a very lucky escape with a crevasse: 'only held myself by my elbows on the brink . . . a very big fellow indeed'. To make the point, a tin mug, loosely fastened to my rucksack in our hurry to pack up Camp 6, continued its journey into the crevasse, echo-sounding its depth as it went. We reached Camp 5 in darkness. Never have I felt more thankful for the friendship and help of our waiting companions, who guided our last steps with hurricane lamps, helped us remove our boots and fed us, rather oddly, according to my diary with hot milk and bacon. The storm continued for three days more and it was providential that we returned safely to base. A third ice avalanche of séracs had swept across the Peak 36 col while we had been on the mountain.

With a great deal of luck, we had paid lightly for our inexperience, nothing worse than persistently numb toes which betokened mild frostbite. But we could feel that because, rather than despite, the treatment accorded us by the mountain and the weather gods, who granted us only seven fine days out of thirty and never more than three of those days in succession, we had done rather well to reach 24,500 feet and to find a line up a Karakoram giant which others would follow. But it would be twenty-four years, in 1959, before a Japanese expedition finished the job on Peak 36, now dignified with the name of Saltoro Kangri.

For me, the climax of an expedition is often in its aftermath. We were southward bound across the mountains towards the Vale of Kashmir, superbly fit and totally relaxed after all our earlier anxieties; it was in a kind of ecstasy that we wandered up the valleys, crossed the cols and wandered down the other side. In the big village of Khapalu we were fêted by the Rajah, who presented us with the gift of a sheep, rice, flour, sugar, butter and cherries; the village was summery and smelt of clover. At another village we fell upon the mulberry trees and gorged ourselves with the ripe fruit. On our journey home we were in a paradise of green alps and flowers. Wild roses, saffron and pink, adorned the hillsides and, on a high ridge before the big peaks disappeared from sight, we had a last view of K2, the Masherbrum and the other Baltoro giants. There, too, was Peak 36, taunting us against a clear blue sky in the distance. I have never lived more intensely than during that journey back, savouring every living moment, seeing every living thing afresh.

There was a tailpiece which gave Brotherhood and me special satisfaction. During the final stage of the trek down the Liddar valley we turned aside to look for a mountain named Kolahoi (17,799 feet). We had no map to guide us, but we found it, saw its impressive and unclimbed south face and, in one long day, involving ten miles of distance and 5,000 feet of ascent, made a direct route up a steep rock buttress 2,000 feet in height. Everything went right for us that day. It was a particularly good effort on Brother's part for that expedition was his début in mountaineering. And I am no different from any other climber in treating as trophies my first ascents.

We arrived in Srinagar to read the headlines in the *Statesman* of Calcutta: 'CLIMBERS ORDEAL IN BLIZZARD'; 'MOUNTAINEERS ESCAPE FROM

AVALANCHE'. Even the London *Times* struck a note of melodrama in its leader commenting on our effort; the editor wrote of '. . . The mystery and the thrill of travel in the Himalayas. But the mystery is awful and the thrill is sometimes a shudder'. Apparently we were heroes and it was heady stuff. Among many lessons I had learned in the Karakoram, and many more I was still to learn, I had yet to understand the truth that it is better to travel than to arrive.

1935 was an *annus mirabilis* for, when I returned to England to spend the balance of my leave, I was elected to the Alpine Club and the Royal Geographical Society. I was also selected by the Himalayan Committee for the Everest expedition which was preparing to leave in the following year. And to fill my cup of happiness to the brim, I became engaged to be married. Joy was a Middlesex and Wimbledon tennis player, a game for which I had no aptitude, while she had no experience of mountaineering. But while I made no progress to match her on the tennis court, she soon began to show promise in my line of country. When she came out to India we found the birds and butterflies of the plains and hills a constant source of delight, and we have shared a love of mountains through the past forty years.

So for two months I lived on air. But an RAF Medical Board detected a murmur in my cardiograph; it was the first of several occasions when doctors were to advise me to be careful about climbing the stairs. Though they were later proved wrong, the Everest Expedition leader, Hugh Ruttledge, understandably felt that I might be a liability; so I rejoined my regiment at the end of the year. Little though I enjoyed it, I had always taken regimental soldiering seriously; but at that moment of disappointment I could have done with some of that sense of proportion which my commanding officer, in his Confidential Report, had rightly said that I lacked.

3

Peaks, Passes and Yetis

1932–40

IN 1931 I HAD SEEN K2, AT 28,250 FEET THE SECOND HIGHEST mountain in the world. A year later, from our regimental hill-station at Lebong I first viewed Kangchenjunga (28,150 feet), third of the greatest peaks, fifty miles away across the little State of Sikkhim. That view today is almost as famous as that of the Matterhorn from Zermatt and, for those who know both, an even greater source of wonder. But the climber is not content to gaze at the mountain scene; for him, the mountain makes a call for action, its appeal is to his prowess as much as to his aesthetic sense. I was conscious of the challenge, but my response would have to await another day. For the time being, I was content with my liberation from the humid heat of Calcutta and the claustrophobic confinement of us soldiers within the ancient walls of its Fort. While others played tennis and sensibly continued the customary social rounds, I roamed the surrounding hills. My diary records that I covered considerable distances along the great ridges and down to the steamy depths of the Teesta and Rangit rivers. I even persuaded Tiger White to accompany me on a thirty-five-mile walk to and from the neighbouring hill-station of Kalimpong, a journey which I have since covered with less effort but far less enjoyment in a jeep. Wherever I went I found enchantment: in the girls with baskets on their backs, picking the leaves from the terraced bushes in the tea gardens; in the village folk drinking tea at a *basti* by the wayside; in the butterflies drinking from the puddles on the rain-soaked path; in the scarlet and yellow minivets flitting among the trees. And beyond the foreground was Sikkhim, its ridges and valleys beckoning me towards those stupendous mountains in the north.

The chance to travel further came in the autumn of 1937. I was shortly to resume my duties with the Bengal police, but was granted leave for another expedition. Through the Himalayan Club Joy and I had met C. R. Cooke, a senior official with the Indian Posts and Telegraphs, who had made the first ascent, solo, of the North Summit

of Kabru (24,075 feet) a close neighbour of Kangchenjunga. We began
to pool our ideas for our next venture: to Kangchenjunga itself. I was
attracted to Peak 1 (25,525 feet), one of the summits along its East
Ridge, from which a rock and ice buttress descended the southern face;
it was clearly visible from Darjeeling and, from that distance, looked a
reasonable alpine proposition. Nowadays the huge scale of such a
Himalayan face climb no longer daunts our leading mountaineers;
but in the 'thirties we lacked their modern equipment and techniques
and I was more inhibited than Reggie Cooke by the prevailing beliefs
as to what was in the realm of the possible. So, on reflection, we
decided to base ourselves on the Zemu Glacier, beneath the East Face
of the mountain and, in view of our limited resources, to content ourselves with prospecting a new route. Two notable German attempts
had been made to climb Kangchenjunga by that face, led by Paul
Bauer in 1929 and 1931; but we believed that there might be a better
route via the North Col and the North Ridge which would avoid the
great difficulties they had experienced. We were also keen to try out
climatic conditions in the early part of the winter, after the end of the
monsoon snows. Up to that time Everest had already resisted no less
than six attempts, all of them made before the monsoon, in May and
June. It was time, we thought, to seek an alternative time of year when
the elements might be less hostile.

So it was with these objectives, particular and general, in view that
Joy, Reggie Cooke and I travelled up the deep gorge of the Teesta
river in October 1937, accompanied by some doughty Sherpas. There
was Rinsing, with high testimonials from two Everest expeditions in
his record book; Dawa Thondup, my companion in the Karakoram,
and Pasang Kikuli who had been, with him, the only survivors from
the disaster on the Silver Saddle of Nanga Parbat in 1934; Pasang
Chakadi had done well on a recent French expedition; Pasang Sherpa,
a likely looking lad who, as Pasang Dawa Lama, was later to become
one of the most renowned among the Sherpa climbers, had just
returned from the first ascent of Chomulhari with Freddie Spencer-
Chapman. And there were two others, of no repute, who soon became
close friends: Hawang, an endearing simpleton, and Ang Kitar, a
lively boy who was to win his spurs with us and then tragically to die,
with Kikuli, on K2.

I like to think that the Mount Everest Foundation would have
approved the credentials of Cooke and myself; but they might have
looked askance at the record of the girl in the party who, at that stage
in our partnership, had accomplished only a few rock climbs on Kern
Knotts, the Napes ridges and Gimmer Crag, while we were honey-
mooning in the Lake District. But as we walked up the path beside the

The Everest massif from Nepal Peak.

Climbing to Camp 3 on Nepal Peak, with Kangchenjunga in the distance.

An impression of Mount Athos sketched by the author in 1945.

The monastery of Iviron.

river, Joy and I had no thoughts about climbing; we were brandishing our butterfly nets, adding to the collection we had made during our year together in Burma. Later, when we reached the glacier, she exchanged her butterfly net for an ice-axe 'and felt very adventurous'.

In the village of Lachen we met a German party on their way back from the Zemu glacier. Ludwig Schmaderer, Herbert Paider and Ernst Grob were fresh from their triumph in making the second ascent of Siniolchu (22,600 feet) which Freshfield once described as 'the most beautiful mountain in the world'. Under the stimulus of national socialism German climbers were very active in the Himalayas and the Caucasus in those years before World War II; those I met could not have been more delightful people and this trio was no exception. We spent a convivial evening together, poring over maps and drinking *marwa* through straws from bamboo tumblers. Like Bauer's parties, they had been climbing during the monsoon; they had not been troubled by wind, but had suffered appalling and dangerous snow conditions, which had defeated them in an attempt to make a second ascent of Nepal Peak, first climbed by Bauer's party. I made a mental note that it would be worth our having a go at that mountain.

I was surprised that their Sherpas made our own men look positively pallid; their faces had been blackened by sunburn. We, too, were to suffer considerably from the exceptionally fierce sunlight, reflected from the snow, during our stay. Apart from severe blistering, our faces swelled up incongruously despite the special cream prepared by Elizabeth Arden, which had proved effective in the Karakoram. The inventive Reggie solved the problem by cutting out face masks from leather which he had brought to repair our boots.

In the following weeks the words 'snow conditions' were to be graven on our hearts, coupled with the word 'wind'. We set up a base camp at 16,000 feet beside the glacier, near a little ice-free lake, Green Lake, which is fed by hot springs. We were surrounded by fantastic peaks which towered above us on every side. At the head of the glacier was the dominating presence of Kangchenjunga, its summit ridge seemingly impregnable above the 10,000 feet high East Face. An attractive summit named the Sugar Loaf, only 21,300 feet, stood invitingly between two feeder ice streams: the Twins and the Nepal Gap glaciers. On the left of Kangchenjunga a great gash in the ridge which connected it with Simvo was the 19,275-feet Zemu La, which had been named by Kellas 'Cloud Gap'. And downstream from our camp rose the graceful Siniolchu. The effect on myself was overwhelming, for the whole scene was closer in, even more imposing than had been those Karakoram mountains on which I had climbed two

4

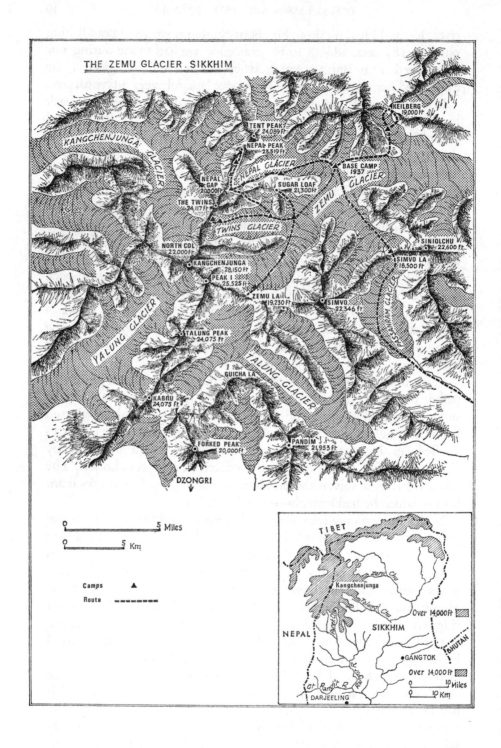

THE ZEMU GLACIER. SIKKHIM

KEILBERG
19,000 Ft

TENT PEAK
24,089 Ft
NEPAL PEAK
23,519 Ft

BASE CAMP
1937

KANGCHENJUNGA
GLACIER

NEPAL GLACIER

NEPAL
GAP
20,000 Ft
THE TWINS
24,117 Ft

SUGAR LOAF
21,300 Ft

ZEMU
GLACIER

SINIOLCHU
22,600 Ft

TWINS GLACIER

NORTH COL
22,000 Ft

SIMVO LA
18,500 Ft

KANGCHENJUNGA
28,150 Ft
PEAK 1
25,525 Ft

YALUNG GLACIER

ZEMU LA
19,230 Ft

SIMVO
22,346 Ft

PASSANRAM GLACIER

TALUNG PEAK
24,075 Ft

TALUNG GLACIER

GUICHA LA

KABRU
24,075 Ft

FORKED PEAK
20,000 Ft

PANDIM
21,953 Ft

DZONGRI

0 — 5 Miles
0 — 5 Km

Camps ▲
Route ------

TIBET

Zemu Chu

Kangchenjunga

NEPAL

SIKKHIM

Gt. Rangit R.

GANGTOK

BHUTAN

Over 14,000 ft

Over 14,000 ft

0 — 10 Miles
0 — 10 Km

DARJEELING

years earlier, which stood back in the vastness of their wide glacier basins.

Certainly there was no lack of peaks on which to test high climbing conditions. Reggie and I registered an early success by making a first ascent of the 19,000-foot snow dome of the Keilberg, immediately above the camp. The wind had rocked the tents of our high camp all night and we had very little sleep. 'Wind really terrible' I wrote at the time. So violent and demoralising were the gusts next morning that, below the final snow-face leading to the summit, I sat down and wept. But we were mightily pleased with our modest achievement as we descended a long ice couloir on the way down to Base. Then Reggie was struck down with a bout of sickness which was to plague him at intervals throughout our stay; so Joy and I set forth to attempt the Sugar Loaf. On our first effort we so exhausted ourselves floundering in waist-deep snow that I foolishly decided to take a short cut to the crest of its North Ridge; this involved me in the same ordeal as I had experienced on Peak 36 in 1935; I found that the only way of making progress was to plunge my arms up to the shoulder above my head, and lever myself up in order to stamp out the next two footsteps. We reached the ridge so tired that we could not face the task of continuing to the top, which was only some 300 feet higher. When we returned to the fray a few weeks later, we climbed that slope with ease in crampons, on board-hard snow. But hardly had we reached the ridge again when, with an all too familiar 'wumpf' the entire slope by which we had climbed broke away with startling suddenness in a windslab avalanche, over a distance of fifty feet and to a depth of nearly one and a half feet; it went thundering down to the glacier with terrifying speed, or rather, according to Joy's diary 'I was too astonished to be terrified'. It was one of the most providential escapes I have had in fifty years of climbing. This time, however, the wind was unbearable. I was able to make some progress, climbing steep and unstable rocks on the sheltered side, before we had to tackle a big rock *gendarme* on the crest itself. In a matter of seconds our hands became numbed by the cold—I developed a large frostbite blister; for Joy it was too much of an ordeal and although I said to her, 'If you climb this we've climbed the mountain', I was in no state to press the matter. But we were even closer to the top, and this double defeat was a big disappointment. Back at our high camp we were hounded down to the Zemu glacier by the tremendous force of the westerly gale; at least it provided some indication that the second half of October might be too late in the year for high climbing. But perhaps the best of it was that we had shared our first big climb. 'Joy has done amazingly well,' I wrote that night.

When Reggie and I took a mini-expedition to attempt Nepal Peak on 5th November, we were forewarned about what to expect. We camped beneath the 20,013-feet Nepal Gap, 'surely the windiest place in the world', and climbed it the next day. The ferocity of the wind was such that at one moment I was literally lifted out of the steps I had just cut in the steep ice slope. Reggie's favourite felt hat was plucked off his head and after making an adventurous journey to the Nepal glacier far below us, was caught up again in a gust and sailed many hundreds of feet up to the North Ridge of the Twins, to disappear into Tibet. But fortune favoured us on the following day, for we were climbing by a steep, sheltered couloir in the East Face of our mountain. The climb reached a fitting climax when, just beneath the ridge, I cut a hole through the cornice. I was braced for the brutal blast which struck me and which made it quite impossible to struggle out on to the crest; but I was staggered by the view which was spread before me. There was Jonsong Peak, Ramthong, Cross and Wedge Peaks, and White Wave; they were names I had read in the writings of Freshfield and Smythe. There, away to the West, was Makalu; beyond it Lhotse and Nuptse. And there was Everest. For the first time I was looking at the top of the world. An eagle was soaring nearby, at over 23,000 feet.

Unable to get higher, we spent that night comfortably in a snow cave which we excavated under the sheltering cornice at the top of the great couloir we had climbed. The following morning the wind mercifully relented and we pushed on for another 1,500 feet up the ridge. There was some quite exciting ice climbing as we cut steps across the ice flutings beneath the crest and up one of the gullies which separated them; my clinometer reading was 62 degrees. We fixed a hand-line for the Sherpas at this point. At 22,300 feet we stopped at the foot of the dangerous snow slope which had defeated the Germans; but now the avalanche which deterred them had fallen; the slope was hard as concrete—and safe. Fortunately we were able to pitch the tent in a snow scoop, for on 8th November the wind had resumed its onslaught; I was hurled back each time I tried to mount on to the slope, and it was not until midday that we could make a start. Having scarcely set foot on the big slope, Reggie felt unwell again and had to return to the tent; it was cruel luck. But the chance of getting up was too good to miss and I decided to continue on my own. Using crampons on the hard surface I went up the 800 feet at a good pace and, taking a little more time and trouble where the upper slope became much steeper, reached the summit ridge in no more than an hour; a few feet to my left was a snow dome and I headed towards it; I had arrived on the South-West Summit of Nepal Peak, 23,350 feet. If it was a great moment, I scarcely appreciated the fact at that time; I was clinging for dear life to my ice-axe, driven hard into the snow as I crouched just below the crest. Had I raised myself a little higher I risked making an aerial journey back the way I had come. The highest peak, 23,442 feet, was only three or four hundred feet away to my right and one hundred feet higher; but to get there was quite out of the question; such was the force of the wind. Thankful to escape, I paid scant attention to the stupendous view from my peak and retreating to the relative protection of the big slope below, I returned quickly to the tent. Next day we found that our camp on the Nepal Gap glacier had been collapsed by the wind; even one of the aluminium poles had been broken. But we could record another success, and a second ascent at that.

During the following two days we improved on the record by making a first crossing from the Nepal Gap glacier to the Twins glacier, over the ridge connecting the Twins with the Sugar Loaf. It included some splendid mountaineering and gave Reggie Cooke some consolation for his disappointment on Nepal Peak. There is always a large element of uncertainty and suspense about descending an uncharted mountainside, especially when this involves the negotiation of a steep glacier. You may be able to see your way just so far, but then the angle becomes more abrupt and the ground below the change in gradient is hidden from sight; there may be a cliff, or even an overhang, and your further progress may be checked. You may decide to retrace your weary steps, perhaps a very long way back and over the ridge you have crossed. Or you may resolve to dismiss discretion, burn your boats and abseil down the obstacles, hoping for the best. This is what we did that day. We were kept on tenterhooks till the last for, as we plunged on down, roping off small icecliffs and traversing sometimes on the mountainside away to the left to avoid the more precipitous areas of séracs, mists crept up to conceal the flanks of Kangchenjunga; the view down was blotted out. We went on blindly, and then, all of a sudden, our weariness and anxiety were dispelled as we discerned the level moraine of the Twins glacier beneath us, just as the light began to fail. We had won through. 'A memorable day,' I wrote, 'and a magnificent supper of tzampa, pemmican, biscuits and butter.'

To economise our time and efforts Reggie and I now divided; he, with Kikuli and Dawa going up the Twins glacier to prospect the approaches to the North Col; myself, with Pasang Sherpa, to make the third ascent of the Zemu La between Kangchenjunga and Simvo. My mini-expedition with Pasang was the coldest and most arduous in all my experience. The snow surface was atrocious; for three days we wallowed, sinking through the surface crust to our waists and occasionally, where there were boulders on the medial moraine, even up to our shoulders. It was killing work, but could have been made much easier had we brought skis or racquettes with us, as we had on Peak 36. The wind, fortunately behind us, gave us no rest and more than once I had to remove my boots and restore circulation to my numbed feet.

But our arrival on that 19,275-feet col was one of those great moments. It is a striking place, a narrow thread of ice linking two great ridges, one thrown down by Kangchenjunga, the other from Simvo. And the view was tremendous. Southwards I looked across the greens and browns of Sikkhim to Darjeeling, fifty miles away but clearly visible. In the opposite direction, my possessive eyes rested on Nepal Peak beyond the big ice buttress of the 'Bauer' Spur, by which the Germans had carved their way to a height of 25,000 feet beneath the North Ridge of Kangchenjunga six years before.

At the foot of the final slopes below the col, Pasang and I had been surprised to come across what appeared to be human tracks, raised above the surface by the action of the wind. An odd feature of this discovery was that one pair of steps was larger than the other. And they were placed side by side, despite the danger of breaking through into one of the numerous crevasses. That evening I noted: 'The Germans again!' But Grob later insisted that they had not climbed to, or near the Zemu La. Moreover, Pasang had shown signs of alarm and foreboding. 'Those are Yeti tracks,' he said. The Sherpas are superstitious; they associate the sighting of a Yeti with impending misfortune. And indeed Pasang went on to tell me of one such sighting in 1931 in this same area, which had been followed by the deaths of a German climber, Schaller, and a Sherpa, members of Bauer's party. Maybe Pasang was right.

Tilman, who visited the Zemu glacier in 1938, also saw tracks below the Zemu La. From accounts which I have had since from travellers and local people in the eastern Himalaya, I am more persuaded now than I was at that first sighting that the Yeti, if he does not now exist, has done so at some period. From the descriptions given to me by the anthropologist Professor Tombazi of Athens, in 1939, the acting Abbot of Tengpoche monastery in 1953 and a yakherd at Chukkung, beneath Lhotse twenty years later, it would seem to be a large ape, possibly an orang-utan, which may have existed until fairly recent times in small numbers, at the upper limits of the forests in a few Himalayan valleys. And the memory of these creatures has been perpetuated in stories told to the children in Sherpa homes. Indeed, Tenzing once told me of one such story related to him by his father, during his boyhood in the village of Thami.

There was a happy reunion at Base Camp. Reggie had reached a point only a few hundred feet below the North Col, abandoning the route only when he was convinced, by the bombardment of ice and stones which swept the slope, that it would not be suitable as a line of communications for a serious assault on the mountain. Joy had made a journey to Lachen with two of our Sherpas who had been seriously ill and needed to be evacuated; it had been a big responsibility on her part to do this on her own. By the same kind of coincidence as had occurred twice during the Peak 36 Expedition, all three parties arrived, after an absence of nine days, within five minutes of one another. It was good to rest and tidy up and, above all, to eat big meals for the next forty-eight hours. Everyone was in good spirits with the prospect of returning to the valleys. We also had visitors: a raven and several choughs were with us regularly and a covey of snow cocks glided by. A lämmergeier was picking at the carcase of a sheep which we had slaughtered after our arrival and kept in cold storage for this occasion.

For the last time we separated again. Reggie and I climbed for the second time towards the Simvo La. At the beginning of our stay beside the Zemu glacier we had returned from this easy climb defeated and dispirited from the sheer physical struggle of ploughing through the appallingly deep and heavy snow. This time it was no better, but we were much fitter. Next morning I bade him farewell on the 18,500-feet pass, for his adventurous journey down the Passanram gorge, a feat only accomplished once before and, as was usual at that time in these parts, by a German, Karl Wien; Pasang Kikuli and Dawa Thondup went with him. A blanket of cloud filled the valley, hiding all but the higher summits, among them Siniolchu (22,600 feet) which towered above me, resplendent in the early sunlight. Reggie's party were to run out of food while hacking their way through the dense rhododendron forest and might never have come through but for the incredible fortune of finding a wild pig, which had recently fallen from a cliff and lay dead at their feet. Joy and I returned to Lachen with the main body of porters carrying the expedition luggage.

Our journey homewards was full of delights. It was good to meet other people again. We came upon a party of Tibetans, pig-tailed and high-booted with tall fur-rimmed hats; among them a woman playing a fascinating string instrument with an ingenious wooden bird affixed, so that it bobbed up and down to the movements of her bowstring. We were permanently hungry, but almost out of cash; we took our meals cheaply in the local bastis, choosing only what we could afford, counting our pennies. 'Black tea, flat breads, suet meat rolls and macaroni' was our staple diet. In Gangtok, capital of the State, we watched the annual ceremony of dancing by the monks in front of the monastery, before an audience which included the Maharaja. There was a sumptuous dinner: 'soup, beckti, goose, wild pig, strawberries, cheese, fruit and coffee' which fortunately, we did not have to pay for, being the Maharaja's guests.

This made us eager to see more monasteries and, to finish the journey, we decided to cross the centre of the little mountain principality and pay a 'flying visit' to the monasteries of Pemionche and Rinchinpong. My diary entry was apt for, superbly fit, we covered forty miles in two days, climbing 13,000 feet and descending as much again; I noted with evident satisfaction that our rate of climb was even faster than had been mine in the Pir Panjal in 1932 – 2,500 feet in an hour. On 5th December we arrived in Darjeeling: 'the end of the expedition and the regrets are only just beginning'. But the regrets were not on account of what we might have done; they were for what we were leaving behind. In fact, we felt well satisfied with the results. We had achieved both our general and our particular objectives; we had reached conclusions, negative in both respects, on the questions of high climbing in winter, and about the North Col of Kangchenjunga as a route to its summit. We had recorded two first and one second ascents, climbed up to all three of the major cols on ridges surrounding the Zemu glacier system. Most important of all, we had been a happy band of friends. It was for the pleasure of travelling again with Dawa Thondup, Pasang Kikuli, Pasang Sherpa, Hawang and Ang Kitar that we looked forward to other visits to Sikkhim.

By 1973 thirty-six years later, four Everest expeditions had come to the same conclusions as we had reached regarding the overwhelming handicaps of cold and wind in mid-winter. On the other hand, Bonington discovered, as Bauer and Schmaderer had done, that climbing in the late monsoon up to the early days of October, provides a good chance for the mountaineer at high altitude.

In 1938 I was stationed in the District of Rangpur, in North Bengal. At the end of the monsoon rains you could see Kangchenjunga from our garden at a distance of nearly a hundred miles. Its base was obscured by haze; the mountain appeared to be floating, an etherial magnet, in the sky. It was irresistible, and we continued our exploration of Sikkhim during short periods of leave. At the end of 1938, entrusting our three months' old daughter Sally to the care of friends, Mr and Mrs Jameson, a judge and his wife at Rangneet tea estate, Joy and I met Dawa Thondup, Pasang Kikuli, Pasang Sherpa and Hawang at Ghoom and, amid great rejoicing, made a rapid march along the high ridge which marks the western frontier of Sikkhim with Nepal. This time we were making for the southern precincts of Kangchenjunga, our objective being the 16,000-feet Guicha La. Our familiar enemy the west wind was in terrific form, but this did not diminish our sense of elation as we traversed those frozen, grassy highlands at 13,000 feet north of Phalut, with the great mountain looming larger almost hour by hour. From the Guicha La we looked straight across the Talung glacier to the Zemu La, where Pasang and I had stood just over a year previously. Straight above us was a most attractive peak, Pandim 22,010 feet; it would be well worth another expedition to climb it.

On our way back, partly from sheer youthful exuberance, partly because we were pressed for time and, most of all, in Joy's view, because we were now anxious and responsible parents, we covered prodigious distances at irrational speeds, to reach Darjeeling. In military parlance, it was both a raid and a reconnaissance, and it was highly satisfying.

A few months later, this time with only three days to spare during a break at Easter time, we made a wild dash for Sikkhim's eastern frontier with Tibet. From Gangtok we climbed twenty-four miles up the trade route towards the Natu La, caught a glimpse of Chomulhari from the pass early next morning before the swirling mists drew a veil over that splendid summit; traversed southwards on the Sikkhim side of the border to visit the main crossing of the yak caravans, the Jelep La, and returned via Kalimpong to pick up our baby daughter. In those three days we had travelled eighty miles over the mountains involving us in 10,000 feet of climbing and descents. Both of us damaged our feet as we slid and skidded in the pouring rain down the endless, slippery, cobbled track. One night we slept in a butcher's shop, its walls decorated with blood-bespattered ancient newspapers, the gory carcases visible in an adjacent cubicle. It was a joyful kind of madness, in which the snags, recorded in my diary as 'misery' and 'no ordinary torture', were nicely balanced against the fun. It was in this area that fierce fighting took place during the Chinese invasion across that frontier in 1962. Roads have been built to replace the rough bridle tracks; Kalimpong is a garrison town. When Joy and I next visited the place in 1973 with mountaineers who were attending an international conference in Darjeeling, Kalimpong had lost the charm it possessed in its heyday; with the pony caravans and their noisy, pig-tailed drivers dicing away their earnings on the side-walks; with the shrill voices of Tibetan women attractive with their earrings and necklaces of coral and turquoise.

The opportunity for that promised closer look at Pandim came in 1940. Though about to be posted back to my regiment, I was that May still serving with the District Intelligence Branch in Midnapur. The date of my departure for the war in Europe was uncertain: I was able to get the Presidency and Assam District to agree to let me go on one more expedition, on condition that I would be within five days' recall. So Joy and I, with Reggie Cooke and his wife Margaret set off for the Parek Chu to attempt Pandim, arranging a chain of fast runners, located in various hamlets along our route, who would relay any messages from Headquarters: the timing would be crucial, but it seemed worth the gamble. In 1938 I had made a close inspection of the approaches to the South Ridge of the peak which, if it were reached, offered a promising route to the top, though some hard climbing might be involved.

Once again, Dawa and Pasang Sherpa were awaiting us, and with them was Reggie Cooke's companion on Kabru, Ang Tharkay; by that time he was one of the leading Sherpa climbers. But two friends were not there. In 1939 an American expedition had attempted K2 in the Karakoram. One of their team, Wolfe, had remained at the highest camp, a very sick man; Pasang Kikuli and Ang Kitar had volunteered to climb up from the Base Camp and bring him down. None of them was seen again. It was an act of gallantry, typical of them and of their people, which would have won them medals in a war. We missed them sadly. I think there is little doubt that, had he lived, Pasang Kikuli would be numbered with Tenzing Norkay, Pasang Dawa Lama, Dawa Tenzing and Ang Tharkay among the foremost men of his race. Like these others he was a natural mountaineer, swift and sure-footed on steep ground, quick and intelligent in learning the skills of tackling steep snow and ice. And unlike most Sherpas of that period, Kikuli seemed to enjoy mountaineering for its own sake.

This time, our march was up the valley of the Rangit rather than along the Sandakphu ridge; as we climbed up the path past Yoksam and Dzongri to descend into the Parek Chu, the rhododendrons — magenta, scarlet, mauve, pink and white — were in their full glory. And I will never forget our first sighting of that miracle of loveliness, a fire-tailed, yellow-backed sunbird, flitting from blossom to blossom and trilling a song as he flew.

Anxious as we were about the possibility of recall, we lost no time in beginning the climbing programme. Opposite Pandim, and immediately above our Base Camp rose another good-looking mountain named Forked Peak, 20,000 feet. It, too was still unclimbed and we welcomed the opportunity of attempting a first ascent which would also provide us with a grandstand view of the major peak on the other side of the valley. We climbed by a rock buttress and its flanking couloir to a point above the rocks where open glaciated slopes appeared to lead, without technical difficulties, towards the summit;

the weather was bad and we had little view ahead. We dumped our loads: a tent and stores, intending to return and finish the climb in the next two days; the height must have been about 18,000 feet. When we returned to base we were tired; it had been a long hard day's climbing. But we were very confident about the prospects, ate our supper and were about to turn in.

Outside the mess tent we heard a long, low whistle. There were a number of woodcock around, whirring and drumming in the dark; was it a bird? But I had ominous forebodings. A moment later Sonam, one of our men, put his head into the tent and handed me a message. It was the order of recall. The date was 13th May.

The order was dated three days previously, which left me only two days in which to fulfil my promise to return within a five-day limit. There were about seventy miles between us and Darjeeling, and some very big hills along the route. We had a hasty conference; I must leave at once, and Joy insisted on coming with me; Pasang would accompany us. Reggie and Margaret sensibly decided to stay. There was no time to lose and, despite our weariness we packed at once and started off in the darkness for Dzongri, ten miles away. When we arrived on the little alp 2,000 feet above the valley at midnight, we were very tired indeed and, without ceremony, we went into one of the huts occupied by yak herdsmen. The scene was weird. Around a big fire in the centre of the floor space were seven or eight wild-looking men and some women and children; one or two men rose to view the strangers, their naked torses shining whitely in the flames of the fire. Outside the circle were a number of young yaks. Somehow we wriggled our way through the tangle of men and beasts and found space near the blaze and, to the unmelodious music of yak grunts and human snores contrived to get a few hours' sleep.

Next day we covered a distance of thirty miles, which, even now, I think of as best forgotten. A single redeeming feature of wild rasp-berry bushes laden with ripe yellow fruit was nearly our undoing, for there was not a minute to spare. That night we knocked on the door of the police head-constable at the village of Gesing; the good people inside, seeing our sorry state, made space on a table for us to lie and bathe the numerous leech bites on our feet; they made us tea, cooked rice and eggs, and generally ministered to our needs. On 15th May after putting a further thirty miles behind us—the last ten, we were not ashamed to accept, on ponies up the hill from Singla Bazar—we arrived at North Point. There were still two hours to go before the five days grace was up. I spoke on the telephone to the appropriate staff officer at District Headquarters. 'Oh,' was the casual reply, 'there is no question of an immediate sailing, but you will embark at the earliest

public opportunity.' It was a cold douche of anticlimax after that
marathon journey. But my diary noted, 'The world news which greets
us makes any personal feelings of this sort, out of place.' The news was
the evacuation of the British Army from the beaches at Dunkirk, and
the triumphal entry of the Germans into Paris.

But when, three weeks later, I sailed from Bombay on my way to
Europe, I could not help thinking ruefully of the private opportunities
we had missed during those weeks of waiting.

4

War in the Mountains

1941–44

I WAS IN DARJEELING IN SEPTEMBER 1938 WHEN NEVILLE Chamberlain returned to London from Munich waving a piece of paper signed by Hitler's hand, purporting to reassure his anxious fellow countrymen that a war was not imminent. Joy was expecting our first baby in a few days' time; I suppose the relief we felt was shared by millions of others, some of whom were only too ready later on to condemn the Prime Minister for being naïve and pusillanimous. Like all those others, we wanted to be assured of a secure future together, with our future family. Two days later, when Sally was born in the early hours of 1st October, I left the hospital and walked at great speed the ten miles distance and 3,000 feet in height between the town and Tiger Hill, to view Everest, eighty miles away to the west, in the clear morning air at the end of the monsoon rains. It was as good a place as any to offer a prayer of thankfulness for the safe arrival of our first-born child, and for the promise of peace. No thought was in my mind at that moment that Everest would become a highlight and a turning point in my life one day.

Such were my thoughts that autumn. Yet when, less than a year afterwards, I listened to the awesome words of the Prime Minister over the radio, informing the nation that we were committed to war against fascism, I suppose I was no different from any other self-respecting soldier in wanting to be involved in the fighting. While waiting on a troopship in the Clyde on 3rd September, laden with reinforcements for the Middle East where the 1st Battalion of my regiment was stationed, I remember my bitter disappointment when a launch came alongside with orders to transfer me to the M.V. *Britannic*, bound for India. My instructions were to resume my secondment to the Police in Bengal. Here indeed, was the converse of the sentiments which had moved me to leave that same battalion in Calcutta nearly six years previously, for active service with the Police! At Port Said I went ashore and telephoned the Commanding Officer,

begging him to arrange for me to join the battalion then and there.
'Strafer' Gott, who was to command an Army Corps in the desert and
died tragically in an air crash after being nominated to take over
Eighth Army, was typically positive and provocative. He pointed out
that there would be no time for him to obtain official permission and
that, in any case, it would probably be refused; but 'why not jump
ship and come along. We could fit you in and would be delighted to
have you back. We will sort out the awkward questions afterwards.'

But with the initiative and the challenge in my hands, I let it pass.
Natural caution and an innate respect for orders prevailed and I
returned to Bengal for a while. Life for me in the war and afterwards
would have been very different, had I taken the plunge and absconded
during that brief spell ashore. But looking back, I have only one regret
about exchanging the experiences which I missed for those I was to
gain—this was the chance to serve under 'Strafer' Gott. He was a
brilliant and lovable person, one of the few members of our mess in
those dreary days in Calcutta whose buoyancy, intellect and wide
interests dispersed my unsocial gloom and drew me out of self-
imposed seclusion.

On my return from India in 1940 there was another period of
frustrating service in England with two of our territorial battalions
which, to the chagrin of all the fine men who served in them, were
never to see battle. Training was, of course, the order of the day; we
lived in hopes that it would be put to good use on the field of war. It
provided me with the opportunity to experiment in my own belief in
the value of mountain terrain for preparing troops for war. I wrote a
memorandum on the wider theme of its relevance to the education of
youth in general, drawing also on my experience with the young
Bengali schoolboys, and sent it to the President of the Alpine Club,
Geoffrey Winthrop Young. From him it found its way into the
hands of Dr Kurt Hahn, then headmaster of Gordonstoun, a passionate
advocate of developing outdoor adventurous activities as personal
tests of youthful character, which he believed to be a necessary complement to the academic aspects of formal education. That document
was to become a passport for me to another sphere of activity later
on.

I was tremendously impressed, both by the performance and self-
confidence of our soldiers when called on to negotiate steep and rugged
mountain country on Cader Idris without any previous experience.
I carried the experiment further by persuading the Brigade Commander to let me run a toughening course for elected officers and men
in Snowdonia, with the help of a few mountaineers. They included

Wilfrid Noyce and Alfred Bridge. Wilfrid, a schoolmaster, was at the beginning of the war one of our leading young climbers. Alf Bridge, a generation older than Wilf, belonged to a select côterie of outstanding rock climbers who were in the van of working-class interest in the sport. Tough, uncompromising and intensely loyal to his friends, he talked the language of the soldiers and fired them with his passionate love of the hills. We did some hair-raising things on that course; its success was a revelation to everyone who took part. Not least surprising at that time was the notion that all of us, ranging in rank from trooper to major, could happily share the crowded hospitality of a small mountain hut for a fortnight, eating, sleeping, sharing washing up and all the other chores together, with no detriment to essential discipline. Indeed, I allowed the patrols into which the field training was organised to choose their own leaders irrespective of rank, but with due regard to their natural competence to cope with the testing conditions of wind and weather on this precipitous mountain terrain; some officers found themselves under command of other ranks for the duration of the course. An abundance of mutual understanding and respect was generated in those two weeks, and some surprising friendships were made. I am not sure how much the Brigadier knew about this; I doubt if he would have approved.

That course at Helyg set me thinking about mountain warfare and its relevance to the future course of the war. In the Far East some of our troops under Orde Wingate had become specialists in jungle fighting. In the Middle East our forces were seasoned experts in mechanical manoeuvre across the waste lands of the Western Desert. The Special Services Brigade was undergoing thorough training for the future assault landings somewhere along the coasts of Europe. When the time came to invade that continent most of the terrain in the West could doubtless have been simulated by the varieties of countryside in Britain. But there were other possible fronts such as Italy and Greece, picturesquely, if inaccurately, described by Churchill as the 'soft underbelly' of the Axis, where specialised training and equipment suitable for traversing high mountains might be an important, perhaps decisive factor. When the opportunity came to fill a vacancy as Chief Instructor of the Commando Mountain and Snow Warfare Centre at Braemar I jumped at the chance. I was accepted.

The Commandant of the Centre was the famous mountaineer Frank Smythe, who had taken a notable part in all the attempts on Everest from 1933 onwards. He was author of a number of books about his climbs and expeditions. Frank and I got on well together and I think we made an effective partnership. He was a gentle, most unwarlike character, whose main contribution to the work at the Centre was to impart his deep, poetic love of the mountains to the tough, high-spirited wearers of the Green Beret. His achievements and his obvious sincerity won him respect, the more so because of his very slight physique. I was able to supply an element of military pragmatism to the exercises, which had tended to be rather aimless mountain walks which Frank so much enjoyed. With the support of an able and enthusiastic staff, I put the commando units which were sent to us through a rigorous programme of all the permutations of action in all weathers and seasons, both on ski and on foot, in the testing vastness of the Cairngorms. The troops moaned a little about the amount of plodding through endless heather-clad slopes to reach the high tops—some wit planted notices along the road up the River Dee announcing 'you are now in Khad* country'. But at the end of each period of six weeks, which included a spell of rock-climbing in North Wales, they were good movers over difficult ground, inured to the vagaries of weather and cold temperatures, knowledgeable about Arctic rations and mountain equipment; superbly fit; their leaders skilled in navigation through dense mist and driving snow. Above all, they had had their baptism of that most demoralising element, the wind. I have experienced high winds in the Arctic and the Himalayas; I know of nothing worse than being caught in a blizzard on the peaks and plateaux of the Cairngorms. On one occasion, climbing up the track towards Loch Etchachan carrying skis and heavy packs, I saw Frank Smythe, who was just ahead of me, lifted off his feet by a violent gust and deposited several yards away in the burn. Those troops would have been a match for the crack German Gebirgstruppen and the Italian Alpini. Their toughness was, of course, an asset for no matter what eventuality, but it seemed, to those of us who trained them, wasteful of our skills and efforts that the commando units, and the 52nd Highland Division which was trained on Speeside, should have been committed to the battles in the low country of the Netherlands. I strongly argued for the formation of a mountain division reserved for use in an appropriate theatre of war on the European mainland. But the War Office, while drawing on the experience of our Centre to produce manuals in the subject, was not persuaded that this kind of training had any practical bearing on the conduct of the war, except as a kind of recreational morale-booster.

Six weeks after leaving Braemar, in September 1943, I was to find myself in one of those theatres of war where sufficient troops with that special experience and equipment might have made a significant

* An Urdu word meaning mountain slope which became slang for any hill, with a strong overtone of dislike for plodding up it, among British troops in India.

difference to the strategy and conduct of the campaign. I fought in
Italy with the 2nd battalion of my regiment in the bridgehead when
Eighth Army reached the River Sangro in November 1943 and was
stopped in its tracks by the German 65th Division on the high ridge
to the north, on which stood the towns of Lanciano and Guardiagrele:
this was the Gustav Line, which stretched across the spine of the
Apennines between the mouth of the Garigliano river and Pescara.
On this line the American Fifth Army on the left and Eighth Army on
the right of the peninsula were held firmly throughout that winter and
well into the spring of 1944. Shortly afterwards I took over command
of our 11th Battalion on the banks of the Garigliano river, in the
sector allotted to 1st British Division, under American Army command. We spent a most uncomfortable few months there, our forward
positions on the bare rocky slopes of Monte Damiano, impeded by
wire obstacles and numerous minefields; our every movement was
wide open to the watchful enemy observation posts. We were
spectators of the bloody battles to the east, where American, New
Zealand, British and Indian troops successively stormed, and failed to
dislodge the defenders of the fortress monastery above the town of
Cassino, at the junction of the Liri and Garigliano rivers. The 4th
Indian Division alone suffered more than 4,000 casualties in their
assaults. All along that well-prepared line the Germans withstood
every attempt by the Allied forces to advance. Trained and equipped
for fighting in conventional warfare as they were, scope for manoeuvre
appeared to be restricted to flanking movements from the sea. A
limited 'right hook' movement was made by landings on the Adriatic
coast at Termoli, and a much more ambitious operation was mounted
at Anzio; they failed to roll back the Germans and to enable the Allies
to liberate Rome by Christmas, which Montgomery had confidently
predicted.

   Much opinion has been expended on Anzio. Churchill was very
disappointed. 'I had thought we would be landing a wildcat ashore,'
he wrote. 'All we got was a stranded whale.' To the soldier at the
front, battles are perceived only in a tactical sense; they are either won
or lost. We viewed Anzio as a costly failure at the time. I remember
Monty, his famous fly-whisk in hand, paying a flying visit to the 4th
Armoured Brigade to give one of his morale-boosting exposés of the
situation and his future intentions. To the soldiers gathered round, he
said that but for the extra pressure exerted on the right flank of the
peninsula when the Anzio battle became critical, which drew off
German armour from the beleaguered bridgehead, the crisis might have
ended disastrously. The inference was obvious, and it certainly helped us
to feel, as soldiers of that proud Army, even more superior than before.

5

Strategically, it was seen differently. Sir David Hunt, an Oxford historian serving at that time on General Alexander's headquarters in Caserta (whom I was to meet later as High Commissioner in Lagos during the Nigerian civil war), points out in his book *A Don at War* that the landing fulfilled the requirements of Allied strategy. It was all a part of the grand design that as many German divisions as possible should be drawn down into Italy, and held there so as to reduce the available build-up of enemy forces to oppose the forthcoming invasion of the continent of Europe over the Normandy beaches. From that angle, Anzio can be seen as having served a useful, though costly purpose. So did Cassino and all the many small-scale battles and aggressive patrolling along the eighty-five miles of the Gustav Line. The speed of our advance, including the political and moral value of an early capture of Rome, was not a matter of paramount importance. Indeed, it did not matter how much we got bogged down in the appalling mud of the Italian plains and valleys, how unable we were to cope with the exposed and rocky mountainsides during that terrible winter, provided that we were engaging the enemy actively and keeping him committed to opposing us. Of course, that depended on German willingness to stand and fight on ground which gave every advantage to the defenders; the Germans obliged with strong and skilful opposition.

In my opinion, however, it was precisely in this small-scale warfare over that rugged terrain — especially on Monte Cassino — that strong contingents of mountain troops would have made all the difference; they would have added a dimension of mobility in that inhospitable land. They would have been able to skirmish ahead and loosen the tight hold of the Germans on the heights, thus assisting the inexperienced American formations and our own troops, too. Our First and Eighth Armies, confident though they were, flushed with the great victory which culminated at Tunis, were also battle weary; they were unused to fighting in the enclosed European countryside; they were quite unversed and unequipped for manoeuvre on steep mountains. I remember the deprecating attitude of some officers in the 2nd battalion of my regiment when I joined them at Taranto, full of enthusiasm to teach them the battle training skills we had been perfecting at home in preparation for fighting in Europe; they did not want to know.

In the following spring the Goumiers of the French Algerian Corps, mountain men of the Atlas range and fresh from North Africa, swept through those same defences on the Aurunci and Lopini mountains which we had found impregnable in the course of one murderous night. True, there were a few units in the theatre, including the Lovat

Scouts who had trained in the Rockies and the 2/7 Gurkhas who had undergone training in the Lebanon similar to that provided at our Braemar Centre; but they were too few and were never employed as mountain troops. It went against the grain for me to see the Gurkha soldiers careering around in Bren-gun carriers. They were certainly adept in the use of modern military equipment, but their native skills of swift manoeuvre on steep slopes and their familiarity with the mountain landscape, were largely wasted. A Greek mountain brigade which had fought in the Western Desert, was being prepared for operations in Italy, when it mutinied; I was to make its acquaintance later. This formation did, eventually, take part in the Italian campaign, but too late to make any impact on the impasse we had reached in the winter and spring of 1943–44. It is my belief that, with more units prepared for the conditions in central Italy, to infiltrate, silent and sure-footed, in those rugged mountains and break through the crust of the German defences, Anzio would not have been necessary and the campaign might have been completed more quickly.

Before leaving the subject of the two sea landings, I was myself involved in an incident, in the immediate aftermath of the Termoli battle, which might have had considerable repercussions, not least on myself. While moving up to the River Sangro the advance of 4th Light Armoured Brigade was held by the fighting ahead of us. I decided to make use of the pause by giving some shooting practice to the anti-tank guns of my battalion; what better than the charred hulks of three or four German tanks on the high ground overlooking the coastal plain? All went well with the exercise until one shot, missing its target, continued its journey uninterrupted until it struck the coast road at a bend, about half a mile away. A few minutes later the Army Commander passed that exact spot, on his way up to the front. I trembled to think of the scene which would have ensued, but for the fortuitous mistiming of that misdirected shot.

The following spring was, for me, the least disagreeable period in my limited experience of actual warfare. My battalion had been moved across to the eastern part of the front. I was back not far from the bridgehead area which held poignant memories for me from the previous winter, memories of several hazardous crossings of the swollen river, its bridges shattered, under heavy fire. This time, we were positioned further up the Sangro at a bend in the river immediately beneath the imposing, snow-covered summits of the Monte della Maiella, which rises over 9,000 feet above the sea. Here indeed, was mountainous terrain which presented me with a challenge! The opportunity was the greater in that I was given command of a larger force holding a 'gap' of over twenty miles of the Apennines between the American and British armies. I handed over my battalion temporarily to my second-in-command, Major Tom Mitford, and established my headquarters in the little hill-top town of Casoli.

'D' Force comprised, in addition to my own battalion, two armoured-car regiments, a machine-gun battalion, a field regiment of artillery, an Indian mountain artillery regiment and a light anti-aircraft battery. It was an extraordinarily inappropriate array to confront a high mountain defended by genuine mountain men. Apart from the Indian gunners, none had any experience of fighting in this type of country and, needless to say, the armoured cars were precious little use. We were, to say the least of it, operating at a disadvantage in numbers and expertise, compared with our adversaries, the German 5th Mountain Division which was mainly composed of Austrians and Bavarians. They occupied the heights and were supplied by rope hoists in their rear. With such a thinly held front, we spent an entertaining two months. When I arrived the Germans held the initiative, patrolling deeply into our positions at night. It was my intention to turn the tables on them. Both sides realised that, until there had been a major break-through by the Allies on the west end of the Gustav Line, there would be no fundamental change on our front.

In addition to stepping up our patrolling on the front held by my battalion, with an occasional reconnaissance in force, I decided to indulge in a limited form of amateur mountain warfare. The Central India Horse had not adjusted themselves well to the European terrain in winter conditions, after rendering excellent service in the Desert, so I withdrew them from the left of the Maiella Gap and replaced them with the Household Cavalry Regiment. Armoured cars having no rôle for the time being, I told its commanding officer, Lieut.-Colonel Eric Gooch, that his troops must take to their feet and train to be mountaineers within a fortnight. Understandably, he did not like the order and there were even dark hints that a complaint might be sent to the King. But I had no doubt that they would rise to the occasion, and of course they did so magnificently. I sent for a cadre of American instructors from a mountain school at Benevento and watched with a quasi-professional eye as those sergeants, naturalised immigrants from the Austrian Alps, gave basic training in movement on steep ground to the cavaliers of His Majesty's mounted bodyguard. At the end of the course patrols from the unit were probing upwards towards the distant summit, playing a game of hide and seek at altitude with the real professionals. Communications with headquarters of the regiment at the mouth of the Fara Gorge were primitive. The wireless sets of the unit being much too heavy for the purpose, simple flare signals were used; even carrier pigeons were resorted to! These amateurs had some interesting encounters with the enemy, and I well remember the day when a patrol came down the mountain in triumph after ambushing an observation post, carrying an officer's cap, complete with Edelweiss insignia, as proof of their exploit.

Years later, while travelling by train to Vienna to give a lecture about the first ascent of Everest, I sat opposite a man wearing a small Edelweiss badge in his button-hole. We fell into conversation. Where was I during the war? I mentioned Italy. So was he. Where were we both in the spring of 1944? Why, he was in the village of Pennapiedemonte, which nestles at the foot of the Maiella and was immediately in front of my battalion. More than once, on that wide open front, I had wandered alone up the mountain slopes behind that enemy-held village, trying to observe signs of activity. My companion and I clasped each other warmly by the hand; he unpinned his badge and handed it to me. It was the insignia of the Old Comrades of the élite Gebirgstruppen.

When the battalion was ordered out of the line in June 1944 to rest and retrain in Palestine, we paraded for an inspection by Lieut.-General Charles Allfrey, commanding the 5th Corps. The parade ground was a field outside the little town of Scerni above the south bank of the Sangro which, with the 2nd Battalion, I had entered in triumph eight months earlier, after a hard-fought action to dislodge the German rearguards. We were doubtless in need of a rest after that relentless period of relative stalemate; but our morale was high. We looked forward to returning in time for the big advance which was now confidently anticipated, and to having a share in the victory ahead. Little did we know that the battalion would soon be confronted with very different problems, in a different country.

For myself, I was sorry to exchange the mountains of central Italy for heat and dust in the Levant. Spring-time had been beautiful on the slopes of the Maiella: the primroses provided a link with home and the wild cyclamen were a reminder of my childhood in the woods beside the Lake of Thun. Like others, I had experienced the kindness of villagers and farmers as we advanced towards the Gustav Line. I remembered the rapturous reception by the townspeople when we entered Scerni as conquerors. I had witnessed the sad little groups of dust-stained, forlorn and fear-stricken refugees plodding southwards along the roads and rail tracks as we moved north. And there were those brown-uniformed partisans who worked with us on the mountain front during the spring; a trifle unpredictable and decidedly unorthodox, their enthusiasm and courage commanded our respect. Everyone who had seen and experienced these things must have felt, as I did, some commitment to the Italian people.

And there was more to it than that. From both battalions I had lost good companions in the fighting along this river, some of whose graves were in a temporary war cemetery near the village. There was a feeling of being parted from them afresh. War is a crude, uncivilised business, but for those involved in the fighting, life at the personal level gives real meaning to the word brotherhood. Men are less selfish, more caring, more united across the social barriers which tend to divide us in peace. It matters not whether that bond is made by a belief in the ideals of destroying evil, or of defending basic freedoms, or by the more gut instincts of survival, of protecting hearth and home. Regardless of the motives which kept us together under discipline, all were agreed on the need to see it through and finish the job. Would that we could re-capture that spirit today! It was Kurt Hahn who once observed: 'We have yet, in peace, to find the moral equivalent of war'.

Nor, I think, was there any hatred towards the enemy soldiers opposing us. That was the property of the propagandists in the home country. Often there was respect, as was accorded to General Rommel in the Western Desert; sometimes there was gratitude, as when the German artillery ceased a heavy bombardment of the shattered bridge across the Sangro to allow me to bring back our dead and wounded during a carry of supplies into the bridgehead. And did the men of both sides not share a common sweetheart to console their separation from women in, Lili Marlene?

5

Crisis in Greece

1944–46

INTENT AS WE HAD BEEN ON THE BATTALION'S CONTINUING
commitment to the campaign in Italy, from which our sojourn among
the orange groves near Gaza was, to the best of our knowledge, no
more than a breathing space, an urgent order from Cairo in early
September to move across the wreck-strewn battlefields of the Western
Desert, surround and disarm a mutinous Greek Brigade, came as
something of an eye-opener to the turn of events on the enemy-
occupied mainland of Greece. I knew little about the situation in that
country. I was, of course, aware of the whirlwind advance of the Axis
armies three years earlier during which a British force, despatched in
haste, in inadequate strength and too late to stem the German tide, had
been swept back into the rescuing arms of the Royal Navy. But few
people knew of Force 133 which was operating with rival partisan
bands in the mountainous interior of the country, keeping them
supplied with money, equipment and arms, air-dropped into their
hide-outs. Fewer still were aware of the conflicting political allegiances
and aims of these freedom fighters, or Andartes, and their increasing
tendency to involve themselves with fighting one another instead of
harassing the Germans. Least understood of all was the intention of a
left-wing political group, the National Liberation Front (EAM) to
seize power through the medium of their own guerrilla forces, the
Greek Popular Liberation Army (ELAS), supplant the government in
exile and prevent the holding of free elections. Despite the clearest
possible warnings given by Brigadier Myers, senior British liaison
officer with the Andartes, British military and political leaders appeared
to be confident that, whatever complications might develop later on
with the Soviet Union over its future policies, all parties would
co-operate in Greece in the initial stages of its liberation and until
elections could take place; credence had been given to this by an
agreement between the guerrilla generals Sarafis and Zervas with the
Supreme Allied Commander, at Caserta in Italy.

The Greek Mountain Brigade, against which we were required to act, had fought in the desert and was being prepared for operations in Italy. But like units of the Greek navy in Alexandria, it had been infiltrated by left-wing agents from the mainland and in April 1944 it mutinied, declaring in favour of the communist government in hiding, EAM. It had promptly been ordered by the Commander-in-Chief to move to an isolated camp near Sollum, and had done so. But with the impending Allied return to Greece it was deemed prudent to disarm this formation. As we advanced at high speed across the desert road and crept forward in darkness to throw a cordon round the camp, my mind went back to those anti-terrorist operations in Bengal; there were, of course, several important differences, not the least being that instead of one or two desperadoes armed with revolvers, we might find ourselves at some disadvantage against 4,500 armed Greeks. The event was sheer bathos. Private Andriotis who had instigated the revolt, agreed to hand over the weapons and to the transfer of the formation to the Delta where there could be security vetting, sorting out of loyalists from revolutionaries and a reforming of the brigade for future action.

That, we thought, was that; but we were wrong. A few days later I was supervising the loading of the battalion's equipment and vehicles on to the cruiser *Black Prince* in Alexandria harbour. We were bound for Piraeus, port of Athens. I cannot say we were pleased by the prospect. It seemed like a sick joke to have pamphlets handed out to all ranks entitled 'You are Lucky to be going to Greece', just as though it was a peace-time commercial cruise. For me, fate seemed to point to a different destiny. At the moment of embarkation, a signal from Italy assigned me to the command of the 11th Indian Infantry Brigade, in the 4th Indian Division, under whose orders I had served as Commander of 'D' Force in the Maiella Gap. So I was going back to Italy after all. Sad though I felt to be taking leave of my battalion, it was most satisfactory to be getting back to the real business of war, and to the liberation of Italy.

It was doubly pleasing that I was to serve with Indians and Gurkha troops whose soldierly qualities I had learned to appreciate in Bengal. There, like the British, they had been aliens in a strange land, but with Bengalis and Britons alike they had had a marvellous gift for making friends and making the best of a difficult and distasteful job. I liked and admired them and consider our magnificent Indian Army the finest legacy we left to that country when our rule ended in 1945. Now I was especially happy to be attached to a division whose name had become a by-word for gallantry; against the Italians in Eritrea, the Afrika Korps in the Desert and on the slopes of Monastery Hill above

Cassino. I was proud to wear the Red Eagle flash on my battle-dress. But I had hardly assumed command when the division, resting near Lake Trasimeno after fighting on the Gothic Line, was ordered to Greece in its turn. After three weeks during which I had begun to organise a training programme, hopefully for the final advance to the Alps, I was flying instead to Athens to receive instructions from General Scobie. The Germans had finally withdrawn from Greece, leaving a trail of devastation behind them. Aid and relief were the order of the day. Our task would be to support an organisation known as Military Liaison (Greece) in helping the authorities establish administrative order and in bringing supplies to meet the desperate needs of the people whose country had been ravaged, and many of whom were in destitution and near-starvation. My troops were to come directly under Scobie's command in 3 Corps, spread over a distance of nearly 200 miles on the islands and along the coastline of western Greece from Corfu to the Peloponnese.

For a formation with the fighting reputation of the 4th Indian Division, this was a tall order. When I returned to Athens on 10th October after a five-day reconnaissance of my area I told Scobie, with due deference but with all the emphasis I could command, that his orders were not only tall but unwise in the extreme. I had travelled by naval launch to Préveza in the north and back by jeep through the hinterland of Epirus, down to Pyrgos on the coast of the Peloponnese, and back to my intended headquarters at Patras. Everywhere I had received clear indications, from the earnest warnings of friendly Greeks and the menacing attitudes of others, that a civil war was imminent. The atmosphere was very different from the rejoicings which had greeted Lord Jellicoe and his Commandos when they had landed at Patras in September. In the circumstances, to disperse my soldiers in penny packets over that wide area with such poor communications, would be asking for trouble. Scobie, a soldier of great serenity, was tolerant and calm. He said little. His Brigadier General Staff, Robin Springhall, was voluble and emphatic; dispersal among the population was of fundamental importance to the job we had to do. Scobie expressed his confidence that a recent agreement at Caserta between the opposing guerrilla generals, Sarafis of ELAS and Zervas of the Greek National Republican League (EDES), to co-operate under British command, would be honoured by both sides. The Andartes had agreed to disarm and hand over their para-military rôle in the areas they controlled to the new National Guard, which was about to be formed by calling up the Class of 1936.

There was nothing for it but to comply with my orders; but Scobie suggested that I have a word with General Sarafis himself. So off I went to Thebes, where he was addressing a meeting. At this long interval of time my recollection is of a lean, earnest, somewhat insignificant-looking person, humourless but with a burning fire within him as he harangued the crowd from a balcony overlooking the town square. His appearance and character certainly contrasted strongly with the rival partisan leader, General Zervas, whom I met a few days later: a big bluff, laughing cavalier. Notwithstanding the name of the organisation he served, Napoleon Zervas had by that time agreed to support the provisional government of Mr Papandreou, and favoured the return of the King from exile; and Sarafis must have given me some reassurance to allay my fears. By 17th November my Brigade had sailed across the Adriatic and were moving into their scattered positions. The 2nd Camerons went to the Pyrgos area in the south; the 3rd/12th Royal Frontier Force Rifles into the troubled region north of the Gulf of Corinth. Detachments of gunners were despatched to the large islands of Zante and Cephalonia and the 2nd/7th Gurkha Rifles were shortly to be moved from Taranto to Corfu and Préveza, far away in the north. In Patras, with only the 21st Field Company, Royal Engineers and some supporting units, I had no effective reserves; it was a set-up wholly abhorrent to any commander of fighting troops. Colonel Kenneth Hicks arrived with a detachment as Head of Military Liaison (Greece), to advise and administer to the needs of the long-suffering Greek people. But that samaritan task was to wait awhile, for events began to move with startling speed and suddenness.

On 24th November 900 men answered the call-up into the National Guard in Patras; there were similar responses in Pyrgos, Agrinion and elsewhere in Greece. Scobie fixed 1st December as the date for the new Guard to take over responsibility for law and order and for ELAS and the Andartes to disarm. A conference was called with Colonel Tsikliteras, the commander of 3rd ELAS Division and his staff, which included the somewhat sinister, bearded figure of his political Commissar, Capitanos Akritis, who was all too evidently in effective charge of the party. It was arranged that the new Guard should be accommodated in the same barracks in the town with 12th Regiment of ELAS; indeed, there was nowhere else for them to stay during the short interval before they took over. Hardly had that been done when the ELAS leaders began to procrastinate about the delivery of their arms. They said they had received no instructions from their own headquarters; then they claimed to have orders contrary to what had been agreed at Caserta. But Colonel Tsikliteras insisted that 'we are all working in close harmony'; it was agreed to defer the date for hand-over until 4th December and to seek urgent clarification. I liked the grizzled little Colonel, a first-war veteran who wore the ribbon of the British Distinguished Service Order on his battle-dress; but our daily conferences were becoming increasingly tense and acrimonious, a sketch made by a member of my staff of that time testifies to this.

The crux came on the night of 3rd/4th December when ELAS troops, acting in concert with their forces in Pyrgos, Agrinion and elsewhere, surrounded the defenceless National Guardsmen and carried them off to the mountains. In the morning I found no more than 150 frightened men out of the full complement of 900 who had come to the colours. It was a treacherous trick, carried out in total bad faith.

Shortly after the ELAS coup I received the following signal from Athens. It was from General Scobie and dated 5th December:

> Prime Minister has given me full powers to act in dispelling communist attempt to overthrow constitutional government. This power I delegate to you as far as your area is concerned. If possible arrest forthwith ring leaders of ELAS and politicals. I rely on you to prevent to utmost any bloodshed, but you have authority to use force should this be necessary.

I immediately planned a coup myself for the following day, which had a touch of skulduggery about it, but which seemed justified in the circumstances. I invited Colonel Tsikliteras, Capitanos Akritis and the ELAS staff to yet another conference. Some of my staff officers took up positions outside the door of my office, their revolvers at the ready; my own weapon was in the drawer of my desk. The ELAS men arrived jubilant; they had heard an announcement by the BBC that Papandreou's government had resigned and it was clear that they foresaw a political victory for the National Liberation Front (EAM) which would pre-empt further British grounds for resisting ELAS. Hurriedly I withdrew to consult with my Brigade Major. If the story were true (it turned out to be false), it would be unwise in the extreme to proceed with our plan. The conference was resumed and somehow I managed to raise a few mundane matters before we adjourned; the whole episode must have seemed somewhat suspicious to the ELAS officers. I signalled to Athens my decision not to carry out the arrests; it was now late at night and I have seldom felt so exhausted, defeated and deflated.

Later that night, and on the following day, came three return signals* which, while they were a welcome endorsement of my decision,

* The following are extracts from the signals from 3 Corps: 'Relations with ELAS should not repeat not be broken off until you consider it necessary . . .' (6th December); 'Until further notice no repeat no attempts to be made to disarm Andartes who are not disturbing the peace . . .' (7th December); 'As far as disarming is concerned, we are not in a position to enforce this at the moment . . .' (7th December).

required me to return to ELAS any arms which might have been seized. In fact this had also occurred both at Pyrgos and Agrinion; my headquarters had not been able to communicate my own decision in time to prevent it. Humiliation was added to deflation.

But if the pretence was over, the perilous situation in which we were placed was all too apparent. Militarily, we soldiers in Greece were unimportant to the Allied advance against the retreating and hard-pressed German armies elsewhere in southern Europe. But in political terms it was quite a different matter. The central issue was the outcome of the fighting in Athens, where the new provisional Government had only just been set up when hostilities had broken out. If the leftist guerrilla forces, which had heavily infiltrated the city and its port, were to win the battle for Athens, the consequences might not have affected the main war effort against the Germans; but it would have severely damaged British prestige, making it impossible to honour our pledge that the Greek people should freely choose their form of government at the polling booths, and decide on the controversial question of the return of their King George II, by a plebiscite. And there were further implications only now beginning to be understood by those of us who had daily contacts with the communist capitanios commissars, for the eventual balance of power in the aftermath of the war. My Brigade, and 7th Brigade in Macedonia, had the thankless but vitally important task of holding firm, without allowing our-selves to be embroiled in actions which might call for outside support. No reinforcements could be spared for Greece; and in Greece, Athens was the focus of the communist drive for power. We in the West were in a military backwater, conducting an essential political side-show on the Greek stage. It was also a lonely as well as a thankless job. There was little understanding of our position among the public in both Britain and the United States at that time. The British press was openly critical of the actions they were reporting by British and Indian forces against the gallant partisans. For the first, but not the last time, I was to realise the harm which the media can cause to the morale of men carrying out a difficult, dangerous and vital job during a critical situation; especially when pressmen are not, for whatever reasons, kept fully informed about the background and the reasons for the policy being pursued. It is a situation I have since experienced in the course of missions to both Nigeria and Northern Ireland.

In this extraordinary situation, the following six weeks were the most tense and difficult period in all my experience, before or since. There was no question of reinforcements. Parts of the 4th Indian Division, with some Commandos and an armoured brigade (which included the battalion I had been commanding only a matter of weeks

previously) were engaged in a desperate struggle to defend the remaining few streets in Athens not already in ELAS hands. Difficult though
physical communication had now become, an Auster aircraft was sent
to fetch me to Athens, where Scobie impressed on me the need to
avoid getting involved in fighting, subject only to securing my own
force. A subsequent signal confirming this conversation read: 'Maintain status quo as far as possible without prejudice to security.'

Tolerance of provocation almost beyond endurance was the hallmark of the greatness displayed by all ranks during those anxious and
delicate times. I can only hope to impart some sense of the extent to
which our patience was tested by a scant narrative of events. The first
task, after the dramatic coup by ELAS against the National Guard, was
to concentrate my troops in Patras. I ordered 2nd Camerons to come
in from Pyrgos, where Lieut.-Colonel Alistair Noble and his 'Jocks'
had behaved splendidly under very trying circumstances. I called back
an RAF detachment from the airfield at Araxos, abandoning two large
passenger aircraft to be sabotaged by the Andartes. The Gurkhas, who
were about to embark for the north, came across directly from
Taranto. The position of the Royal Frontier Force Regiment was more
difficult. Separated from Patras by the Gulf of Corinth, they were in
the process of moving into widely spaced positions in Epirus, which
was a main stronghold of ELAS and EAM. There, the guerrilla
leaders had made no pretence of recognising the orders to hand over
to the National Guard. I ordered the battalion to concentrate at the
little port of Missolonghi, where Byron is revered for his part in
supporting the Greeks during the first stage of their liberation wars
against the Turks. This was the signal for open hostilities to be launched
against the unit to which, as ELAS had doubtless appreciated, I had no
power to respond effectively. Beginning with an ambush of a patrol,
and the capture of a party which went forward under a white flag to
negotiate its release, two ships were blown up in the entrance channel
to the port, which had been cleared of mines by our Navy only a
few days previously. Casualties were heavy: more than 120 dead and
wounded, and 100 vehicles and much other equipment lost. On 13th
December ELAS opened a full-scale attack on the depleted battalion.
A signal from 3 Corps authorised me to withdraw it with such
shipping as might be available in Patras harbour; none could be
spared from the Piraeus. The Naval Officer-in-Charge of the port,
Captain Kalergis, rose magnificently to the occasion and we managed
with a motley assortment of caiques and other small craft to bring the
men across the Gulf with their weapons, but without their vehicles, in
the course of the day. It marked a very low point in our misfortunes,
which continued to pile up. I sent caiques to the offshore islands of

Zante and Cephalonia to fetch the detachments posted there, only to learn that they had been captured, in one case after a fight in which they had suffered casualties. It was rumoured that they were somewhere in the mountains on the mainland.

I now had my force concentrated in Patras, where the Military Liaison Group joined me to form PATFORCE, with Colonel Hicks as my second-in-command; all thought of relief aid had, perforce, been postponed. For the following month we lived in a strange world of make-believe. We took up defensive positions to protect ourselves and defend the town from an external attack; for we were surrounded by the 3rd Division of ELAS, which was well equipped with captured German and Italian weapons and had some artillery trained on our strong-points. But the defence of Patras was illusory. A signal from Scobie had warned me that 'many of the opposition are not in uniform and may mingle with and fire from crowds containing women and children and considerable skill will be required by local commanders in dealing with them'. Indeed, I had reliable reports that within Patras some 2,000 armed guerrillas had infiltrated, masquerading as civilians; the citizens were in constant fear. Many acts of intimidation and several murders were reported. A general strike was called; when volunteers came forward to man essential services they were threatened and intimidated. Marches and demonstrations, in which we British were vilified and the provisional government denounced, were almost a daily occurrence. Almost every day, in observation of my orders to maintain the status quo, I held conferences with the ELAS leaders and the leftist police commander; on the agenda were shooting incidents, including the occasional attack on British and Indian soldiers. To test the seriousness of our opponents, I ordered units to drive outside the town and carry out field training; when they were attacked training had to be suspended as a matter of expediency.

One major issue was the future of a local security battalion, part of a force originally set up by the Germans to maintain order in the occupied areas, some of whose members were accused of atrocities against their fellow Greeks. They were the special object of hatred for ELAS. I went out to the camp where they were held under a joint guard of British and ELAS troops at Pappas Point, and was appalled by the inhuman conditions prevailing there. Among the prisoners was the young and attractive wife of a captive officer, who did her pathetic best to give me the glad eye, in the hope that I would extract her from the squalor in which she lay—doubtless in return for services to be rendered. But to add a Greek mistress to my entourage in those circumstances—or in any event—would hardly have been appropriate. I decided to move the whole party from the camp into Patras, for their own protection and to improve their lot. Those against whom war crimes were alleged went into the local orphanage, the remainder were taken good care of by the Gurkhas. But feeling in the town ran high; the convoy bringing them in was fired on. Fearing that it might spark off serious disorder I signalled Scobie, asking that the whole unit be taken away from Western Greece, some to await trial, the rest to fend for themselves in an area where they were not known. I must admit to having derived pleasure at the fury of Capitanos Akritis after he had seen the ship conveying the security men sailing westwards out of the Gulf.

If the troops were models of puzzled patience, the inhabitants were stoic beyond words. Knowing that the enemy was in their midst, they none the less carried on with their daily jobs. They turned out in thousands to mourn the victims of the landing craft and the *Empire Dace* which had been sunk at Missolonghi. I treasure a resolution signed by the Nomarch, and the town council, expressing gratitude and confidence in the troops and their commanders. I wish I had kept the moving petition I was given, signed by fifty per cent of the male population, after addressing the public from a balcony at the Town Hall. My speech reassuring the people of continuing Allied support in those difficult days was greeted with fervent, almost frenzied, enthusiasm.

The other essential element in the situation was the forbearance of the soldiers themselves. In a number of statements made to them I tried to convey the importance of what would today be called playing it cool, and doing everything possible, consistent with our obligations, to avoid bloodshed.

As a corollary to courage and forbearance, there was the need to build good relations between the soldiers and the civilians. As Christmas approached, units were encouraged to give parties and organise dances to which the citizens were invited. £200 was raised in response to an appeal by the Nomarch, to provide food for the poor. It was ironic, as we discovered only later, that food was being requisitioned by ELAS at the same time, from those very same people, to provide rations for their men. In a gesture to reduce tension at a higher level I entertained the Bishop of Patras, the Nomarch and other senior officials, as well as Colonel Tsikliteras, Commander of the 3rd ELAS Division, at dinner. At a Christmas party given by the garrison for a thousand Greek children there were three Father Christmases: Kenneth Hicks, an Indian commanding officer and myself. We put on a performance of *Red Riding Hood*, in which the Big Bad Wolf was played by a Gurkha who brandished his kukri at the moment when he leapt out of Grandmother's bed. It was the ultimate in make believe.

On New Year's Day 1945 I held a parade of the whole garrison, accepting the risk that our defensive positions might be seized by ELAS during our absence. Apart from marking the occasion, the idea was to raise morale among the troops and to strengthen the fortitude of the Greek population, who turned out in large numbers to witness the ceremony. An unforgettable sight was our British Consul, Ken Nicholl in morning dress and top hat, at the saluting base. It was all part of the game of winning the war of nerves.

The exercise of command can be a lonely business. In those fraught days my constant companion was my Greek interpreter, Captain George Athenogenes. Tall, thin, bespectacled and scholarly, George was an untypical warrior. He was the product of a wealthy Athenian family whose roots were in trade. He was a most cultured and civilised man, possessed of both humour and good horse sense. Wherever I went George was at my side, performing the exacting task of turning one language into another with swift and easy fluency. His knowledge of the crisis in his country, his understanding of his own people, were an incalculable source of help to me in assessing up the situation and sizing up personalities. He knew as well as I did that, had we failed in our objective of repairing the foundations of democracy in Greece, his life would have been forfeit.

It was also a saving grace for me to be made welcome among friendly Greek officials, officers and civilians, in the beleaguered town. I would pay calls on Bishop Theoklitos and the Nomarch, sipping turkish coffee and ouzo while we discussed the grave situation. There were occasional calls of a purely social nature. Captain Leon Kalergis and his wife Penelope made me feel at home in their cosy flat within the precincts of the port. Charming hosts too were Mr and Mrs Lekas, whose seventeen-year-old daughter Daisy had been awarded a BEM for her gallantry in coming openly into a street when the first British officer entered the town in September 1944. As he advanced with a patrol, she called out in English, 'Don't go any further. The Germans are just ahead in the main square.' She then insisted in leading the patrol to a house where they could fire on the enemy. Daisy worked for Kenneth Hicks in Military Liaison (Greece); later they were to get married. Perhaps most of all I enjoyed relaxing over a glass of Mavro-daphne with our Consul, Ken Nicholl. He had produced a touch of pure Gilbertian farce when he arrived on being posted to Patras, at the height of our troubles in a destroyer; he was wearing plus-fours, carrying a golf bag and he demanded to know the whereabouts of the local course.

But behind the genuine caring, the building of confidence, the fun and games and such gentle moments as these, there was serious business to attend to. Scobie had signalled to warn me to expect further pressures and threats, and to be 'prepared for any eventualities'. Aside from standing firm, there were also the alternative possibilities that we might be allowed to attack, or ordered to withdraw from Patras. Despite the hazardous nature of the journey, I tried to send Kenneth Hicks to Athens in a Fairchild aircraft which I had requested from 3 Corps headquarters. It crashed on take-off from the makeshift air strip constructed by my Sappers, so I asked Admiral Mansfield, commanding a naval force, CS 15, which had just arrived, to despatch him by destroyer. But the ship sailed into a minefield as night was falling and had to turn back before it could reach the open sea; it was also blowing a gale at the time. Next morning the intrepid Colonel Hicks again boarded an aircraft which had been sent from Athens to replace the wrecked plane; this time he was able to take off without mishap. I had asked him to press once again for reinforcements in order to enable me to break the deadlock in our situation. Permission was not granted. Instead the Brigadier, General Staff, came round in the same destroyer with orders to prepare for evacuation by sea. It was vitally important that such a withdrawal should remain top secret, unknown both to ELAS and to our own men. Both for our sakes and that of the civilian population I prayed that it should not come to pass.

In the event, my proposed alternative was adopted. By 10th January the tide had turned in the capital. A British division and a new Corps Headquarters had arrived from Italy; this and a hammering by the RAF, forced the demoralised and exhausted ELAS troops to retreat in disorder towards the north, carrying many hostages with them. The cruiser *Ajax*, with three attendant destroyers, one of which had been so helpful in an attempt to take Hicks as envoy to Athens, were standing off Patras under the command of Rear-Admiral Jack Mansfield. The presence of this famous ship gave a tremendous boost to our morale; I shall not forget the sheer bliss of relaxing over a drink, after a hot bath in the Admiral's comfortable quarters.

On 5th January I received a signal from Lieut.-General 'Ginger' Hawksworth, commanding 3 Corps, stating that reinforcements in the shape of a British infantry brigade, two squadrons of tanks and a new National Guard battalion were on their way by sea. Brigadier Adam Block, commanding the 139th Brigade was my senior and would take command of operations on arrival. It was tremendous. But it was also a bitter moment for me, despite a typically generous and appreciative personal message from General Scobie. I had planned this moment of the break-out, which would release our pent-up energies and avenge the insults and injuries we had endured all these past months. It was hard to have the leadership and the initiative taken from me at that time. Admiral Mansfield who, with his ships' companies, had been a marvellous source of encouragement to me and my sorely tried soldiers ashore, was furious. He had a penchant for writing doggerel verse and promptly composed a poem full of bitter sarcasm, of which it is perhaps as well that I remember only the appalling pun 'Block blocks Hunt's elevation to Peer'. But it mattered not at all to the outcome.

Adam Block was a man of little finesse and no nonsense. He was not attuned to the niceties of personal relationships which I had been at pains to cultivate during the all-important state of seige and status quo. Unlike ourselves, he and his troops had come straight from a triumphant hot pursuit of the ELAS forces retreating pell-mell from the capital city. Brushing aside the protests of Colonel Tsikliteras and the entreaties of the Bishop and the Nomarch, fearful as they were about the prospect of bloodshed among the innocent civilians, Block brusquely ordered the ELAS commander to get his disguised guerrillas out of the town and his units away from their positions surrounding the enclave by first light on the following morning. And he gave me free rein to implement my long-laid plans.

Before dawn on 11th January tanks were rumbling along the road from Patras leading towards the wine factory at Klauss, where we knew the main ELAS force and headquarters were situated. A wide encircling movement was beginning along the coastal road on both sides, which was to be directed inland after some miles so as to sweep our opponents within a huge circle in the mountains; two destroyers steamed eastwards along the Gulf, bombarding the retreating guerrillas. The Cameron Highlanders drove straight into the hills to relieve Kalavrita, a mountain village which had been martyred by the Germans and which was a symbol of the true Greek resistance. To the Gurkhas I gave a special rôle: that of making a rapid night march to bypass Klauss and cut off the retreat of the main ELAS force as the tanks approached. Those swift, silent little men did a most effective job; on a small scale, it was the story of the Goums on the Garigliano all over again. Late in the afternoon of January 11th I rode on a tank into the wine factory and drank a toast to our success.

It was all over and we began to smarten ourselves up before embarking for Salonica, where we were to rejoin the Division in their task of searching for hidden arms, helping the Greek authorities to restore order, distributing the deferred supplies in the villages and training for active operations in the real war. I was to have the opportunity to set up a school on Mount Olympus where I could indulge my enthusiasm for training for mountain warfare. During those last days in Western Greece I had the satisfaction of crossing the Gulf in a landing craft to pick up my officers and men who had been taken prisoner off the islands of Zante and Cephalonia; they had some extraordinary tales to tell. And it was flattering to receive a visit from Harold Macmillan, the Government's Minister-Resident in Cairo, who spoke warmly about the value of our stand at Patras.

In a Special Order of the Day to all ranks at the conclusion of our task in Western Greece I praised them for their forbearance under continual tension, but equally for their behaviour when the long awaited chance came for action. 'I want you to know, therefore, that my admiration for your conduct during this second phase has been no less great than it was during the first. The speed and skill with which you have carried out tasks, both mounted and on foot, on mountain roads and in difficult terrain, in the worst possible conditions of weather, have been magnificent.' And so it was. We had been involved in a Balkan brawl not of our making, with far wider ramifications. We had played it cool and had won a battle of nerves.

With Theo Nicholson, a Lovat Scout who had been one of our instructors at the Commando Mountain School in Scotland and who had joined the Brigade staff, I climbed up to the snow level in the Panachaikon mountains carrying some skis we had managed to borrow in the town. Turning downhill we glided swiftly towards the blue water of the Gulf of Corinth. It was just what was needed to forget, for a while, the stresses of those three months.

Holy and Roman Mountains

1945–48

FOR THOSE WHO DO NOT WANT TO CLIMB, ONE MOUNTAIN MAY look very like any other. To the mountaineer, who insists on getting on to intimate terms with steep ice and rock, especially on the less frequented and preferably unclimbed peaks, each mountain is different. But mountaineers do not always enjoy climbing because of technical difficulties alone; a mountain may be easy, its attractions different. So, at any rate, I found with the mountains I climbed in Greece and Egypt.

In 1945 Mount Olympus was still relatively unknown. First climbed in 1913 by two Swiss, long after the age of exploration in the Western Alps had ended, it was rarely visited, partly because the principal hazards lay in being captured and possibly killed by bandits who had their hiding places in its forests. Fortunately that risk had receded at the end of the last war, but there remained the menace, not to be under-rated, of being savaged by fierce shepherds' dogs; it was as well to make the climb with a stout stick and a pocketful of stones.

After the Rebellion I spent fifteen months with the 4th Indian Division in Northern Greece. Our main tasks were to round up armed bands, search for caches of weapons and ammunition and distribute food in the destitute villages. But there was also time to organise training in my Brigade; Mount Olympus was an ideal area in which to initiate my soldiers in mountaincraft. I had also hoped to establish a ski school in the Vermion mountains, part of the main Pindus range. I went there with Ted Peck, our Consul in Salonika and, using borrowed skis, we spent two days exploring the region, in poor weather. Those plans had to be abandoned when we learned of the existence of communist guerrillas in the area. So mountain warfare training, mainly in the basic skills but also for such experience of skiing as could be had in the sheltered gullies where the snow remained through June and July, was concentrated on the upper reaches of Olympus.

By great good fortune the Lovat Scouts, who took the place of the 2nd Cameron Highlanders as the British unit in the Brigade after we had moved from Patras, had trained in the Canadian Rockies under Frank Smythe after we had both left the Commando Snow and Mountain Warfare Centre in 1942. They arrived from Italy complete with their special clothing and equipment and, no less fortunately, their skis. So my old friend from Braemar days, Theo Nicholson, was the ideal man to run the training course. The gear was all to hand. It only remained to acquire a suitable base on the mountain. I approached the President of the Hellenic Alpine Club, who generously offered the use of their club hut, situated at 7,000 feet at the top of the tree-line on the eastern side of Olympus and 2,500 feet beneath the summits; it was an ideal site.

Theo applied himself with his usual enthusiasm to the four courses we ran during that summer. In turn, Gurkhas, Pathans, Dogras and Jocks went up the mountain, escaping from the fierce heat around the Bay of Salonika and, though they may have learnt little about mountain warfare, they hugely enjoyed each others' company. Theo told me that caste and other religious scruples were set aside; Hindus and Muslims bargained jointly with the shepherds for goats, then killed, cooked and ate them together, sitting round a camp fire outside the mountain hut. The men of 2nd/7th Gurkha Rifles, natural mountaineers, had previously undergone a course in the mountains of the Lebanon similar to those we ran from Braemar; they were by far the best performers on steep ground; their speed both up and downhill was phenomenal. The courses provided me with a carefully contrived excuse to absent myself from my headquarters in Salonika at least once a month, ostensibly to inspect the training. In those days when the roads were potholed and the bridges blown, it was a rough ride in a jeep of three or four hours to reach Litokhoron, a village near the edge of the sea, at the foot of the Mavrolongos glen, up which a path leads towards the summits. A mule track, at that time unfit even for a jeep, took me up some 2,000 feet through thorn and holly scrub to a little grassy alp named Stavros, where shepherds grazed their sheep and goats in summer, and where the first encounters were likely to take place with those ferocious dogs. This was always a climb in burning heat; but soon afterwards came a welcome change as I entered dense forests of firs, beech and walnut trees which flank the glen on its northern side. The walk would become wholly delightful, the path traversing high above the torrent, full of pools and rushing water. The scenery was rugged, with limestone crags and pinnacles towering on either side of the valley, to which clung a few hardy pine trees. I first went that way in May, on a reconnaissance. At that time of year the beech trees were a wonderful sight: in the full, dark foliage of an English summer low down in the glen, their leaves shading off into the delicate pale green of early springtime two or three thousand feet higher up. Beyond, at the limit of the forest, the branches stood naked, the tree trunks still buried deep in snow. I passed a point where one path branches off, to descend into the bottom of the valley where stood the ruins of a fine monastery, Ayios Ioannis. Like almost everything else in that tortured land, it had been wantonly destroyed by the Germans before they pulled out of Greece. While there may have been military sense in the shattered bridges, the burnt rolling stock and twisted rail tracks, for this vandalism there was no excuse.

I was now ten miles from Litokhoron and the path had become less distinct. I descended into the gorge to a place named Prioni, much haunted by shepherds; it is the last place where running water can be had. We used to find the sheepdogs particularly frightening here and I must admit that the owners also looked daunting characters, wild and uncouth. They did nothing to protect us, and several of my men were bitten while trying to cross the stream to the southern side. The final rise of 3,000 feet was quite an effort through the thinning trees, but I was always happy there. The scenery became alpine in character, snow was banked beside the path. Alpine flowers were springing up beneath the limestone boulders. Spotted eagles and griffon vultures were often circling overhead; the summit crags were in view. There was that indefinable feeling of being more free as I climbed higher. Though the top was not much more than an hour's walk away, the snow was still deep from here onwards and, with eight hours climbing behind me, it was enough for that first day.

The peaks of Olympus: Profitias Elias (on which there stands a small chapel); Stefani which, although it is not the highest point, is called the Throne of Zeus; Mitika (The Needle) which is the summit (9,574 feet); and further south, Skala and Skolian, all form a magnificent amphitheatre of limestone cliffs around the head of the Tigania glen, on the west flank of the mountain. There is some fine climbing to be had hereabouts; but for me, at that time, it was enough to be there, the war over, the Rebellion crushed, my worries far below and out of mind. Westwards I gazed towards the wooded skyline of the Pindus range, along which I would walk one day; maybe the germ of that adventure was sown as I sat there on the summit rocks of Mitika. And eastwards was the shimmering expanse of the Aegean Sea. In the horizon haze I would just discern the three peninsulas of Kalkhidiki, from the farthest of which rose high above the water the dark silhouette of a perfect snow-capped pyramid; it was the Holy Mountain of Athos.

At the beginning of August with George Athenogenes and my batman

Rifleman Hull I boarded a caique at Nea Potidhia, one of the refugee settlements which were built in the 1920s for Greeks who had escaped from Asia Minor after the destruction of Smyrna by Kemal Ataturk. We were heading for Mount Athos, or more accurately, the Akti peninsula, which is a self-governing state under the spiritual authority of the Patriarch in Istanbul and under the political protection of Greece. Its unique feature is its exclusive masculinity; no female of any species is permitted to go there and even eggs have to be imported.

It was getting dark and it was dangerous to round the southern tip of Sithonia, central prong of the three peninsulas, until next morning

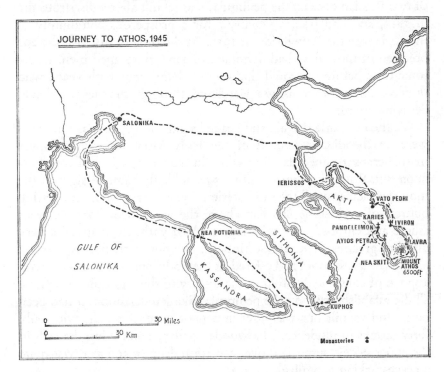

because of still unswept enemy mines. So we headed off for a tiny land-locked harbour, Kuphos, almost at the extremity of Sithonia. Chugging across the gulf in the gathering darkness we watched the glow of many forest fires, common enough occurrences in Greece at that time of year, lighting up the hilly skyline to the north. It was nearly midnight when the caique turned into the little cove between a Scylla and Charibdis of vertical promontories guarding the entrance on either hand. A caique is not designed for comfort, so we took our bedding and spread it out on the sand. Lulled by the gentle lapping of the water, we were soon asleep. At sunrise the bay was so beautiful with its sheltered waters reflecting the rim of golden strand that I

would gladly have lingered. But I had given myself only three days'
leave and we would need every minute of that time.

Rounding the point, our little craft rolled and pitched in an uncomfortable swell; I am a poor sailor, and only by concentrating on
imaginary routes up the big cliffs above me, over which three golden
eagles were soaring, was I able to take my mind off my queazy
stomach. But the sea became calmer as we headed eastwards towards
the lee of the Akti peninsula and in two hours we stood off the wooded
coastline opposite the huge Russian monastery of Pandeleimon, its
golden cupolas reflected in the waters at its foot. The monastery, one
of two Russian ones on the peninsula, was rebuilt after a disastrous fire
in 1812, and had been a sanctuary for a prosperous community of
monks before the Revolution of 1917. At the time of my visit the 200
brethren of those days had dwindled to some sixty aged men. It was
some time before we could find one of them, bent with years, who
shuffled ahead of us as we wandered through the neglected and
decaying rooms.

We then embarked again and headed south along the coast; my eyes
were on the distant summit of the Holy Mountain, whose upper
marble crags gleamed dazzling white in the strong glare of the afternoon sun. Rounding a promontory we suddenly came in sight of the
most spectacular of all the monasteries, Ayios Petras, built on a jutting
buttress of rock some 800 feet above the sea. Once more we went
ashore and climbed up a winding, cobbled path, to be given a very
different greeting. The Abbot himself came out to receive us, ushered
us into the guest room and offered us the traditional glass of ouzo with
a spoon of conserve. He told us the history of this most picturesque of
all the establishments on the peninsula; like Pandeleimon, it had been
burnt and rebuilt but was now in a poor state of repair, with only
forty monks in residence. The wooden gallery connecting the cells in
the upper storey, suspended over a vertical drop of 200 feet, was quite
a nerve-racking gangplank to tread.

I wanted above all to climb the mountain, so to shorten the long
climb we landed again, this time at Ayios Pavlou, whence an obliging
Brother led us up behind his mule to a dependency of the lower
monastery, a hermitage named Nea Skiti, about 1,000 feet higher up
the hillside. On our way he persuaded us to pay a call on an ancient
hermit, whom we found engrossed in his life work, sculpting a most
remarkable and intricate ikon. The old man told me that he had
devoted the past fourteen years to this work of art; he enquired
anxiously whether I would buy it, or bring its merits to the notice of
some art collector in Salonika. I admired his skill, but declined the
opportunity to acquire a work which deserved a place in a church or a

museum. In the economic circumstances of the time, there seemed little prospect that he could dispose of it.

Nea Skiti, when we reached it, turned out to be a scattered group of cells, built in a circle around a church. The monks, who live a very simple existence in dire poverty, seldom received visits from strangers; delighted by our arrival, they set about clearing one of the houses for our use, and preparing a modest meal. Sitting that evening on our veranda, trellissed with vines, looking westward to the dark outline of Sithonia silhouetted by the setting sun, I experienced a deep sense of peacefulness. Like very many others, I had been living for several years under a certain amount of stress, practising, in war, the profession for which I had worked and trained in those far-off days which we then called peace, but which even then were anxious times, as the shadow of war grew longer year by year, then month by month. Like others, I had known fear on the battlefield, responsibility in command, the loneliness of separation from a wife and family. All this was commonplace, shared by millions on both sides of the conflict. But very few, I thought, could have experienced this moment of timelessness, or a stepping back in time through some ten centuries. For a few hours the momentum which had carried my life along every 'unforgiving minute' of all the years before had come to rest; and I was still.

It was on 4th August that Hull and I climbed Mount Athos; we set out on our private pilgrimage at 5 a.m. and, climbing in the coolness of the morning, reached the top, 6,500 feet above the sea, soon after 10 a.m. For the final few hundred feet I left the path for the pleasure of scrambling up those white marble slabs which had attracted my attention as we sailed along the coast on the previous afternoon. At the door of the little chapel, which is visited annually at Easter by the more agile monks from all the twenty monasteries on the peninsula, was a cistern of clear, ice-cold water, drained from the melting snow which covers the roof in winter. It was a most welcome find. We stood surrounded by sea on three sides, only the narrow spine of the forested promontory linking us with the mainland of Greece. A summer haze obscured the far-off coast of Asia Minor. We rested for one glorious hour, brewing tea, then ran down fast into the heat below to join George Athenogenes who was waiting for us on the bridle path which traverses the southern end of Akti at a height of about 2,000 feet above the sea. Frequent springs, rare in the Greek highlands, crossed the track and at every turn there was a new perspective to admire in the landscape. Even so, it was difficult not to be aware of the heat and the hard cobblestones beneath our feet. I am ashamed to say that we passed Lavra, the oldest of the monasteries, with no more than an admiring glance and plunged down the steps to its harbour, where our caique was riding at anchor together with a few other fishing boats. The water was so clear that we could see the bottom at thirty feet. We stripped and swam under the shadow of an ancient keep; it was a perfect finish to a memorable day.

Iviron, several miles up the east coast, was to be our shelter for the night and we chugged our way northwards through the limpid water, the low sun now screened from us by the mountain; I made a sketch of it as we went. The views shorewards were no less striking than on the other side of the peninsula and there were signs of human industry: great stacks of timber, the only export from Akti, stored in caves, waited to be shipped to the merchants in Kavalla in exchange for clothing and food. The monastery, an impressive pile of eleventh-century buildings standing at the water's edge, is easier of access to visitors than those at the southern end and is therefore, with Vato Pedhi, the best known of all the monastic communities. Its harbour is the terminal for the only track which, at that time, was almost a road, although it was used only for mule traffic. It leads to the village of Karies, the administrative capital of Akti, seat of the Monastic Council, and residence of both the Greek government administrator and the representative of the Orthodox Patriarch.

After a comfortable night in the well-appointed guest quarters of Iviron where we were attended most hospitably by an English-speaking monk, we walked up to Karies, where the monastic councillors entertained us to lunch. Afterwards we called at a studio where several Fathers were busy painting traditional religious subjects, a stylised, somewhat crude and florid art. There was a small shop where we purchased some beautifully carved crucifixes; we also visited the oldest church on the peninsula, dating from the ninth century. A detachment of the Greek police had recently arrived to fill the place occupied since 1941 by the Germans, whose task, courageously and skilfully foiled by the monks, was to prevent the use of Akti as an escape route for British servicemen left behind in the hasty retreat of the force which Churchill had despatched, too small and too late, in a vain attempt to stem the tide of German invasion, during that low point in the Allied fortunes in 1941.

Back in Iviron, we made a detailed tour of the monastery, took leave of our kindly hosts and sailed for Vato Pedhi, the last big monastery on the east coast. It was appropriate that this should be our final port of call, for Vato Pedhi excels all the others, with the possible exception of Lavra, in the magnificence of its buildings and their setting, and in its ancient treasures. It stands on a high bluff above the water, on steeply rising ground; the courtyard is sharply tilted. The principal church, among several within the precinct, is full of beautiful mosaics and possesses a priceless collection of gold and silverware. The library is the showpiece, with numerous old manuscripts, many of them marvellously illuminated and in an excellent state of preservation. I was especially interested to inspect an eleventh-century reproduction of the original atlas drawn by Stravos in 50 BC, a work quite astonishing in the accuracy of its broad coastal outlines. We also inspected the guest book, which recorded the visit of our King George V as a young lieutenant serving in a British cruiser in 1880. We dined sumptuously with the brethren, sipped Turkish coffee and ouzo on a verandah overlooking the sea, then sailed northwards again as darkness fell. The monks of Vato Pedhi, eating and drinking well, enjoying their cigarettes, were far removed in their cultured ways from the humble hermits who subsist in caves at the southernmost tip of Akti, fed only by baskets lowered down the cliff by monks from Lavra.

It was too far to reach Ierissos, the nearest village in Kalkhidiki and beyond the border of the religious domain. After rounding Cape Platiou we put into a sheltered cove and, as we had done on the first night of our journey, contentedly stretched ourselves out to sleep on the sand.

Domestic and social life on the Suez Canal was very much what one could make of it; in our family centres there was much mutual support and plenty of self-made entertainment. I used our old pre-war gramophone and records to run monthly concerts in the Centre's communal dining hall. One winter Father Christmas arrived, impersonated by myself, riding on a camel; it was Joy's idea and created great excitement for the children. We made miniature gardens on the sand outside our living quarters, mixed with mud from the Sweet Water Canal, and supplied with a strictly controlled water ration. We fertilised our plants with camel dung which we gathered with bucket and spade from the Canal road. The swimming was superb and there were picnics to the beaches at Suez at weekends. I organised a cycle club, hiring a fleet of machines from Ismailia, which was popular with the other ranks; the choice of journeys was limited for they were mainly along the Canal road, on which we were speeded one way and hampered the other by a stiff northerly breeze. A family camp at Famagusta on Cyprus provided a pleasant change of scene and Joy and I spent several delightful weeks during summer holidays in a former monastery at Mesapotamos, in the forest halfway up the southern flanks of the island's Mount Olympus, which had been converted into a simple inn. Those were the happy times before the Enosis movement grew into a state of hostility against the occupying power; when both communities lived overtly at peace with one another and were on good terms with the British. We could entrust our babies to friends in Fayid and could safely leave our two elder children to be cosseted and spoilt by the friendly management at the inn, while we roamed the wooded hills, climbed on the limestone crags of the coast range, with monasteries as our welcoming overnight resting places.

And there were opportunities to travel further afield. In the spring of 1948 a party of eight of us, officers and wives, decided to spend the period of the Easter of the Orthodox church in the monastery of Saint Catherine, among the mountains near the tip of the Sinai peninsula. In more recent times it has become a tourist attraction, easily accessible overland or by air, and the coast of the Gulf of Suez has been developed by the oil industry. But just after the war we were in the happy position of feeling quite intrepid travellers. It was, in fact, an exciting moment when, armed with a permit from the Governor of Sinai and a letter of introduction to the Archbishop resident in the monastery, we set off in two somewhat dilapidated cars hired from an Ismailia taxi firm. We crossed the canal at Kubri, submitted to a rigorous examination of our baggage, and headed south along a rough track.

Our first stop was at Moses Wells, believed also to have the first staging post of the Israelites after their miraculous crossing of the Gulf of Suez. The scenery was monotonous, featureless sand and camel-thorn; but later we entered the Wadi Gharandal, supposedly the Elim of the Old Testament where palm trees grew. Water was already becoming a serious problem, for the car radiators repeatedly boiled over and by the time we arrived at the mining port of Abu Zenima, we had used no less than 24 gallons on refilling them. We began to wonder whether our enterprise bordered on the foolhardy.

Onwards next morning along the coast, over another alleged biblical landmark, the Wilderness of Sin where, we are told, the Israelites murmured against Moses and Aaron. It was bleak enough in motor cars and we rather sympathised with the grumbles of those early trekkers. The landmark we were looking for to turn eastwards from the coast towards the hills was a lone tree—not difficult to identify in that empty landscape, and we turned into strikingly different scenery. The crumbling escarpments we had passed gave place to sounder rock; we entered a narrow gorge, its sides scoured by winter torrents; high cliffs towered above us. It debouched into a wider valley, the Wadi Mukattab, with a small oasis and a Muslim burial ground, at the head of which rose a splendid mountain wall of red granite, the Gebel Banat, for which our maps gave a height of 5,000 feet. We came upon a maze of tracks which were used for mining turquoise in the nearby quarries, and temporarily lost our way by

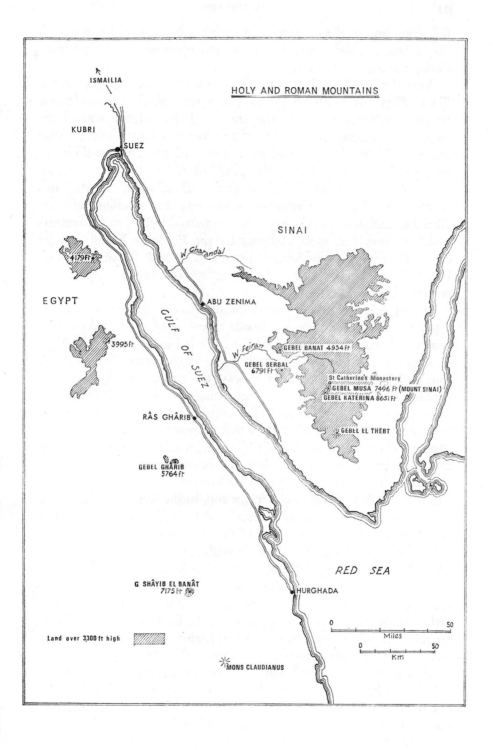

HOLY AND ROMAN MOUNTAINS

ISMAILIA

KUBRI

SUEZ

SINAI

4179Ft

W Gharandal

EGYPT

ABU ZENIMA

GULF OF SUEZ

3995ft

W Feiran

GEBEL BANAT 4954ft

GEBEL SERBAL
6791ft

St Catherine's Monastery
GEBEL MUSA 7496 ft (MOUNT SINAI)
GEBEL KATERINA 8651ft

RÂS GHÂRIB

GEBEL EL THÉBT

GEBEL GHÂRIB
5764ft

RED SEA

G SHÂYIB EL BANÂT
7175 ft

HURGHADA

0   50
Miles

0   50
Km

Land over 3,300 ft high

MONS CLAUDIANUS

following one of these, rather than steering by map and compass; it was a lesson which would be impressed upon us more than once during the trip.

From the Wadi Mukattab we drove on into one of the principal Sinai valleys, the Wadi Feiran, and passed through the first settlement we had encountered since leaving the Canal area. Pharan was a large oasis with running water sufficient to support a large forest of date palms, which reminded me of villages in Baltistan. This would be an excellent base for exploring the peaks of Gebel Banat and Gebal Serbal, on which there should be good rock climbing. In the cliffs around the village were numerous caves, once the dwellings of early Christian anchorites, until they were massacred by the early converts to Islam. Survivors were sheltered by the Emperor Justinian, who caused the monastery of Saint Catherine to be built for that purpose. Pharan is also held to be the place where the Israelites sinned by worshipping the Golden Calf.

Leaving this delectable place we climbed to a wide plateau at about 3,500 feet and turned south towards a barrier of rock peaks which appeared to bar our progress; yet the track led us on, across the Plain of Rephidim, where the Israelites, if the site is correctly identified, fought the Amalekites. Indeed it was easy to conjure up the scene described in Exodus 17 where Moses, standing on the barrier ridge, his arms supported by Aaron and Hur, urged his people on to victory. Soon we reached the Watia Pass, which dramatically cleaves the rocky barrier and leads into the Wadi el Sheikh. Here, not for the first time that day, but inconveniently late, as the sun was setting, we ran repeatedly into soft sand and both car crews had a hard job shoving. But it might have been more serious and, in the last of the light, we turned finally into the Wadi Safsafa: and there, barely visible in the dim light was the monastery, just a kilometre away.

Soon we were beneath its ancient walls, surrounded by a group of friendly monks. One of these, introducing himself as 'Father Nile' examined our credentials and led the way through a low doorway in the north wall. When first constructed as a refuge for the persecuted early Christians there was no entrance to the fortress at ground level; a kind of pulpit, or penthouse, 20 feet higher, on the east side, was used to hoist up the refugees by a rope and basket. We were very weary and had entertained hopes that our hosts might offer us food, as Joy and I had received hospitality in other monasteries. But this was not so; though they grew vegetables in the monastery garden and owned other gardens in the Wadi el Lega and in Pharan, the brethren depended for their own supplies on a monthly consignment from Cairo: in those days before the advent of tourism, no allowance was made for occasional visitors like ourselves. But they gave us the run of their kitchen and soon the girls in our party had a hot meal ready. As we ate and relaxed, Father Nile, who spoke excellent English, regaled us with stories about the monastery.

For Joy and me, a main attraction of this journey was to climb the famed Gebel Musa (7,496 feet), reputedly the Mount Sinai on which Moses received the Ten Commandments from the Almighty. In fact, we had a more ambitious programme: to go on from its summit to climb the highest point in the peninsula, Gebel Katerina (8,651 feet). For the first of these summits we were supposed to be accompanied by one of the monks, but we managed to slip away unnoticed next morning, heading for the famous steps, the painstaking work of holy men over many years which lead the climber, also not without much monotonous labour for there are about 3,500 of them, towards the top. At the top of a gully we reached a small chapel, said to have been used as a refuge by the monks centuries before, when they were smitten by a plague of fleas in the monastery. Soon we came on another chapel, in a hollow in the mountainside, dominated by a single cypress tree; this is built over a cave where Elijah is believed to have sheltered from Jezebel's vengeance after he had slain the priests of Baal, and where he recognised the Lord not in the wind, earthquake or fire, but in the still small voice.

A third chapel, new, brash, ugly and surrounded by a hideous iron railing, greeted us on the top of Gebel Musa. We had come up 3,000 feet, it was still early and we were reasonably fresh. But across a wide valley far beneath us stood our next destination, Gebel Katerina. It was about a thousand feet higher than our position, and seemed to be a very long way off. There was no time to lose and we realised that, by descending into the Wadi el Lega we would be burning our boats. But down we went, following a good track round the south flank of Musa which then descended into the Wadi, past the wall of the garden which is an appendage of the monastery, to the foot of Gebel Katerina; there were now 4,500 feet to climb.

The next three hours required a good deal of dogged determination; but at that time of year the ground was not yet parched; green bushes, which had recently been in flower, covered the sides of the gorge by which we were climbing; quite a variety of birds: crows, rock pigeons, bee-eaters, martins and a grey partridge helped to distract us from the tedium and toil. Unfortunately, it was only on the way down that we discovered a pool of clear, ice-cold water in a cavity cut out underneath a rock close to the path. But it was well worth the effort to have persisted to the top. There, on either hand, were the Gulfs of Suez and Aqaba, the one a long streak of indigo, the other a sheet of silver in the

setting sun; behind the former we could see in dark outline Gebel
Shâyib the highest point on the Egyptian mainland amid the Red Sea
hills. I made a mental note that we should climb that, too. Beyond the
Gulf of Aqaba, well lit by the sun now low in the west, were more
mountains in Saudi Arabia. Much nearer was a bold peak, the Gebel el
Thebt which seemed to outrival Katerina in height.

We would have liked to enter the little summit chapel, for according
to legend it was built over the place – marked by a granite slab in the
form of a human body – where St Catherine was miraculously transported after her martyrdom. She was killed for professing her
Christian faith in Alexandria by barbaric torture on the wheel which is
commemorated for all time by the firework called a Catherine wheel.
Her remains, it is claimed, lie in one of the coffins we saw later in the
monastery church. Catherine the Great of Russia, anxious to obtain
the custody of her illustrious namesake, sent a silver casket, with a
beautifully executed portrait of the saint embossed in enamel on its lid,
to transport the remains to Moscow. It was still in the monastery for
our inspection next day.

Back with our friends later that night, we were able to observe a
procession of monks round the inner walls, symbolising the burial of
Christ. It was a moving and colourful scene; the body represented by a
large tapestry held at its four corners by monks, the procession led by
novices supporting a big lantern, the whole illuminated by tapers held
by the congregation. In daylight next day we were taken on a tour of
the buildings by Father Nile: first to the fifth-century church dating,
like the walls of the fortress, back to its origin in the time of Justinian.
Its appearance is spoilt by a tin roof and peeling plaster, which masks
the old granite walls, but it houses the three coffins provided for the
saint, one of which was pointed out to us as that containing her mortal
remains. Adjoining it is an even more ancient chapel, built, we were
told, by Helena mother of Constantine the Great over the roots of the
Burning Bush. 'And there,' said Father Nile, 'is the Burning Bush
itself.' True, it must have indeed been a plant of great antiquity, for its
trunk had grown through those ancient walls; it was still a flourishing
tree, some of whose trefoil leaves are before me as I write.

The relative newness of the library building did not match its
priceless contents: the Codex Syriaticus; a copy of the Codex
Siniaticus – the original is in the British Museum: Bibles of the fourth
and eleventh centuries; an Order, over the signature of Bonaparte and
dated 1799 during his occupation of Egypt, exempting the Fathers from
taxation. We made a rather less enjoyable visit to the charnel house in
the garden, which, to solve the problem of lack of soil in these rocky
wadis, is used to hold the bones of all monks of the Sinai Order after

St Catherine's monastery with the Gebal Katerina behind left, and, right, the Gebal Musa, Mount Sinai.

The Roman quarry on the slopes of Wadi Um Hussein, Joy seated on a column of red porphyry.

Evans and Bourdillon setting out on the first summit bid in the 1953 Everest expedition.

a sufficient spell of internment in the limited graveyard until they can
be removed to make room for more corpses. There, row upon row,
neatly stacked separately, skulls in one place, the bones piled together
to a height of about six feet in another were many hundreds of forebears of the living generation of monks who were our kindly hosts.
One skeleton alone was intact: that of St Stephen, not the martyr whom
St Paul watched being stoned, but a fourth-century inmate of the
monastery, and he was seated in a corner upon a chair, still clothed in
his original garments. We were glad to emerge from this dismal scene
into the well-watered, but neglected garden; and later, to witness the
interesting and ancient custom of distribution of bread, baked in the
monastic kitchen, to bedouin, from settlements in neighbouring
valleys. A number stood beneath the walls to greet the Fathers on the
occasion of their Easter celebrations. But over the centuries, we were
told, it had been the practice to lower the bread in baskets two or three
times a week from the penthouse on the wall which had formerly
served as the only entrance. It sounded like some kind of Danegeld to
keep on friendly terms with these now peaceable people, whose
ancestors had driven the forebears of those Fathers within those same
walls. Now the relationship was different; we met the chief and a few
notables among the visiting tribesmen, who had been invited to take
refreshment in the guest room.

Before leaving Joy and I, unable to resist the buttresses and boiler-
plate slabs which defended the fine row of peaks dominating the
monastery opposite Gebel Musa, spent a happy day finding an
interesting route to the crest, and then traversing all five summits. The
rock was uncomfortably hot to the touch, but it was good to be on a
rope together once more and, though I have not verified the point, we
may well have been the first to climb those peaks; certainly our chosen
route would have been original. However that may be, it was a highly
satisfying day.

On our last morning, wandering down the Wadi Safsafa to have a
last view of the monastery in its grandiose mountain setting, we met a
small shepherd girl coming down the path with a herd of goats.
Giving us a friendly 'Sa'idah', she sat down and proceeded to play a
plaintive little tune on a brass flute. She asked nothing of us; indeed, we
might not have been there. Perhaps she came there daily and whiled
away the hours with her music. But the child with her flute and
behind her, the monastery and above it the great red peaks, made a
moving picture. It was pleasant, if erroneous, to accept her tune as her
'adieu' to ourselves as we turned to go.

Mons Claudianus. It sounded an intriguing kind of mountain and

7

seemed to us, with a week's leave from duties at Middle East Headquarters, a good enough reason for travelling 300 miles down the
western shore of the Gulf of Suez to have a look at it. 'Having a look'
is not usually a sufficient reason for enjoying mountains, but this one is
unusual. It is, in fact, a Roman *castellum* built, it is believed, towards the
end of the first century AD in the reign of the Emperor Hadrian as a
garrison for the Roman soldiers who supervised the granite-quarrying
industry in the hills forming the watershed between the River Nile and
the Red Sea. Alec Bangham, a young pathologist serving with the
RAMC in the Canal Zone, had been there during the summer of 1948
and he suggested that we should join him and his wife, Rosalind, in
making another visit, under pleasanter conditions, in December of
that year. The Banghams were a delightfully unconventional pair. We
took an immediate liking to them and were all the more attracted to
their idea by our Easter memories of the beckoning view west from
Gebel Katerina across the Gulf of Suez. The nearest I had been to that
jagged skyline of granite peaks, the highest of which was the Gebel
Shâyib, was sailing home from India through the Canal some years
before the war. They had looked quite high and I had wondered whether
they had been climbed. Later, I read an account by George Murray in the
Alpine Journal of his two ascents, in 1937 and 1943, of the Gebel Shâyib
(Shâyib el-Banat, 7,170 feet), the highest mountain in Egypt outside
Sinai, which had first been climbed in 1921. So we agreed to look at
Mons Claudianus, but we would climb Gebel Shâyib.

That little expedition stands out in my recollections as one of those
happy interludes, mainly because of the haphazard and care-free way
we set about it. We knew that at least one third of the track to the oil
station at Hurghada, where the journey into the mountains begins, was
over very rough going; for this reason we thought at first of hiring a
taxi, as we had done for our trip to the mountains of Sinai the previous
Easter; but the cost, which worked out at £25 a head, deterred us, so
instead, we decided to travel in our own transport. Joy and I had a
somewhat down-at-heel, second-hand open Standard coupé with
suspect steering; the Banghams possessed a motorcycle and sidecar
which was not in its first youth. The night before our departure, Alec
worked on it until 2 a.m. repairing its gear box and in the haste of
getting our gear together he forgot to bring a spare inner tube.

By the evening of that first day, rattling over the appalling potholes
and corrugations of the track, Alec's chain broke; it was easily mended,
but worse was to follow when, in pitchy darkness, the valve of the
inner tube of his front wheel was torn away from the rubber. Here was
a pretty pickle! We had omitted to bring torches, but fortunately the
mishap befell us as we were passing only the second bay along the

whole coastline where there was an abundance of drift wood. By groping around on their hands and knees, Rosalind and Joy gathered fuel and, while Alec and I laboured to force the much larger inner tube of my spare wheel into his tyre, filing out the hole in the rim to fit my valve, they kept our operations illuminated with a huge blaze. After two and a half hours the job was done, and soon afterwards we found a sandy hollow to protect us from a bitter wind and huddled together for a few hours' sleep.

The scenery all that day had been superb. We had travelled close to the shore, passing little sandy bays ringed with red sandstone. Across the wind-whipped waters of the Gulf we could see, clear but dwarfed by distance, the familiar peaks of Gebel Musa and Gebel Katerina. For a time a school of porpoises frolicked along beside us, seeming to enjoy our company, or the competition we provided for their speed. Inland on our right was a high escarpment of red rock, with some impressive mountains, Gebel el Galela and Gebel Ghârib, towering above it. All this had helped to take our minds off the hours of bone-shaking and our anxieties for the vehicles.

After passing one oilfield, Ras Ghârib, we reached another one, Hurghada, the turning-point in our journey to the Roman mountain. Our arrival was expected, for we had needed permits to travel along this route. The manager of the oil field, Mr Hopper, made us welcome and placed the company's guest house at our disposal. Dirty, dishevelled and hungry, we were quite unbothered by our incongruous appearance in such cosy luxury. Next morning, well fed and rested, our only worry was the final stretch of fifty miles or so to reach the ruined settlement; for we knew from Alec that the track onwards was even worse, in places, than what we had encountered so far. But Mr Hopper, charmed by Alec's gift of whisky and, I have no doubt, by Rosalind and Joy, generously lent us an American desert utility truck with a powerful engine and balloon tyres. This, and a reliable Egyptian driver, solved our problem. After visiting the Marine Biological Station a few miles away, where we were fascinated by the giant sea turtles, sting rays and a rare bull walrus, we headed off westwards in the early afternoon, skimming at speed over the bumps and ridges of the track. The mountains I had first seen in 1935 rose above us as we drew nearer; they looked magnificent and the further we went the greater our excitement grew. Then came that dramatic moment when, after crossing a low pass, we swung south into a side valley, the Wadi Um Hussein; and there, close at hand on its northern slope, was Mons Claudianus.

It is a most impressive place; a fort or more accurately, a barracks, measuring eighty yards along each side, its outer walls several yards thick, with small towers at each corner. Inside the enclosure a main street led through the quarters with alleys leading at right angles which divided the honeycomb of little dwellings or cubicles. Their roofs had collapsed and so had the door lintels, but the dividing walls still stood, at places as high as ten feet above the street level. There was a communal bath house, still covered in places with plaster; one of its basins, Rosalind noted, had a plug hole. I suppose that should not have surprised us, but it made it look strangely up to date. Further up the northern slope was a temple, dedicated to Sarafis, with inscriptions in Greek and Latin; one of these, in the reign of the Emperor Trajan, identified the name of Mons Claudianus.

But it was the evidence of the industry for which the garrison had been stationed here nineteen centuries before that made the deepest impression on us. In the *wadis* surrounding the settlement to the north and west were the quarries, a track with deep groove marks showed that some kind of conveyance—probably a huge sledge—must have been lowered under gravity when full, and hauled or winched back empty up the slope. Thousands of dressed blocks of red porphyry lay around everywhere; on the vertical rock faces from which the crude material had been prized, were rows of chiselled recesses, into which the craftsmen had once hammered wooden wedges, soaked them with water until, by expanding, they split chunks of granite from the bedrock. Most astonishing of all was the sight of a number of granite columns, some still roughly hewn, others smoothly polished and seemingly ready for export. Joy and Rosalind climbed on to the biggest monster to improve a photograph; it measured sixty feet in length, with a diameter of eight feet. On its base was a Latin inscription: 'Valvennius Priscus, Centurion, 22nd Legion, by the architect Heracleides'.

L. A. Tregenza, who inspected the site in the year following our visit and who furnished this translation noted, as we did, the extraordinarily 'fresh-looking' aspect of the quarry and its materials. It was as though the work was still in progress, the workmen having knocked off for their lunch break. The workmen, according to the chronicler Aristides were 'malefactors and Christians'* whose living quarters we could see still faintly defined outside the garrison walls. It was not difficult to conjure up the scene as they toiled in this airless, arid place under a scorching sun, their productivity ensured by the slave masters, who sat perched on high stone cairns, which still stood at intervals

---

* Aristides' opinion was quoted in the journal kept by John Wilkinson who accompanied James Burton when the latter revisited the site in 1832. Burton, a noted Egyptologist and elder brother of Decimus Burton, was the first known European to visit Mon Claudianus, in 1830.

alongside the recumbent columns. From Mons Claudianus the finished artifacts – tablets, baths, plinths and pillars – were transported, probably by sledge, down to Qena on the Nile, eighty miles away. It must have been a back-breaking journey; that biggest column alone weighed well over a hundred tons. But the workmen were not away eating their dinner; they had left their jobs long ago. What brought their toil and tribulation to a halt, we wondered? and then we surmised that it must have been a lack of water sufficient to provide for so large a community. It was a strange experience to stand there, denied of any evidence of change to mark the passage of time, in this still, dead place. It was as if time had stood suspended all those nineteen hundred years.

But for us, with only three days left before we were due to report back for our military duties, time did not stand still. All too soon we had to leave, for the Gebel Shâyib lay some twenty miles back along the way we had come and this was our next mountain.

That long day on Shâyib, during which Joy and I made the sixth ascent of that mountain, provided us with an experience more familiar to desert travellers than to mountaineers. We camped at 2,000 feet beneath a pass at the head of a *wadi* on the east side of the mountain and, making an 'alpine' start in the dark next morning crossed the pass to descend into a wide valley, the Wadi Abu Abid, which runs down from the southern escarpments of Shâyib. At the head of this valley Alec and Rosalind left us and returned to our camp site; we began to climb the mountain, following a boulder-filled gully; a wide terrace at about 5,000 feet beneath the cluster of turrets which comprise the summit; the highest point was still depressingly high and distant, and there was nothing to cheer us, or take our minds off the heat and the sheer sterility of the scenery; no green shrubs or living things. Yet it was hereabouts that we began to come across animal droppings: ibex, of which we picked up a small horn; wild asses and, if my diary is to be believed, marmots. After dodging round their vertical walls for a long time we eventually arrived, on the stroke of midday, on a huge flat boiler plate of granite slab which is the highest point in Egypt; and there was the cairn built by Murray eleven years beforehand.

It should have been a good moment, There was a tremendous panorama all around us, with the Sinai peninsula 130 miles to the north, sprawling map-like upon the ocean between the containing arms of the gulfs of Aqaba and Suez. Away in the west and 100 miles distant, we could see the desert beyond the Nile; far below us were sand-filled valleys, white in the bright light, looking for all the world like the glaciers of the Karakoram. It was a stupendous scene, which we were scarcely in a condition to appreciate, for our senses were dulled, not by lack of oxygen, but of liquid; we were severely dehydrated. By ignorance and lack of foresight, we had had with us only one orange apiece and a pint-size waterbottle. As we descended the boulder-filled gully towards the Wadi Abu Abid I began to seize up with painful cramp in both thighs; I could barely move. Not for the last time on our climbs together, Joy was in better shape than I was, and such was my plight that I felt no qualms in accepting her offer to carry my rucksack as well as her own. Then, on the climb up those 600 feet to reach the col below which our friends were waiting at the over-night camping place I suddenly felt a resurgence of energy. The light was fading and it seemed sensible to forge ahead to alert Alec and Rosalind that we were safe. While Joy plodded up with a double load I topped the col and shouted. One moment I will not forget was the response to that call; I saw car headlights switched on in acknowledgement. Half an hour later we were swigging mugs of tea. It had been a grand day's mountaineering, none the less satisfying for the fact that it had involved us in nothing more than scrambling. In thirteen hours we had covered about twenty-eight miles and climbed 5,000 feet.

Mr Hopper had come out to escort us back and a little later that night we were in his comfortable house, being entertained, as Rosalind recalls: 'with cocktail food; just the sort of food that disappeared in a twinkling'. It was a great kindness, and it made a welcome appetiser for the gargantuan meal we ate even later, in the guest house.

7

The Generals at Peace

1946–52

WHEN I HAD PASSED THROUGH THE STAFF COLLEGE IN 1946 I was posted to GHQ Middle East Land Forces, which after a brief spell in Cairo, was moved early in 1947 to hutted quarters in Fayid, on the banks of the Suez Canal. This massive exodus would scarcely have been possible but for a large labour force of about 100,000 German prisoners, most of whom had been captured in the surrender at Tunis in 1943, and many of whom we detained for several years after hostilities had ceased as part of the retribution exacted from Germany for Hitler's war. Some served as mess waiters and batmen and with two of these, who worked for my family, Joy and I remained in touch long after they had been repatriated. Those were interesting and, on the whole, good years for Joy and myself, with our three young daughters. Our fourth, Jennifer, was born at Ismailia while we were stationed on the Canal. My duties as GSO I (Operations) took me to Cyprus, where I had to inspect the camps established to control another exodus, that of Jewish refugees from all over Europe towards the land of their fathers; to Iraq, where the Persian Premier Moshadeq was threatening our oil supplies; and to Palestine during the last year of our mandate as administrators for the erstwhile League of Nations. I went to Jerusalem with the Commander-in-Chief, General Dempsey, for urgent discussions with the High Commissioner, Sir Alan Cunningham at a critical moment in the terrorist campaign of Irgun Zwei Leumi. As Staff Officer to his successor, General Crocker, I flew to Haifa for an immediate investigation into the circumstances in which the Arab community of that city had been summarily evicted by the Jewish patriots, shortly before the British left Palestine.

Some involvement at 'the sharp end' in the business of warfare and rebellion was one thing, planning the strategy for possible future wars, and the immediate action to deal with emergencies arising from some political crisis, or a disturbance which might call for military aid to civilian power—was an interestingly different experience. As GSO I (Plans) at Middle East Headquarters and as a member of the Joint

Planning Staff with representatives of the two other fighting Services, I was engaged in laying plans for a variety of contingencies, from the 'Fire Brigade' kind of rôle of despatching relatively small forces to deal with emergencies in Iraq or elsewhere, to the grand strategy for stemming a Russian advance on the Delta through Palestine. It was my first experience of serving on a headquarters as a staff officer at any level; like most officers accustomed to the responsibilities of command, I found it at first difficult to adjust to the sense of remoteness from the realities of coping with actual problems 'up front'. But it was a cockpit position from which to survey the kaleidoscope of trends and events in the shifting political sands of Eastern Europe and the Near East.

On a large headquarters the focal figure is the Chief of Staff; our Army has never lacked the men to measure up to that demanding job and war has produced some brilliant exponents, with the requisite qualities and proven experience. Major-General Pete Pyeman joined GHQ Middle East Land Forces at the same time as I did. He had been one of Monty's outstanding young senior officers in 2nd Army Group and might be described as a disciple of his master. Although only forty at the time of his appointment, he found youthfulness no handicap in dealing with older officers on the Staff with more experience of the area, who were now his juniors in office; he quickly established his ability to manage the huge staff. Pete was a person of extraordinary breadth of view and sharpness of intellect, He had acquired from Monty the knack of grasping essentials and discarding everything else, in reaching important decisions. He devoted all his waking hours to his profession; I doubt if he ever read any literature in those years other than official reports; a good husband and father, his main relaxation was discussing the manifold problems of the huge area covered by the Headquarters candidly and informally in his caravan with his Personal Assistant, Sheila Drake. A disciple of Monty, he had rather irritatingly adopted some of his former Chief's mannerisms and modes of speech. I have since thought of Pete Pyeman as a military edition of Harold Wilson in the power of his intellect, his toughness and resilience and somewhat subtle turn of mind; but also for his friendliness and warmth, and his lack of formality in his dealings with colleagues and juniors alike. He had the great gift of trusting and delegating responsibility among his subordinates; once you had earned his confidence, you had his total support. Pete was a person whom you either liked and forgave his tiresome bumptiousness, or you strongly disliked him. For a while I was his GSO I (Co-ord) — the equivalent of a Chef de Cabinet; being privy to almost everything that went on. I learned to like and respect Pete Pyeman.

★   ★   ★

Shortly after the war, the Western European Powers: the United Kingdom, France and the Benelux countries established the Western Union to co-ordinate their defence plans for an eventual future con-flict; for it had soon become clear that the Soviet Union, our war-time ally, might one day exercise its military might against Western Europe. An Allied headquarters was set up at Fontainebleau under the joint command — unusual, if not unique at the time — of a committee of high Allied commanders: a French General, de Lattre de Tassigny, and a Rear-Admiral, Jaujard; a British Air-Chief Marshal, Robb. Its Chairman was Field-Marshal Montgomery. I served on the staff of this headquarters between 1950 and 1952, first as a member of Mont-gomery's staff in his capacity as Chairman of the Commanders-in-Chief Committee at Headquarters Allied Forces, Central Europe. I had the opportunity to observe, with some involvement, the growing-pains of Allied co-operation in peace, planning for the eventuality of a major invasion from the east towards the Channel ports. It was, at my level, a most stimulating and enjoyable exercise in mutual relationships; we managed to achieve integration without many difficulties, despite the differences in the organisation of our respective forces and com-mand structures. I enjoyed the opportunity to speak French, in which language all joint discussion between the Belgian, Dutch, French and British staff officers was conducted at that time. The Allied Officers' Mess at Fontainebleau was a happy place where understandings grew easily, greatly assisted by the popularity of Scottish dancing at our social occasions. Life outside my desk work in the Cour Henri Quatre, where the British staff had their offices, was delightful.

Joy and I rented a house, 'Les Perriers', in the village of Fontaine-le-Port, situated on the Seine at the northern outskirts of the forest. Our second daughter Susan was admitted to the Lycée at Fontainebleau and quickly became bi-lingual; our third daughter Prudence trotted along to the village *Maternelle* with a small French friend from a neighbour-ing farm; her limited vocabulary included as many French words as English.

The forest was our playground: a place for picnics, for finding edible fungi, a place where wild daffodils grew in spring and lilies-of-the-valley in early summer. Above all, it was a place to meet our Parisian climbing friends, fellow *bleausards* and amuse ourselves struggling up the smooth sandstone boulders and crags: the circuits jaune and rouge, the Eléphant, the Dame Jeanne and other delicious places. Best of all, perhaps, were the long breaks for lunch at some forest restaurant, drinking Pernod and red wine, amid much light-hearted chatter. What fun it was!

At the higher staff echelons things were less happy. I was never sure

that the orthodox and serious-minded senior Allied officers of the three
fighting Services quite approved of Monty's Chief of Staff, Major-
General R. F. K. (David) Belchem, not being aware, from my less
exalted view, of the true relationship between him and, in particular,
Général Clément Blanc, Chief of Staff to Général d'Armée de Lattre de
Tassigny. I now know that, but for the moderating influence of
Belchem and Blanc, things might have been even worse at the top.
David was meteoric, dashing and brilliant, refreshingly unlike the
stereotype of a British General Officer. He carried his responsibilities,
which involved a heavy load of work, with a touch of the carefree
university undergraduate. A fluent linguist, he mildly shocked his
French colleagues, who cherished the proper usage of their language,
with his liberal use of *argot*—I am not sure where he picked it up. But
this colourful young man with a streak of the devil in him, kept us on
our toes and added a spark of fun to the work of the staff, though
sometimes at the expense of the sensibilities of our French hosts.

David Belchem was subsequently posted to Rhine Army in 1951 to
take command of an armoured brigade in his substantive rank of
Brigadier. I was a member of a visiting party of General Staff officers
from Fontainebleau who attended the manoeuvres in the Rhineland
that August. We paid a call at David's tactical headquarters in a
German village. The Brigade Commander was delighted to see us and
over the bonnet of a jeep we studied our maps while he explained the
state of the battle. He then excused himself and left us, saying that he
had other work to get on with. When I looked for him to say goodbye,
I found him behind a barn having his nails manicured by an attractive
flaxen-haired fräulein, while dictating orders to a clerk/stenographer.
Provided that there are not too many of them, characters like David
Belchem, who contrive to combine hard work with a touch of gaiety
and fun, are a valuable object lesson to others who, like myself, are
less endowed with the means to off-set the pressures of work and
worry with a little light relief.

Relationships at the very top cast a slight shadow on all members of
the staff during the first two years of the new High Command. Monty
was the soldiers' General. He had inspired me, as he had tens of
thousands of others, with his brisk and breezy appearances at some
battalion or brigade headquarters, or in his staff car drawn up on the
verge of some dusty road as we advanced towards the front in Italy
during September 1943. But he was not ideally cast in the rôle of
Chairman of a committee of Allied Commanders-in-Chief, sharing
the decision-making with colleagues, which that office demanded. Nor,
for that matter, was Général de Lattre de Tassigny, later hero of Dien
Bien Phu, an easy person to work with. The French were under-

standably touchy at that time about the collapse of their country's armies before the German onslaught in 1940, and the rule of Pétain which followed it. As a major European power they had been unable to share fully in the fruits of victory in 1945. Their pride rested on past military prowess, seemingly presided over by the ghost of Napoleon Bonaparte. I am told on some authority that the trouble between the two great men started early on in the Allied partnership, when de Lattre attended a meeting in Dover House, Whitehall, which was Monty's London headquarters at the time. De Lattre, it appears, used the words 'j'insiste' to emphasise a point he was making, which even Monty, despite his linguistic limitations, was able to understand. 'Nobody insists with me,' he retorted.

There was a basic difference of view between de Lattre and Monty about the appropriate structure for High Command in a future war. It was implicit in the existence of a committee of Commanders-in-Chief with a presiding chairman that there would be a Supreme Commander in Central Europe with subordinate commanders-in-chief for each of the three fighting services. For the French, and de Lattre in particular, the traditional dominant arm in the land battle was the Army; the naval and air forces were in a subordinate rôle. By implication, Monty was also superfluous. Monty naturally had no taste for this concept. The disagreement between the two great men simmered on, exacerbated by their strong and contrasting personalities; apart from their undoubted qualities as military commanders, they seemed to share in common only a lack of modesty and diplomatic skill. De Lattre, like Monty, did, however, possess a peculiar magnetism. I remember a meeting in his headquarters to discuss a forthcoming staff exercise, when he appeared to focus his considerable powers of persuasion about a certain point upon myself, perhaps because I was fluent in French. His gaze was mesmeric, but flattering rather than embarrassing.

The antipathy between the two men continued. Fortunately, however, the other Service Chiefs were able to paper over the cracks in Allied harmony, and personal relationships between us smaller fry were excellent. Eventually the two men did reach agreement: they would each mount a staff exercise, purporting to demonstrate to their staffs, if not to each other, which was the preferable system of high command. I think that it was by virtue of seniority that Monty's staff were called upon to run the first exercise; there was, however, some tactical advantage for de Lattre in taking up any weaknesses revealed by Monty's demonstration, during his own presentation. The onus of laying on the British staff exercise fell mainly on the Brigadier, General Staff, John Dalton, and myself as GSO I (Ops and Plans); David

Belchem, of course, sketched the main guidelines, but he was not often at Fontainebleau, dividing his time between that place and Monty's rear headquarters in Dover House, Whitehall, and the capitals of the other three nations involved; he was a fast mover. When the appointed day arrived the Allied staffs assembled and Montgomery cordially invited Général de Lattre to take a seat reserved for him at the front of the hall; he declined and ostentatiously placed himself at the very back. The exercise was deemed to have been a success and Monty was pleased; in conciliatory mood, he again invited de Lattre to come forward, and to offer his views. De Lattre declined.

A few weeks later the game was repeated, this time in French staff territory. Their exercise was immaculately conducted by Général de Brigade Jean Beaufre; it went far to persuade any unbiased observer that the French system of high command, at the appropriate level, was workable, even right. De Lattre was pleased; he invited Monty, who had sat throughout the demonstration at the front, to come up to the stage and offer his opinions. To say that there was an air of expectancy in the audience when the famous figure stepped forward, would be a masterpiece of understatement; he took his place opposite the rostrum occupied by de Lattre. 'Mon Général,' said Monty (and I was thankful that he did not proceed to spoil the effect by continuing in his execrable schoolboy French), 'you and I have wasted two valuable years in disagreement with each other; we have wasted the time of our staffs. I would like to offer you my sincere apologies, here and now, for my part in this affair. Let us bury the hatchet.'

It was like the dénouement of a great piece of theatre, with two fine actors on stage. De Lattre strode across the stage, tears in his eyes; he embraced the Field-Marshal, whose face registered quite a range of emotions: surprise, pleasure, embarrassment. We, the audience, British, Dutch, Belgian and French officers of all three Services, rose to our feet as one man. There were cheers and thunderous applause. It was as though a dam of pent-up tension had burst. I suspect that de Lattre was not the only one to have a tear in his eye. Never, in any Service setting, have I seen the like. Monty, whose word was treated by nearly all of us as the gospel he believed it to be, who delighted in being right, who did not suffer fools and who sometimes enjoyed the game of de-bunking other high commanders, had actually shown humility and regret. It was, I believe, his finest hour.

The problem of the best system of high command in a future European war was solved shortly afterwards by the arrival of the Americans, and the establishment first in Paris and later at Versailles of a Supreme Headquarters, Allied Powers in Europe (SHAPE), embracing the northern and southern sectors—from Norway to the shores of the Mediterranean, in addition to our own Central Command. General-of-the-Army Eisenhower came to fill that supreme post, and Monty was appointed as his Deputy. Marshal Juin succeeded de Lattre, taking command of all three Services in Central European command at Fontainebleau. I was transferred to Juin's staff as head of his Training Branch, in the rank of Colonel. There was a feeling of deep doubt and suspicion before Eisenhower arrived. He was preceded by his Chief of Staff, General Al Gruenther, who came to speak to the staff at Fontainebleau about the new set-up. Gruenther made a most favourable impression; he spoke modestly and tactfully, evidently very conscious of our sensitivity; I think that by the end we were all much relieved, and confident that the management of the top headquarters was in very competent hands. General Eisenhower came to us shortly afterwards and, aided by the searching questions of his Chief of Staff, did a first-class job of public relations in smoothing any ruffled feathers, especially in the French camp.

I had the honour of being received by President Eisenhower, as he became, when some of my companions of the Everest expedition were bidden to the White House to receive a gold medal—the Hubbard Medal—with replicas for each member of the team, which was awarded by the National Geographic Society of America. The room in which the presentation took place was banked with photographers, as well as members of the President's staff; light bulbs flashed as Eisenhower led us in, after spending a few minutes in delightfully informal chat, in an anteroom. Ike presented me with the gold medal on behalf of the whole Expedition and spoke a few gracious words. 'Do it again, Mr President,' shouted the photographers. The President dutifully complied and I followed suit. 'Just once more,' they demanded, and again the President repeated the performance. President of the United States he may have been, former Supreme Commander of the Allied forces in war and peace. But the President and General-of-the-Army was very definitely under the orders of the communications media at that moment in time.

With the arrival of American staff officers at our headquarters in Versailles, a change came over the climate of our working and social relationships. We had become accustomed to one another at the personal level, we understood the permutations in our respective command systems and 'order of battle'; not least important, we had accepted French as our common tongue and, by and large, it was spoken well by most of us. The integration of a fifth element with different organisation, coming from outside the European cultural traditions, was not going to be easy. The newcomers and their families were very numerous; new buildings sprang up in the forest, the Allied

mess became extended, less cosily intimate. Later, with the arrival of
the West Germans, the staff became bigger still. But at about the time
the Americans arrived I was moved to 1st (British) Corps headquarters
in Germany at Bad Oenhausen, where my job was concerned with
putting a tactical interpretation on the high level strategic planning in
which I had been involved in France.

After the Everest expedition, Hillary and I were invited to come to
SHAPE to tell the story. General Gruenther, by then Supreme Commander in succession to Eisenhower, was in London on official business
and we were received at the door of the headquarters by the Deputy
Supreme Commander in person. Monty gave us a smart salute, which
Ed appeared to take as a matter of course in his delightfully breezy
manner, while I did my best to conceal my own sense of the ridiculous
in the situation as it applied to myself. I tried to put on an act of looking
gracious and dignified; but I was feeling quite queer inside. After the
lecture, Monty addressed the assembled staff. 'Well,' he said, 'you have
now heard the story and I want you all to buy a copy of Hunt's book.
Turn to Appendix III, and you will find the basis on which the whole
operation was planned. Brigadier Hunt served as GSO I (Ops and
Plans) on my staff at Fontainebleau before taking charge of the
Everest expedition.' The inference was lost on no one—audience and
lecturers alike: it was Monty who had planned the ascent of Everest.
This was vintage Monty, if not in his finest hour, he was certainly at
his typical and endearing best.

8

1953 and All That

'OH, WELL; IF YOU CAN GET KILLED, IT MUST BE WORTH DO-
ing,' remarked a boy when a youth leader was trying to work up
enthusiasm among an indifferent audience of his club members, to
whom he was explaining the Duke of Edinburgh's Award Scheme.
There had been some publicity at the time about a lad who had
collapsed on an Award expedition and had subsequently died of
exposure; it was one of the very rare tragedies attributable to the
Scheme. In chapter 9 I have touched upon the philosophical debate
between those who are rightly concerned to protect young people and
who place their priority on safety, and others who, while not dissenting
from the general proposition that children should not be exposed to
undue hazards, stress the value of encouraging the spirit of daring, in
which an element of risk is inescapable. It may seem a paradox to some
people that those who lean towards the latter view, while deploring the
tragedy, will also sympathise with that boy's reaction to it. I was
thirteen when the news of Mallory's and Irvine's deaths on Everest
was made known in 1924, and my own feelings were much the same.
It would be too much to claim that it inspired dreams of climbing that
mountain when I heard the moving and intriguing report by Noel
Odell of how he had seen two figures through the mists moving up
towards the Second Step on the North-East Ridge; but it certainly
made me want to climb.

For a number of years other mountains provided quite enough
challenges to go on with; it was only eleven years later that the name
Everest cropped up again. Edwin Kempson, who came to teach at
Marlborough when I was a pupil and with whom I started guideless
climbing at Chamonix in 1933, was a member of an Everest reconnaissance expedition two years later. I received several letters from him
while I was on Peak 36, at the opposite end of the Himalayan chain.
My experience on that mountain was probably more rewarding than
Edwin's on Everest, but the correspondence put ideas into my head,

for the reconnaissance was a prelude to another major effort which the joint Himalayan Committee of the Alpine Club and the Royal Geographical Society was preparing for 1936.

It was one of the great thrills of my life to be invited to join that expedition after returning from the Karakoram, and a correspondingly bitter blow when I was told that I had to be dropped from the team, following an adverse medical report. There was some consolation in the regrets expressed by the two leading Everest men of the day, Eric Shipton and Frank Smythe. Two years later, Joy and I were with Reggie Cooke on the Zemu glacier, hoping to provide evidence about high-altitude climbing conditions in the early winter months, in view of the failures of both the 1935 and 1936 expeditions to get high on Everest because of an early monsoon, which brought heavy snowfall in May. I probably nursed ideas about trying out our findings on Everest, until the intense cold and the north-west wind drove them from my mind; for it would have been impossible to view the great mountain from Nepal Peak without feeling the challenge of that higher horizon. However that may be, the war years put all such thoughts into cold storage.

After the war, apart from two spells in England to attend the Army and the Joint Services Staff Colleges, I was posted abroad between 1946 and 1952. I did not know the new generation of British climbers; at Fontainebleau, our climbing friends were French. As far as the pundits in the Alpine Club were concerned, making preparations for a fresh attempt on Everest, I was out of sight, and doubtless out of mind. But while we were at Saas-Fee in 1951 Joy and I met Basil Goodfellow, then honorary secretary of the Alpine Club, and three of his friends. We joined forces and together we climbed our way over to Zermatt, traversing Allalinhorn and Rimpfischhorn, and then the Obergabelhorn. We went on to climb the Dom, Schallihorn, Zinal Rothorn and three summits of Monte Rosa. To round off the season, Basil and I traversed the Weisshorn and Bieshorn, bivouacking on our way down, with the lights of Randa twinkling invitingly at us through the darkness. It is in the sharing of uncomfortable circumstances like those that close friendships are made. I doubt whether, if it had not been for our climbs together that summer, I would have been asked in 1952 to go to Everest.

I was serving with the 1st British Corps in Germany when I received a letter from Basil in July 1952. He told me about doubts over the leadership of the forthcoming expedition, after a training expedition had returned from Cho Oyu; these doubts centred on Eric Shipton's organisational ability and commitment to the job. The Committee regarded it as being of crucial importance that a very determined effort

Elbrus, from the summit of Pik Shchurovskiy, with the Shkhel'da glacier below.

Ushba.

should be made this time; always assuming that the Swiss, who had climbed to over 28,000 feet on the South-East Ridge in May of that year, were to fail in the second attempt they were preparing to make in the autumn. Basil said that the Committee would like me to become the organising secretary of the expedition, and to go as a climbing member on the mountain, if the War Office were willing to release me.

I nearly jumped over the moon. After the good years at Fontainebleau, the four months I had spent at Bad Oenhausen had been unhappy ones for me. I had found it difficult to settle into a large, high-level army headquarters; Joy and the children had not been able to join me and I did not enjoy a bachelor's existence in a headquarters mess. I knew nothing of the background to this sudden change of fortune: of the difficult and devious discussions, and the vacillations of the Himalayan Committee which had led to this invitation. But almost at the same time I also heard from its Chairman, Claude Elliott, inviting me, prematurely as it later transpired, to be deputy leader to Eric. I was so excited that it was difficult to concentrate on my job; it was a busy time, for we were getting ready for a big Rhine Army exercise in which, as Colonel, General Staff, I was heavily involved. Then, in mid-August, came a further letter, a formal one this time, inviting me to accept the job as organising secretary and asking me to come to London to discuss the matter; fortunately the Corps Commander, General Dudley Ward was most enthusiastic, and I left at once.

On 22nd August I met Eric Shipton at the Royal Geographical Society. It was a sadly disillusioning encounter. No doubt I was over-keen and showed it. Apart from the Swiss challenge, I knew, as a member of the Groupe de Haute Montagne, that the French were preparing to make an attempt to climb Everest in 1954; as I saw it, something more was at stake than simply that of climbing a mountain. I sensed that after all his years of doing battle on Everest, on which he had climbed so high before the war, and after showing the way towards the top on the Nepalese side, Eric's exploratory spirit, which was so much a part of his nature, was waning on that particular mountain. The meeting was, in fact, a failure and I said as much to Basil before returning, in very low spirits, to Germany; it was almost like 1936 all over again. But the Rhineland exercise got under way and took my mind off Everest for a while.

Then, in mid-September, I received a telegram from the Himalayan Committee. Shipton had resigned; the Committee had decided to appoint me as leader; the CIGS had agreed to second me for the duration of the expedition.

I could hardly believe my luck. My colleagues at Corps Headquarters

8

were almost as delighted as I; at a farewell dinner I was presented with the Corps flag and instructed to place it on top of the mountain. I left my job in Germany and arrived in London to take charge of the Everest expedition in early October 1952. Fortunately I had had no part in the process by which the painful decisions were made, but I felt very sorry indeed for Shipton. He took the blow to his pride with dignity and without fuss. He had been most considerate to me in 1936 and it was now my turn to offer my condolences to him; I tried to persuade him to join the party, but could understand his feelings in declining.

It was also an invidious position for me. The change in leadership affected those whom Shipton had invited and who felt a strong loyalty towards him; especially Tom Bourdillon who, despite his burning ambition to climb Everest, at first declined my invitation and needed much persuasion to make him change his mind. One of the moments I shall always treasure was when, during our walk towards the mountain in March the following year, Tom said to me one evening: 'What a very happy party you've got going.' Charles Evans had said much the same a day or two beforehand. Tom had been with Shipton on a reconnaissance of Everest in 1951 and on the Cho Oyu expedition and he, like Michael Ward, Alf Gregory, George Lowe and Ed Hillary, may well have felt misgivings about the change. But by then that sadness had been set aside; we were becoming a united and contented party, despite the fact that we were twice as numerous as Eric had intended; because, perhaps, everyone had accepted the importance of aiming single-mindedly for the summit. Much as we all preferred climbing in small groups of friends, we agreed that this was going to be no ordinary climb. For the time being, Everest was rather more than a mountain.

The blending process took place while we were walking to Everest; the Approach March in the military terminology of the time, for which I accept some responsibility. It continued during the three weeks when we divided into groups after arriving at the monastery of Tengpoche and went off to train together with our Sherpas. By the time we reached Base Camp on 18th April we were not only very fit, we were very confident about our equipment and our plans—and we were very good friends. It was a partnership strong enough to endure the tedium, and the undoubted dangers, of those wearisome 'ferries' up and down the Icefall and along the Cwm. It was strong enough to stand the tensions and anxieties and the test of our endurance, as the Assault Plan got under way. Of course, there were the occasional tiffs: Griff Pugh our physiologist and Tom Stobart our cameraman waxed indignant with me on one occasion about my neglect of their particular rôles, as I became more and more absorbed in resolving the technical and logistical problems of climbing the mountain; at Base Camp Griff gave me a salutary dressing-down on behalf of them both. It was fair criticism, and their worries were easily remedied.

But behind those discontents there are more deep-seated problems which, fortunately, did not loom large during our expedition. It is natural enough that the viewpoint of scientists on expeditions should differ, both as to objectives and in emphasis, from that of the explorer or mountaineer whose motives are mainly adventurous in origin. The scientific interest is not, or not so much, simply that of getting to the top of a mountain; it is likely to be mainly the effects, psychological and physiological, of demands made on human beings in their efforts under difficult conditions at high altitude. Griff Pugh is a dedicated and distinguished scientist, who has become a leading expert in his field of physiology; he had made a great contribution to the design of our clothing and equipment, the composition and balance of our diet and to the policy for the use of oxygen, as well as the principles of acclimatisation. All this had a powerful influence on my plans, and on our performance on the mountain. Notwithstanding the earlier feats of Everest climbers with far more rudimentary equipment and clothing, I greatly respected his view, which is shared by Michael Ward, that it was the application of science to our problem which was decisive in our success.

Tom Stobart's complaint was a harbinger of much more serious problems which we, fortunately, were spared: those arising from the place and influence of the media on expeditions. Nowadays no major expedition is likely to be able to take the field without some support of a broadcasting or film company; the despatch of film and the radio reporting of events from day to day has become a normal feature of expedition life. Indeed, some expeditions have the making of a film as their *raison d'être*. The consequent need to highlight and dramatise the happenings can place pressure on the leader's judgments and the party's plans; the eye of the camera can make climbers conscious of an audience while they are on some ice slope and during conversation in their tents. I am thankful that we had no such problems, for it certainly simplified the task of helping to harmonise our relationships and co-ordinate our efforts.

Harmony, I believe, was all-important. Discord on some subsequent Everest expeditions must have had some bearing on their outcome. In providing good public entertainment on the television screen, some have left a sad record for mountaineering history and, perhaps more important to those involved, they have diminished the quality of friendship in their aftermath.

A human difference of view occurred at 28,700 feet on the South Summit of Everest on 26th May, when Charles Evans and Tom Bourdillon, conversing through their oxygen masks, argued about whether to continue along the final stretch of ridge towards the top. It is scarcely possible to engage in prolonged debate in such circumstances and, happily for them both, for their relatives—and for the outcome of the expedition—they decided to give up a prize so nearly within their grasp, and came back.

To stress the importance of a harmonious relationship and of team work is not to detract from the personal performance of Hillary and Tenzing; they were unmistakably outstanding at the time, climbing faster and more strongly than any of us. But for that fact, my final dispositions might have been different, and it is a matter for conjecture who might have been the successful summit pair: Ed, with his zest, his tremendous physical strength and purpose; and Tenzing, just as strong and swift as Ed, more quiet and gentle, but with an inner ambition to get to the top which was rare among his people at that time. It had grown from his experience on several previous Everest expeditions, and especially from a new relationship between 'Sahib' and Sherpa which he had found with Raymond Lambert and the other Swiss climbers. The world, in unfairly overlooking the immense contributions made to their success by my other companions, has rightly acclaimed these two men. Of course, those final dispositions were a source of much disappointment to some members of the party, even including myself. Michael Ward, who had accepted to join the expedition as our medical officer, was an outstanding mountaineer who had climbed with Shipton's parties during the 1951 Reconnaissance and the Cho Oyu expedition; it was particularly hard for him to be asked to make his climbing contribution to the Assault Plan below the level of the South Col, in case of illness or accidents to other members of the party. I was in no doubt about his chagrin at the time. Happily, this did not prevent us enjoying three alpine seasons, which included some memorable climbs, in the years immediately after Everest. Wilf Noyce was another strong contender for the summit, but so were Alf Gregory and George Lowe. I shall always be grateful to my companions for making my invidious task easier by taking those hard decisions so well.

Everest, while we were climbing it, was a continuous and connected series of events, most of them anticipated and each contributing to the next. In memory, it comes back to me as a few disconnected highlights. There was the tense, protracted drama as we tried, in wind and heavy snowfall, to solve the problem of climbing the Lhotse Face in order to reach the South Col, during those ten days in the first half of

May, when the momentum so splendidly provided by George Lowe, Ang Nyima and Michael Ward gradually slowed down. My diary records my own feelings at the time:

12th May It is difficult not to feel bitter disappointment in these atrocious weather conditions. Today it has snowed another seven inches and this evening I found the track both up and down the Cwm obliterated. George Lowe . . . was waist deep at times and his hard-won tracks will have been completely filled in. We've got to solve the Lhotse Face problem and must put the best men on to this, regardless of other tasks.

The day after I wrote this I climbed the Face with Ang Namgyal to consult with George. Once on the steep parts, there was no track and work became 'dreadfully hard, ploughing thigh-deep in new snow, made heavy by the heat'. The drastic steps I had in mind when I wrote those words on 12th May took the form of asking Hillary and Tenzing, who were earmarked as the second summit pair, to go up the Face to Camp 6 and give fresh impetus to the Sherpas who were there, on their way with vital loads for the South Col. But for the spirit and stamina of those two men, they could not have undertaken that job and returned to get ready to join the Second Assault only three days afterwards.

There was the thrilling, heart-warming moment when Wilf Noyce and Annullu banished our doubts as they topped the crest, beside the rock buttress which divides the Face, known as the Geneva Spur, on 21st May. There was that unforgettable struggle as Charles Evans, Tom Bourdillon, and I tried to put up a tent on the South Col on 24th May:

The wind was terrible. My oxygen was finished and the others had to take theirs off to help get the tents up. This was a fantastic struggle with each of us falling about with lack of oxygen and unable to work for more than a few minutes at a time. And all the time that fiendish wind – deadly cold – was tearing the tent from our hands and blowing away anything we chanced to lay down on this desert, stony waste. In the end we managed somehow, using rocks and oxygen bottles as weights, and dragged our gear inside. The Sherpas had turned up and we put them in the 'Meade', while we three got into the large Pyramid. Charles struggled with the stove, Tom with the night oxygen, and I handed round the food. Between 5 and 9 p.m. I had no less than nine brews; nothing very solid but all most comforting. In the end we managed to settle down amid a confusion of oxygen gear, Li-Los and sleeping bags, food etc, with the wind outside tearing away at the tent. Altogether an unforgettable experience.

My personal moment of achievement was one I am unable to enjoy, even in memory. My oxygen supply, partly blocked by ice which I was too anoxic to identify at the time, made it a battle of mind over matter to struggle up the South-East Ridge on 26th May:

> I was getting increasingly exhausted; each spell of eight to twelve steps had to be followed by two or three minutes rest. Gasping and moaning for breath was an experience I'll never, never forget: a real fight for life. Bodily self-control vanished as I struggled to get back into my lungs that vital element of oxygen. Never have I been put to such physical strain.
>
> We climbed the couloir, which rises in steepness to 50 degrees near its top and scrambled to the crest of the South-East Ridge at 27,300 feet, where still stand the ragged remnants of Tenzing's and Lambert's tent from last spring. We rested for half an hour. The closed-circuiters had forged ahead and were climbing strongly up the ridge. Da Namgyal and I struggled up another 200 feet* with the weather closing in—it took us another half hour to do so. Then Da Namgyal packed up. I wanted to make another 50 feet, to reach a small ledge at the foot of a steep buttress, whose top—27,800 feet—was my choice for the camp site. But he couldn't. After making a feeble effort to scrape out a platform we dumped our loads; oxygen, tent, food, kerosene etc and started unsteadily down, without oxygen.

But my worst moment of all came the following day, when Charles Evans and Tom Bourdillon, after their great effort in reaching the South Summit, had left the Col to return to Advanced Base. Some time later, Charles returned to tell us that Tom had collapsed, that more help was needed if he was to get down. Whom to send? There we were; Ed and Tenzing, the second summit pair; Greg and George Lowe and Ang Nyima, support climbers for the Second Assault—and myself. I had nursed the same personal ambitions as everyone else, of going to the top. But aside from the question as to whether I had the stamina to do so, I had decided that, as leader, I should not put myself into either of the two summit teams. But I had set my heart on staying in close support of both attempts, to help make difficult decisions and to give encouragement where needed. The decision which had now to be taken, hard though it seemed on personal grounds, was to join Charles in helping Tom down to Advanced Base.

It was soon forgotten, for three days later there was that supreme moment, when Ed, Tenzing, George, Wilf Noyce and Ang Nyima came down into the Cwm and told us the news; my pen is quite inadequate to convey the joy of it, for it was beyond the realm of any other personal experience. Then there was that crescendo of happiness when the news reached the rest of the world, and the universal delight

---

* The height at our turning back point was computed as being 27,500 feet by the Army Mountaineering Association's expedition in 1976.

30 May Our anxieties as
to Ed and Tenzing's safety
were ended when 5 figures
appeared in the colour,
making for PG Traverse;
at least this was the
total number of persons
on or above the South Col.

We had 16 min to [?] till
2 p.m.; however, for
hours of the second
assault when George,
Lowe, Ed & Tenzing
came in to Adv Base.
Most of us went out

to meet them and,
when we realized by
their unmistakable
gestures that they had
been to the top, we
temporarily went mad.

I found myself embrac-
ing Ed & Tenzing,
keeping not a little
and I think the others
did much the same.
James Morris of the
'Times' had come up
and was there in
time to scoop the

was played back to us. Among the many messages was a generous tribute from Eric Shipton. In gratitude for all he had done to make our success possible, we drank his health in the expedition's rum. Tired as we were, we walked on air on our way homewards.

It was sad that as we returned to Kathmandu, a sour note was introduced by a press avid to overdramatise the story. 'Who reached the top first? Was it Tenzing or Hillary?' We were taken completely by surprise, for none of us had thought to ask either of the successful pair that particular question. Yet Tenzing was grilled for hours and hours to say that it was he; indeed in the intensity of rightful pride in his achievement among his countrymen, we passed under triumphal arches depicting a triumphant Tenzing hauling an apparently un-conscious Hillary up the final few feet to the summit. To add to his bewilderment, Tenzing was also asked to declare his nationality: was he a citizen of Nepal, or of India? He was born in Thami, in the district of Khumbu in Eastern Nepal, but he had lived for many years in Darjeeling, India. The question of his nationality had never occurred to him; he was a Sherpa, a people whose ancestors lived in Tibet. Poor Tenzing; it was his first taste of a different, more cynical and sensation-hungry world of which he, until that moment, had had no experience. He weathered it well, and perhaps that special relationship which had been created by those other experiences we had shared together helped him, as it helped us all, to stay together when the meaner-minded press hounds seemed intent on tearing us apart. That, and the rejoicings of everyone, everywhere we went, who could not care less whether it was Tenzing or Hillary who stepped first on to the top of the world, or whether we were natives of India, Nepal, New Zealand, or some part of the British Isles. All that mattered was that man had climbed the highest mountain.

I called my book *The Ascent of Everest*. No doubt an element of presumptuousness could be read into that title; as though it implied, unintentionally, that it was a 'once only' event. Chris Bonington, writing his account of the magnificent achievement of his expedition in 1975, called it: *Everest, the Hard Way*. That too, has been perceived as presumptuous: as a reflection on the first ascent. It also leaves a problem for the authors of stories about future, even harder climbs on that mountain. Our climb has been followed by many other expedi-tions; it is now the standard route to the top. It has even been dubbed by the Sherpas the 'Yak Route'. Our 'Basis for Planning' has, like the route we followed, been adopted as 'standard', a pattern on which many other expeditions have shaped their own plans. But our biggest difficulty was, I think, to overcome, not so much the physical and physiological, great as these were, as the psychological problems, both in general, and particular to each man. Like Bannister's four-minute mile, there was that uncertainty about man's ability to do it: in our case there was that question mark over the last 1,000 feet or so. The Sherpas suffered especially from those doubts, and their superstitions that they should not incur the wrath of the gods by venturing above the South Col. But there was also a climate created by many other doubters, including some in the best position to know. When I went to Switzerland early in 1953 to hear about the experiences of the two Swiss attempts led by Edouard Wyss-Dunant and Gabriel Chevallet Raymond Lambert had left me with no illusions about his doubts as to our competence where they, mountaineers born and bred, had failed. 'Vous aurez de gros problèmes,' he had said, with a wealth of meaning in his voice. When once a man has made a break-through, be it on the surface or the bed of the ocean, over land or in the air, or in outer space itself—that barrier of doubt is down; others can be sure that what has been achieved can be repeated, over and over again.

The acclaim accorded to the first ascent of Everest was due not only to the achievement, but also to its fortuitous timing. I need not expatiate on the near coincidence of the event with the Queen's Coronation on 2nd June 1953; nor on its impact upon a nation still weary after five years of war and standing expectant at the outset of a new reign which was blessed by the youth of the Sovereign and her dynamic husband. In a wider sense, our achievement was seen, as was Gagarin's in 1960, as a unifying influence which transcended national barriers. In mountaineering history it was accounted as an important milestone, although it was greeted by some climbers with a sigh of relief. Eric Shipton voiced the opinions of many when he remarked, with pardonable cynicism: 'Thank Goodness, now we can get on with some real climbing'. There was some truth in that; the mountain had become the focus of so much attention in the urge to attain the ultimate in altitude that it tended to detract from the development and enjoyment of a pastime which had traditionally been pursued without overt competition and free of the glare of publicity. Lucien Devies, then President of the Fédération Française de la Montagne, whose team were to have made a further attempt on the summit in 1954 had we failed, observed: 'Les britanniques ont décapité l'alpinisme.' He appeared to mean that we had destroyed the main incentive to climb, represented by an apparently inaccessible highest point on the earth's surface.

Looking back with the perspective of twenty-five years, I am inclined to say that both Shipton and Devies were wrong. What has happened during this last quarter century? For one thing, our climb to

that ultimate place released a flood of enthusiasm for further exploration and achievement in the Himalayas, the Andes and other high
ranges the world over. Within two years of our success, the second
highest mountain, K2, had been climbed by the Italians and the third
highest, Kangchenjunga by a British expedition. The Germans had
avenged their pre-war disasters on the ill-famed Nanga Parbat by the
astonishing performance of a single member of their expedition in
1953 (in fact he was an Austrian, Hermann Buhl) in getting to the top.
Other high peaks 'fell' in succession during the next twelve years or so
until, with the Chinese ascent of Gosainthan in 1964, all the giants
exceeding 25,000 feet in height had been climbed.

Far from being 'decapitated' after Everest, mountaineering everywhere grew apace. Shipton, too, was wrong if he hoped that its
devotees could pursue their activities without attracting the attention
of the media and of commercial interests. But he was right in the sense
that an obsession for records in height gradually gave way to a search
for new and harder ways up the biggest peaks; the dramas which had
been enacted on the great mountain faces in the western Alps since
the early years of this century, now began on the highest mountain of
all. In 1953 few climbers—myself among them—who had seen the
Muztagh Tower and Amai Dablam, let alone the southern faces of
Annapurna and Everest, believed that these tremendous precipices
could be climbed; especially when they lay between 23,000 and 26,000
feet, or higher. I was proved wrong in my turn as they succumbed
successively to British parties, who were emulated by Polish climbers
on the west face of Makalu, by the French on the south face of Jannu,
the Germans on the Rakhiot and Diamiari faces of Nanga Parbat, the
Russians on the south face of Pik Kommunizma in the Pamirs. Modern
techniques, in particular the use of jumars, have made it possible
to climb at alpine standards even at high altitudes. Annapurna South
Face, Makalu West Buttress, the South Face of Pumori and the West
Face of Changabang provide striking evidence of this. Witness the
Indian triumph on the eastern flank of Kangchenjunga from the Zemu
glacier, and the recent achievements of Bonington and Scott and others
on Changabang and the Ogre and climbs of comparable difficulty.
These deeds raise the standards of mountaineering and at the same
time diminish the credibility of the word impossible. And there is still
a profusion of magnificent new routes for the modern mountaineer.

Since we first climbed the mountain there have been seventeen
further expeditions, not all of them successful, but during which some
sixty climbers have stood on the summit, including two women. The
mountain has been booked with the Nepalese government by climbing
groups from various countries up to the year 1985.

Our ascent of Everest became a symbol of national status, a subject for sermons and for The Goodies, an incentive for export drives, a target for charitable appeals, a trade name for an Italian wine and for double-glazing against the rigours of the British climate. The names of some members of the expedition have been given to schools and school houses, to streets, youth clubs, Scout troops, exploration groups, and even to three tigers in the Edinburgh Zoo.

Everest gave rise to much good entertainment in our honour for many months after our return. We were, for instance, invited to Paris in the autumn of 1953 to receive the congratulations of the President of the French Republic, Vincent Auriol. After the ceremony at the Elysée Palace our hosts, Maurice Herzog and other leading personalities among French mountaineers, took us to a night club in the Pigalle district. There we witnessed an interesting enactment of the ascent of Everest by a troupe of enchanting young ladies. They were roped together in a sort of fashion, with coils round their elegant middles, but that was as far as equipment — or clothing — went, as they danced and sang against a backcloth of snowy mountains. At the end of the song the intrepid leader of this *cordeé* produced, as though from nowhere, a little Union flag. It was a charming gesture by our Gallic friends, which made a small contribution to the *Entente Cordiale*.

'You must be enjoying this kind of weather,' is a remark I have come to expect whenever we have a particularly unpleasant cold spell, in which I shiver like everyone else. To many people those who have climbed on Everest, especially those who made the first ascent, tend to be cast for all time in the heroic mould, and it can be an embarrassing posture. Like most people I enjoy being appreciated, but for things I have done recently rather than a quarter of a century ago. It is somewhat exacting to be expected to live up to misplacedly high expectations of stoicism and intrepidity, which I possess in no larger measure than many other folk.

Yet behind these attitudes there is, I suppose, something good; not about those of us who are on the receiving end of eulogies, but about the people who entertain that sense of wonder and who offer their appreciation. And perhaps the most important thing about our climb was that it caught the imagination of youth and gave a fillip to climbing as a sport, and to expeditions great and small. The joint Himalayan Committee which had sponsored our 1953 expedition, decided to set up a trust fund from the income derived from the Everest film and book, as well as from the lectures given by members of the expedition in many parts of the world. The charitable purpose of this fund, known as the Mount Everest Foundation is to 'encourage, or support, expeditions for the exploration of, and research into the geology, ethnology,

zoology and similar sciences of the mountain regions of the world'
and every year since it was established in 1954, the Management
Committee has considered the applications and plans of many groups,
mostly comprising young people, who need formal approval and
financial help to explore, climb and undertake scientific work in the
more remote parts of mountain ranges.

In mid-May 1973 the Indian Mountaineering Foundation convened an
international conference in Darjeeling to make the 20th anniversary
of our climb and the 8th anniversary of the ascent of Everest by an
Indian expedition. It was appropriate that the venue should be the
Himalayan Mountaineering Institute at North Point, for this training
establishment had been set up at the initiative of B. C. Roy, Chief
Minister of the Government of Bengal in 1953, to commemorate the
first ascent and to encourage Indian youth to learn the rudiments of
climbing and mountain travel. Jawaharlal Nehru, who was Prime
Minister at that time, had himself appointed Tenzing as its first
Director of Training and a number of our Sherpas had joined the
instructional staff. Tenzing and other old friends were still in post
twenty years later, and Gompu, who at the age of seventeen had been
our youngest Sherpa and had twice carried loads to the South Col, was
the Chief Instructor; he had since achieved the unique distinction to be
the only person to have twice climbed Everest. Charles Wylie, Alf
Gregory, Joy and I decided that a pleasant way of marking the
anniversary would be to visit Khumbu, taking the easy way of a
flight from Kathmandu to Luglha, and then to walk across Eastern
Nepal to Darjeeling in time to attend the conference and greet our
Sherpa friends. Apart from Tenzing and Gompu, I was especially
looking forward to seeing Da Namgyal again, and most of all, Dawa
Thondup, who had been my companion on every one of my Himalayan expeditions, including Everest.
    Much had changed in Khumbu and particularly in the precincts of
Everest. A day's march down the gorge of the Dudh Khosi, the airstrip built by Hillary on a tilted plateau at Luglha 9,500 feet above the
sea and 2,000 feet above the roaring river was receiving nine or more
light aircraft daily in the tourist season; visitors were pouring in and
out of this miniature airport and well-worn camp sites marked the
stages from there to our old Base Camp, some of them littered with
evidence of human habitation. Tengpoche itself, which made me gasp
in wonder at the beauty of it when I first stepped out on to the meadow
beneath the monastery, is fast becoming a refuse heap of plastic bags,
paper and tin cans.
    As we travelled in Khumbu, helicopters whirled their noisy way up

and down the valley: an Italian expedition of sixty-four climbers, chosen from their mountain troops, and about a thousand Sherpa porters, was busy invading the great mountain. Ed Hillary, who had visited their Base Camp, gave us a graphic description of the huge mess tent to feed a hundred people; and the comfortable quarters of Signor Monzino, the expedition leader. Superbly situated over the villages of Khumjung at 13,000 feet a Japanese hotel had been built with every modern comfort: heating system, bathroom, internal telephone and oxygen for each bedroom. A special airstrip was being bull-dozed to enable the guests to be speeded even closer to the great mountain, and then taken by jeep for the final 500 feet, gasping for breath, to this lofty haven of modern civilization, and, aided by oxygen, to appreciate the breath-taking view.

Not all was a matter for sentimental regret. A small hospital, staffed by volunteer New Zealand doctors, had been built at Khumde and also a number of primary or intermediate English schools in the villages of Sola and Khumbu. A few modern bridges spanned the rivers, where formerly shaky structures were swept away each year in the monsoon floods. All this was the creative work of Hillary, who has done a tremendous job for the Sherpa people.

Pondering the marks of change, while my companions and I walked east from Khumbu to the Indian frontier during our three weeks' trek, my feelings were mixed as I recollected our previous visit twenty years before. It was a vain hope that we would find everything just as it used to be. We had no exclusive rights to the approach, any more than we could expect to be the only ones to climb the mountain. Commerce has cashed in on public enthusiasm to view the world's highest mountain.

It has offered the Sherpas, for instance, opportunities to earn a living in new ways and attracted some of the experienced men away from expedition work. This in turn has, on some occasions, produced tragic results when their places are filled by men from remoter villages without the expected knowledge of snow and ice craft. We still owe it to these people to safeguard them from avoidable risks and to help train them in mountaineering skills. At the same time we Westerners cannot deny the Sherpas our own opportunities and amenities. Education and the tourist industry are reducing the gap between us, and the Sherpas are not slow to avail themselves of the chances they provide.

Yet man, by seeking adventure and widening the avenues towards the mountains, risks destroying that very thing which he needs to preserve. In bringing education and commercial opportunities to people who have lived for centuries on a subsistence economy, he is helping to exchange a way of life which, for all its hardships, is fundamentally happy, for a different kind of society which, for all its benefits, is competitive and divisive. The prospect cannot be regarded with hope or equanimity.

Such were my reflections as my companions and I travelled through country seldom visited by foreigners. In nineteen days, after crossing eleven passes of over 10,000 feet and covering more than 150 miles, we reached the crest of the Singalila ridge—the frontier between India and Nepal. It had been an unforgettable journey across the rugged foreground of the great peaks. We had passed through a riot of rhododendrons in full and variegated bloom, over open grassy highlands, across and along the turgid waters of the Arun and the Tamur, two of Nepal's biggest rivers. We had stopped overnight in schools, dâk bungalows, Sherpa houses, haylofts and tents.

The journey had brought Charles Wylie in touch with Gurkha pensioners and his knowledge of Nepali had provided us all with some contact with the people—Rais, Limbus, Gurungs, Chetris and Sherpas, farming their rugged highlands along our route.

This is all part and parcel of a mountain expedition. The mountaineers of the future, arriving at the foot of some Himalayan peak by helicopter, or car, will be the poorer, in more than one sense, for having missed the approaches along the rivers, through villages and forests to the uplands on their way.

One thing has not changed. Twenty-five years on, we who first climbed Everest are still friends, keeping in touch with one another as best we may, notwithstanding our various occupations and the distances which separate us; meeting from time to time. For ten years after 1953 we held annual reunions in North Wales. These have since continued every five years. We have just been together once more to celebrate our jubilee in our traditional meeting place, the Pen-y-Gwryd Hotel, with our generous hosts, Chris and Jo Briggs who, with our own families two generations on, have also become a part of our Everest family. Some are no longer the lean and powerful figures of manhood that they were then. Some of us, more fortunately, still climb. But the bond which united us on that mountain has stood the test of time. We are still together.

9

Young Enterprise

1956–66

I WAS LUCKIER THAN THE VAST MAJORITY OF YOUNG PEOPLE OF my own age at the end of the First War. The tradition of foreign travel was then a privilege confined to the middle and upper strata of society and I was in the middle layer. At that time the pound sterling rode high above the debased currencies in most European countries and, although my mother had been widowed in the war and was not well off, she was able to take my brother and me quite cheaply to Switzerland for summer and winter holidays. From 1920 onwards, when I reached the age of ten, mountains became part of my scene. Before we entered our 'teens we were accustomed to exploring up to the snowline and were doing some ambitious walking tours through the mountains. We learned to ski with rudimentary equipment, doing it the hard way by plodding for hours through deep snow up to some distant ridge, in order to earn a single run down to the valley at the end of the day. I soon became wedded to the notion that mountains were there to be climbed precisely because they made demands on my will-power and fitness, and because the effort was so rewarding. I began to realise that there were intriguing challenges beyond that snowline, and up those beetling rock buttresses, which would require skills and entail risks. For me, the satisfaction of these discoveries was the greater for the fact that I was an indifferent performer at competitive games, to which so much importance was attached at my school. It was natural that the successful ones should be held in high esteem, but the high status accorded to games left many others like me with a sense of inadequacy and failure.

Much later on I began to relate those boyhood experiences to other people. Training soldiers in the mountains during the war had brought home to me the fact that a great many other people, whose backgrounds were unprivileged, maybe from the back streets of a large city, could find the same satisfaction through adventurous outdoor activities as I had. Indeed, the shock of discovering their own ability to cope and achieve success was all the greater. The circumstances of birth and background had nothing to do with the matter.

The memorandum on this general subject I sent Geoffrey Young in 1940 was prompted by my beliefs regarding methods of training soldiers for the immediate needs of war. But when he sent it on to Kurt Hahn it was the first link in a chain which was eventually to connect me with the needs of young people in peace. Dr Hahn, Headmaster of Gordonstoun, was already making his mark on the British academic scene. Two years later I invited him to watch some battle drills which, at that time, were a new development in tactical manoeuvre at infantry company and platoon level; I had arranged a demonstration on the slopes of Beguildy Beacon above the Teme Valley, not far from the war-time home of Gordonstoun which had been evacuated from the Moray Firth to Plas Dinam in Montgomeryshire.

This was my first meeting with that remarkable Jewish refugee from Germany who, under duress, had left his own school at Salem on the shores of Lake Constance and founded a new public school in Britain. Here he introduced his ideas, radically new at the time, about the education of boys. I think he was not very interested in the military exercises, but he had come because he was very keen to interest me in his own ideas, maintaining that activities and tests outside the class room should be equally valued with academic studies and examinations; the essence of his creed was that each boy needed a challenge personal to and attainable by himself, rather than being assessed in competition and comparison with the performance of others. He invited me in his turn to Plas Dinam, where I watched some of these 'activities' and learned more about Hahn's theories; in particular, the value of giving outlets to the idealism in young people through the rescue of others in distress at sea and in the hills.

After the war Hahn widened the scope of his ideas beyond his school. He persuaded other educationists to introduce a system of awards for individual enterprise and physical tests of athletic skill which, by training and personal effort, were within the competence of most boys. The scheme was open to all boys, regardless of social circumstances. Known as the County Badge Scheme, it flourished for a time under the auspices of a few local education authorities; but it lacked cohesion and a nationwide incentive. Hahn also founded the Outward Bound movement, with residential adventure schools located on the coast and in mountain areas, providing courses which gave working boys experience in coping with hazardous and difficult situations in all weathers, on the sea and in the mountains. They were a natural development to the Commando and Snow Warfare school and the

Cliff Assault Wing of the war years; for quite a while the regimes at the Outward Bound schools retained the same strong accent on rigorous training and discipline; at the end of the course a commonly held view was that it was an experience worth having, but not a pastime to be pursued voluntarily.

Such was my impression in 1952, on first visiting the Outward Bound school in Eskdale, where I went to give a talk on our plans and hopes for Everest in the following year. At the same time I was impressed by the effect of the experience on most of the boys, in terms of increased confidence, self-respect and comradeship. The regime has long since been considerably relaxed and the sense of enjoyment enhanced accordingly; a quite different atmosphere was apparent when I revisited the school a few years ago for a conference on safety and rescue in the mountains.

A year after that first occasion some members of the successful Everest expedition were again at that school to tell our story. It was a memorable occasion because Eric Shipton was then Warden of the school. The visit was all the happier in that this was the first opportunity for us to meet again, share the discussion which followed my talk, and for me to bring home to my audience the great part Shipton had played in the eventual triumph.

It was also a delight to meet Geoffrey Young again; he had come specially to greet us. Geoffrey was then the Grand Old Man of mountaineering. Although he had lost a leg in the First War and his climbing days were long since over, his achievements at the end of the era of alpine climbing with guides before that war, were a by-word among mountaineers throughout the world. He had that marvellous gift of narrating his exploits, describing his own feelings on a climb and helping the reader to understand why people climb. It was Geoffrey's faith in Hahn's ideas which had led him to send on my paper about mountain training. Later, Hahn was to offer me the post of Provost of Gordonstoun and its preparatory establishment, but I declined. I felt that it would be restricting to remain in a supervisory rôle in the school which had been the nursery for Hahn's ideas when the time was ripe for spreading them more widely.

That feeling was growing in my mind as I continued to meet thousands of young people during visits to schools, factories and youth organisations to tell the Everest story. The demand to hear about it was insistent and the enthusiasm it generated, quite tremendous. There was talk of a new Elizabethan Age and there was, indeed, plenty of the spirit of Drake and Raleigh around at the time. Not many people could hope to climb as high as Everest, but it was obvious that a very great number would jump at the chance to do something adventurous.

9

There was something missing in the upbringing of most of our youth in those days and the moment to supply it was highly propitious.

In the autumn of 1954, when I was Assistant Commandant of the Army Staff College, I received a telephone call from Hahn; he wished to see me that same afternoon. It was typical of the man that his business would brook no delay. I remember his arrival at the portals of that distinguished building, presenting a somewhat cloak-and-dagger appearance to the doorman in his broad-brimmed black felt hat. On being ushered into my room his first act, before offering me a limp hand-shake, was to advance to the windows and throw them wide open; it was a cold November evening and the central heating was on. I think he tended to feel claustrophobic, but it made the interview a trifle unrelaxed. Perhaps it was all part of his technique. He sat hunched in a chair, his bald head slightly bent, his pale blue eyes transfixing me, but contriving to charm me with a singularly sweet smile. He told me in his soft, German-accented voice of his long cherished hopes of persuading his former pupil Prince Philip to give his name to a royal award, which would supersede the County Badge Scheme; the Prince had at last consented. Hahn had arranged a small dinner party in Brown's hotel for the following evening, at which a few people who had agreed to help work out the scheme would be present; would my wife and I join them? He wanted me to give advice on the conditions for adventurous journeys which would be a key feature of the award scheme. Hahn, a confirmed bachelor, was a skilful operator. He knew the value of enlisting the support of the woman in a family ménage, in order to secure the services of someone he needed. He made a lasting impression on my wife, clicking his heels as he bent over her hand. His forte was in choosing men, implanting his ideas in their minds and guiding them from the rear; that was his style of leadership. Guidance often took the form of meetings over breakfast at his hotel, to which his disciples were summoned. Greatly as I admired Hahn, my contrary nature prompted me to resist the spell he cast on some; I think I was a disappointment to him. He appeared to exercise an influence upon some people which can best be described as mesmeric. I was conscious of its bearing on myself and, although I recognised the total integrity of the man and the basic truths behind his vision, I declined to succumb to that influence.

Yet whether Hahn willed it or not, I suppose that moment of his visit to the Staff College marked the beginning of the end of my career as a soldier. I was invited to join the Originating Committee, as it became known, which gradually put flesh on the bones of the Scheme. During the following twelve months it became clear that, despite its potentialities, it was not going to be easy to make it widely acceptable to organisations working for young people; nor would it be sensible to set up yet another youth organisation which, with the prestigious name of the Duke, would be a cause of rivalry with the others. It would have to be on offer as a resource which could be used by any and all bodies capable of operating it. It followed that there was a need for an agency, or focal point, to authorise its use, ensure parity of the standards for gaining awards, and be a general clearing house for developing the Scheme, hopefully in response to increasing demands.

Perhaps the most important need, in a scheme which was so personal in its challenge from Prince Philip, was the appointment of someone to run it who would be generally acceptable. For some time, I harboured doubts as to whether the Award idea would elicit a favourable response; but my reservations were mainly about the prejudices, of which I was aware, in regard to Hahn himself. In 1954 the memories of the war against Germany were still fresh in the minds of everyone. For some, possessed of a surfeit of emotion and a dearth of logic, Hahn, although he was a refugee who had suffered at Hitler's hands and had left his own country out of abhorrence of Nazi atrocities, was identified with the Hitler Youth Movement. For some people the very fact of his former nationality made his ideas suspect and 'alien'. I did not share these feelings. It was true that Hahn had seen and valued the sense of purpose and self-respect which 'Hitler Youth' had engendered in young Germans, but he used the good in it for entirely laudable ends.

I had become entirely convinced of the merits and potential value of his ideas, provided they were suitably adapted to the temperament and needs of young people in Britain. Somewhat presumptuously, it occurred to me that I might take on the job of launching the Scheme. It was a difficult decision to make a final break at that stage in my life from a Service in which I had spent twenty-eight years and in which my prospects for further advancement looked promising, in order to sail into uncharted waters; it seemed crazy to some of my brother officers and the Commandant of the Staff College, Major-General Charles ('Splosh') Jones, thought the venture would fail. On the other hand, I was quite sure that here was an important need which should be met and that this was an opportunity, not to be missed. It was something quite new in the Youth Service; it was fraught with difficulties. There was a lot of persuasion to be done among educationists and social workers, as well as in industry, all of them areas in which I was a stranger. All this made it a risk, and all the more of a challenge.

I suggested to Prince Philip that I might take on the job and, to my delight, he accepted my offer. I have never had less cause to regret any decision.

The general idea was to provide a programme of activities and hobbies within the compass of a single scheme which, with the incentive to gain awards from the Duke of Edinburgh, would help to fill spare time for boys during the awkward period between leaving school at fifteen and being called up for National Service at eighteen. It was a time when it was difficult for lads to settle down and when employers, knowing that their young operatives and apprentices would soon be leaving to join the forces, were apt to take little interest in their welfare. It was therefore, a scheme to be offered after leaving school, with the prospect of progressing through three standards, or levels of performance, of an increasingly demanding nature, gaining a badge and a certificate signed by the Duke at each level. A very wide range of choice was to be given in each of four main areas of performance: the Expedition, Pursuits, Physical Fitness, Service.

The announcement of Awards for youthful enterprise by the Duke of Edinburgh in February 1956 was well received. True, the Scout Movement felt that it amounted to spreading the methods which had been invented by Baden-Powell forty years beforehand; they elected to await the end of the pilot scheme which I was about to launch, before making a decision about using the programme. There was some coolness, too, in the Department of Education and in the Association of Education Committees. The Minister for Education suggested that it should be tried out by the voluntary youth organisations rather than in the schools and the Duke of Edinburgh agreed with him. In retrospect I am sure that the Originating Committee should have consulted at an earlier stage with the local education authorities. However, there were a few Chief Education Officers who felt strongly that the Scheme had great potentialities. At the first full-scale conference of the bodies which were making the initial experiments, held at Ashridge College in September 1956, a powerful plea was made for lowering the age of entry to fourteen thus permitting boys to make a start before leaving school. Otherwise, the argument ran, the majority of lads who most urgently needed encouragement to make constructive use of their leisure and who did not join youth organisations—the so-called 'unclubbables', or 'unattached'—would miss the opportunity. It would be a scheme which would attract only the enterprising ones who needed its stimulus least.

This was a telling point; it was endorsed by the majority of the conference. Caught between the basic principle laid down by the Originating Committee, who did not wish the Scheme to seem to have connections with school in the boys' minds, and the no less compelling need to draw in the under-achievers and lay-abouts who tended to waste their spare time, I accepted the clear view which emerged in favour of the latter argument, and reported our recommendation to lower the age to fourteen. It was a momentous and controversial change, which was not immediately pleasing to the founder and the Patron of the Scheme with whom I had an awkward conversation on the telephone. In the event, I think that its effect was more far-reaching and, on balance, more favourable than most of us foresaw at the time. It did much more than bring in a far greater number and a wider social range of boys; it created a link between secondary schools and youth organisations which was largely lacking at the time. Indeed, the greatest contribution of the Award Scheme, as it has developed over the years, is seen by many people to have been this property of linking together all parties: youth groups, firms, schools and colleges, the Services and civilian bodies, as well as individual people who are involved in it; it has broken down many a barrier between differing allegiances and different social strata.

That first conference at Ashridge, and the second one to review progress a year later, were thrilling experiences. The Scheme was a tool which was common property among all parties represented at the conference, and for many others who might come in later. Collaboration of this kind was a new experience to the youth organisations, which tended jealously to cherish their own distinctive traditions; here was a programme which they could all use without any question of infringing proprietorial rights, and which they could each adapt to conform with their own particular ethos. New again was the prospect that, by making a beginning in their last year at school, more boys might be persuaded to join this or that club or cadet unit with the carrot of continuing their Award progress.

And there was another thing. It became quickly apparent that the Scheme would of necessity be the means of involving a wider circle of adults, whose knowledge about, and enthusiasm for one or other leisure pursuit could be passed on to boys who chose to follow their various fancies: from bee-keeping to ballet-dancing, from motor mechanics to archaeology; for there is an almost endless range of interests from which to select. This was a spider's web of involvement, enmeshing not only organisations of many kinds in both the public and private sectors of national and local life, but older people with the young generation, and young people with one another, irrespective of their colour and social circumstances. The ramifications were breathtaking at that time. Already many organisations, especially local education authorities, were awaiting eagerly the end of the pilot phase; there were insistent demands to devise a scheme for girls; interest was being expressed by countries in the Commonwealth. I have never conducted or attended a conference, before or since, which generated so much enthusiasm and unity of purpose as those two meetings of minds to pioneer the Award Scheme in 1956 and 1957, when its possibilities dawned on those who took part.

It would be wearisome to trace the progress of Prince Philip's Scheme through the ten years of my stewardship. A parallel scheme for girls was launched towards the end of 1958. It retained the basic principles and structure of the Scheme for boys, but Phyllis Gordon-Spencer and her fellow architects were anxious to give it a distinctively feminine touch. Make-up and hair-style, dress design and flower arrangements were a few of the listed pursuits which most girls were then thought more likely to prefer to motorcycle maintenance and potholing. Fitness, as assessed by athletics events for boys, was deemed to be less relevant than activities associated with woman's traditional rôle as home-maker and mother, and when the Expedition Scheme for girls was launched their expeditions were devised so as to be less physically demanding and more widely interpreted. For instance, a group of country dwellers might pay a visit to observe and study aspects of urban life, and vice versa. There were still, however, many other hobbies and many kinds of neighbourhood service which both sexes could usefully and happily pursue together. Over the years, the area of common interest and tastes between the sexes has increased considerably and this has resulted in a major overhaul of the Scheme under the direction of my successor. What has now emerged is an omnibus scheme, in which young people can pick and choose at will from a common pool, within the framework of five areas of activity and levels of achievement. It is an interesting reflection of one aspect of the social changes which have taken place in the past twenty-two years. Hahn, I think, had no interest in including girls in his various schemes. His ideas about woman's rôle in society were as prosaic as his vision for boys was heroic. In them, he maintained, was that germ of leadership on which man's progress would always depend. When he wrote of 'the new aristocracy which would leaven the lump' his thoughts were both élitist and masculine; today they would be dubbed chauvinistic. The Originating Committee's line was more pragmatic. We considered that there was an immediate need to help boys through the 'gap' which then existed in the pattern of their young lives. In any case, it was sensible to simplify the initial testing period through which the Scheme was to be run. The 'gap' disappeared with the cessation of compulsory National Service and the age limit has since been extended from eighteen to twenty-five.

Inevitably, as more education authorities and independent schools, more firms and other institutions, including the various Service organisations became licensed operators of the Award Scheme, our administrative problems increased. So did the costs and the problem of raising money to meet them. Trustees were appointed under Prince Philip's chairmanship, to keep a fatherly eye on our operations; a charter was drafted by Sir Edwin Herbert, an eminent city solicitor who had been Chairman of the Himalayan Committee in 1953 and was my immediate predecessor as President of the Alpine Club. The Award Scheme became a registered charity. Prince Philip's influence, enthusiasm and persuasive skills were mainly responsible for the generous response from many quarters to the Trustees' appeals for funds. But however widely the Scheme was used, it was essential that the administration should retain its character of a service to other organisations and individuals, and should avoid becoming a 'movement' in its own right.

The Award Scheme has now become a universally recognised resource for the younger generation. It is operated almost everywhere in Britain where young people are brought together by work or during leisure. The ideas, and the method of putting them across, have been adopted, in whole or in part, by educationists, youth leaders, community workers, personnel managers and many others concerned with those aspects of training which fall outside the normal curriculum of the school or training centre. From the thousands who have attained that coveted Gold Award a large number of leaders have emerged, some of whom use their experience to operate, advise or help boys and girls with their activities in their spare time. But for all its merits, the Award Scheme has not found a great following in the youth clubs. It needs either a considerable degree of self-motivation on the part of individual young people, which many youngsters lack, or a relatively structured and orderly setting with strong leadership, in which they can feel the advantage of conforming and be encouraged to continue after making a start. By and large, youth clubs cater for young people who prefer to be less socially organised. Nor has the Scheme as a whole drawn in more than a tiny minority of the 'problem' youngsters who have created such serious trouble for many years past, on the beaches and football terraces, in the back streets – the modern vandals in our midst. For them the Scheme is not only too demanding, it is seen as a product of the Establishment against which, consciously or otherwise, they are in revolt. For them something different is needed about which I shall have a suggestion to offer in a later chapter. The real contribution of the Award Scheme has been that of offering a link between many areas of our national life, and its influence in education and the youth service as a pace-setter and standard-bearer. The Scheme upholds values which are still acceptable to most people.

Pioneered by some dedicated people on whose past associations and friendships I traded heavily, the Scheme has spread to many countries of the Commonwealth. Percy Wyn-Harris was a former colonial Governor who had reached 28,000 feet on Everest in 1933; Bill Heald was a former colleague at the Army Staff College both as student and instructor; General ('Dimmy') Dimoline was at that time Secretary of the Inter-Parliamentary Union; and there was Loftus Peyton-Jones with whom, as a joint planner on the Allied Staff, I had spent many happy days both at work and leisure in Fontainebleau.

The programme is not only adapted to match the needs and aspirations of young people from many different backgrounds; in a modest way it has helped to forge a link between the youth of many lands. The international aspect of the Scheme was brought home to me when I visited the first of a continuing series of Commonwealth Gold Award Expeditions in Canada in 1967. It was a heart-warming experience to be with all these young men and women and to observe how quickly they became, during that time and in those circumstances, a Commonwealth family. Some of them have remained close friends ever since and at least one marriage has resulted from those friendships.

When I think back to that tentative start we made in 1956, with myself and one assistant, Norman Charrington, and our secretary Ann Debenham (who had worked as my secretary throughout the Everest expedition) operating, as we were, in two small rooms within the offices of King George's Jubilee Trust, I marvel at the master-mind who placed in our hands the seed which grew into a tree, enthusiastically cultivated by a host of people and tended with zest and critical care by Prince Philip himself. It was also an example of what can be achieved with a little faith and some trusted friends.

It was one of those inspirational ideas which attracted people precisely for that reason and I was more than fortunate in finding myself supported by such a splendid team. In addition to Phyllis Gordon-Spencer, Norman Charrington and Loftus Peyton-Jones, Deric Evans came from a distinguished background in the Colonial Service; David Cobb brought with him from the Navy both his infectious enthusiasm and his sailing skills; he and Loftus gave a tremendous boost to the opportunities for adventure in the Scheme, particularly on the ocean. These, with a Secretariat staffed by some keen and devoted girls, created a most effective partnership in a pleasant family ambiance.

For myself, these were years of enthralling experiences and widening perspectives: work on the Youth Service Development Council and the Central Council of Physical Recreation; investigations into the problems of young immigrants and of juvenile delinquency, as well as involvement with overseas voluntary service. The opportunity to make new friends in various quarters I had not entered previously was among my most delightful discoveries during those ten years. So, too, was the chance to call on some old comrades from past associations in the Army and the mountaineering fraternity. I appointed a number of them as Award Liaison Officers, acting voluntarily wherever they lived and working as points of reference about the Scheme, explaining its rules and encouraging its use. Bill Amory, for example, had been my commanding officer during the crossing of the Sangro River and the fighting on the Gustav Line; he became our man in Devon and Cornwall. Theo Nicholson, one of the instructors at the Commando Mountain school and later Staff Captain at Headquarters of the 11th Indian Infantry Brigade, acted as ALO for Cheshire and Liverpool; a skiing friend, Ken Smith, worked in Surrey and two climbers, Jo Kretschmer and John Baskerville did the job in Berkshire and Bedfordshire. Peter Carpenter, whose father had accompanied Hahn from Salem to Gordonstoun, was another devoted helper. These were a few among many others.

The Award Scheme was one of those inspired ideas which draw in those many people who have something worthwhile to offer the youth of the nation.

In 1953 the floats and fancy dress parades at summer festivals featured numerous miniature Tenzings and Hillarys, perspiring inside their anoraks, muffled in balaclavas and goggles, tied together by mother's clothes lines and grasping Union Jacks. It may well have been mostly reflected parental pride, but the children eagerly played the new climbing game. Among an enormous fan mail after our return from Everest I treasured a letter from two sisters age ten and twelve, which read:

> Dear Sir John,
>   . . . Last year we went with Mummy and Daddy to Wales and climbed Snowdon. Next summer we are going to Scotland to climb Ben Nevis. Will you please send us details about climbing Mount Everest so that we may climb it the year after?

Well, Everest may be getting easier for succeeding generations as more expeditions climb it year after year, but it still isn't as easy as that. No matter, for that was the spirit I discerned in countless boys and girls at that time.

Against that background, I took special pleasure in the task of working out the conditions for the Expedition section of the Duke of Edinburgh's Award Scheme. To help me I invited David Cornock-Taylor, then General Secretary of the London Federation of Boys'

Clubs, and Desmond Hoare, a serving Rear-Admiral at the time, who was also active in a London's Boys' Club and had started a vogue in the London Federation for canoe journeys, under the title, the Fed Afloat. He was later to become the first warden of Hahn's International Sixth Form College at St Donat's Castle in South Wales. Hoare, an engineer officer, had experimented with adventure training for young stokers in the Navy and had already written about his ideas for extending that kind of training. They were enthusiastic colleagues.

Our underlying idea was to provide a framework for journeys by small groups of boys in the hills and moorland areas which would develop initiative, self-reliance and team-work, but which would also call for preliminary training in certain basic skills such as navigation and first-aid, and basic knowledge about appropriate clothing, food and equipment for the arduous business of trekking and coping with the vagaries of climate which even our mountains can produce.

The journeys, and the training which preceded them would, we hoped, give to the young people a respect for and perhaps a growing love of the wilder parts of Britain. We aimed to make the journeys challenging while avoiding turning them into a race or a severe trial of endurance. As with the other sections of the Scheme, it was important that the conditions should be within the capability of every fit boy, provided he was prepared to make the effort. We set minimum distances to be covered: 15 miles at Bronze standard, 30 miles for the Silver Award and 50 miles for the Gold. We also stipulated that, at each level, overnight stops must be made, bivouacking or using a tent: one night at Bronze, two nights at Silver and three at Gold. In addition, some specific but straightforward project was included, like observing and making a record of what had been seen and experienced — something which could easily enough be fitted into travelling across progressively more difficult terrain in a limited number of days.

The essence of the exercise however was that the boys should make and carry through their own plans, subject only to such advice and supervision as was necessary for reasons of safety. This matter of safety from accidents and exhaustion was of great concern to everyone. Apart from the physical hazards of weather and difficult country, we had to take into account what could reasonably be expected of boys at the ages when they were taking part in the various stages in the Scheme. There was also the emotional impact of the environment which, to be deemed challenging by the boys themselves, must inspire a certain amount of awe. To make the journeys too easy, to hedge them round with precautionary measures, to place the leadership in adult hands — would diminish the essential element of adventure and its appeal to the boys. The ingredient of risk was as necessary as that of competition

in organised games. On paper, it was a difficult balance to strike
between retaining the spice of excitement and the avoidance of
accidents. In practice, adult judgment would be of crucial importance.

I needed above all to discover whether we had got that balance right.
I spent a good deal of time in those early years, watching training for
the tests, the arrangements for the expeditions themselves, and observing boys in the course of their journeys; there was a certain amount of
adjustment to be made in the light of experience. It was also a most
heart-warming experience for me. My invariable impression was of
the tremendous enthusiasm of boys from all conditions of living.
Heavy loads, steep hillsides, rain and wind merely added to their sense
of achievement against the elements, the obstacles and all the other
odds. But it was also an anxious time. The differences, both in the
potential dangers and the technical knowledge required, as between
walking over downland and in the mountains was, and still is, far too
little appreciated. On a fine day in summer the way to the top of
Snowdon or Ben Nevis, or any other summit may seem so obvious
that the well-worn track can be disregarded. Other equipment, such
as a map, a compass and warm clothing may seem unnecessary
additions to the load on one's back. Shorts, shirt and light shoes may be
the preferred attire. But a cold, wet blanket of mist surrounds you
from nowhere and, all of a sudden, an icy wind begins to blow. One
or more of the party may quickly become exhausted by the combined
effects of these changes on the mental and physical effort of movement
on steep ground. Only then, and too late, you may realise that there is
more to this journey than a simple country walk. Even if you come
down without mishap, you may not have enjoyed the experience and
you may decide not to explore the mountains again.

Many organisations using the Scheme tended to choose the most
rugged areas in North Wales or the Lake District where the hazards
were greatest. Local mountain rescue organisations found that calls on
their services increased. In some cases they welcomed the opportunities
provided for their samaritan work; in others, there was understandable
criticism. They were quick to point out the need to be less ambitious,
to improve the content and quality of training. It was a salutary
experience when I was invited to meet the Lake District Mountain
Rescue Committee in Coniston after a day spent climbing on Dow
Crag and I was left in no doubt that some Award parties were inadequately prepared. Some disparity of standards was, of course, a
consequence of the decentralised nature of the Scheme's administration. But where risks were involved it became apparent that there must
be nationally recognised standards of competence in mountain travel,
which could be passed on to the young adventurers and by which their

plans would be checked and, if necessary, modified. Many more adults with adequate experience were needed.

When, after three years, the Award Scheme emerged from its pilot stage, we invited expert bodies in other forms of adventurous outdoor recreation to devise comparable conditions for journeys by canoe, or small boat, on cycle or horseback. Special conditions were drawn up, too, in consultation with the medical profession and appropriate national bodies, for children with various physical handicaps; even in a wheel-chair an adventurous journey is possible.

Since 1956 well over one million young people have taken the opportunities open to them through the Award Scheme to make their own expeditions. Large numbers of them have gone on to carry out more ambitious projects, whether within the ambit of the Scheme or independently of it. Accidents, or anxieties caused by young people temporarily missing during these journeys, have been remarkably few. A much publicised incident in Snowdonia in 1973, when four boys were missing over Easter Bank Holiday, did, perhaps, more good for the Scheme than harm when they were found quite safe, because they had followed the training previously given to them. In the twenty years of its existence, the only known fatal accident directly attributable to the Scheme's conditions occurred in 1961, the handful since then resulting from other causes which no rules could have prevented, with no blame attributable either to the Scheme or the adults operating it.

A great deal has been achieved in terms of encouraging initiative, self-reliance and teamwork which we originally laid down as being the basic purpose of this section of the Scheme. Most important of all, the experience has given enormous pleasure and satisfaction to younger and older people alike. While the Scheme as a whole has been found too demanding for some young people who are 'under-achievers' at school and prefer gangs to clubs, the Award expeditions have attracted a number of those who most lack any sense of purpose and who need to be challenged. They found a place in the former approved schools; they are used in some Detention Centres and Borstals. Something may be gained simply by inducing potential trouble-makers to make a start with this activity alone. Social workers and probation officers working with deprived and delinquent young people have also experimented with weekend trips to the hills and courses have been devised and staffed to enable disturbed and difficult boys and girls to benefit from the same range of activities; this training has become one of the resources available to the courts of law under what is known as Intermediate Treatment. The immediate results have been positive, but the longer term effects are more difficult to evaluate.

The value of adventurous training for teenagers and the need to increase the numbers of competent leaders was not, of course, demonstrated only by the Award Scheme expeditions. A number of secondary schools and youth organisations were beginning to develop this kind of activity. The Scheme also coincided with the emergence of outdoor pursuits centres and schools specialising in adventurous outdoor activities such as mountaineering, sailing and canoeing. Jack Longland (later Sir Jack), then Director of Education for Derbyshire, a pre-war Everest climber who had associations with the Outward Bound movement, set up the first Outdoor Pursuits Centre at White-hall in his own county in 1954. In 1955 the Central Council of Physical Recreation invited me to be the first Chairman of a national centre at Plas y Brenin in Snowdonia where mountain activities, canoeing and, for a while, pony trekking was taught. John Disley, the Olympic runner, was the first Chief Instructor and later produced the *Expedition Guide* for the Duke of Edinburgh's Award Scheme, much of the contents based on experiences gained with young people at the Centre. His place was taken by John Jackson, who had been one of the reserve members of the 1953 Everest expedition, and later succeeded Major Jim Milton as Director.

The vogue for mountain activities grew apace; the schools and centres multiplied. Today there are more than two hundred centres and organisations which run courses in mountain leader training. The short introductory courses in which adults had to participate as part of their qualification for the certificate, were having the effect of en-couraging young teachers and youth leaders to pass on their enthusiasm to their youthful charges; but a little knowledge of mountain-craft can be a dangerous thing. By the early 1960s the need for a nationally recognised standard of competence by adult leaders had become urgent and I was one of those who believed that some kind of diploma course should be instituted. Jack Longland was of the same mind; he was at that time President of the British Mountaineering Council and it was with the approval of that body that the Central Council of Physical Recreation took the further step in 1964 of setting up, under Long-land's chairmanship, the Mountain Leadership Training Board, which would draw up syllabuses for a basic course of training, lay down the conditions for the award of a certificate, and authorise approved centres to operate the scheme. In the fourteen years since the Board started this important work, several thousand Mountain Leadership certificates have been granted and a number of men and women have qualified at a higher standard to work as instructors at mountain schools. In Scotland a further qualification can be gained which enables leaders of groups to cope with the severe winter conditions of

snow, ice, wind and low temperatures in the Highlands. In some local
education authorities it is now standard practice not to allow school
groups to undertake journeys in the hills and over the moors unless
supervised by the holder of a Mountain Leadership Certificate.

As one of the original Board members, whose concern arose from
the need to provide essential safeguards for Award expeditions, I have
remained convinced of the importance of maintaining the standards of
adult leaders by means of these courses. But in 1973 voices were raised
within the fraternity of mountaineers expressing no less concern, as
the mountains became more and more frequented by groups of young
people for educational and training purposes, lest this large-scale
development in outdoor education and organised recreation should be
too dominated by bureaucracy; there was a fear that the holders of
these certificates in elementary hillcraft might be tempted to exceed
the limits of trekking over the easier ground and expose young people
to unjustifiable risks; one or two serious accidents gave point to these
fears. Some climbers maintained that mountain training was becoming
too stereotyped and that the true spirit of mountaineering, which is
perceived by some people as more than just a sporting activity, was
ignored. It was suggested that some teachers were seeking to gain
Mountain Leadership Certificates not because they enjoyed the
mountains, but simply because the qualification was useful to their
careers.

In 1974 I was invited by the British Mountaineering Council to
chair a committee to review the Council's position in regard to the
whole subject of training and educational work in the mountains.
The committee reported in May 1975. Our report, which offered some
philosophical views on the nature of mountaineering for the consideration of training establishments and education authorities, recommended that the British Mountain Council should, in the general
interest, assume overall responsibility for training methods and
standards. To this end we advised that agreement should be sought with
the Mountain Leadership Training Board for the Board to come
within the ambit of the Council in regard to its policies. We also
recommended that, while recognising the continuing need for the
basic courses, the granting of certificates should cease and be replaced
by simple course attendance with individual reports on students to be
available if requested by employers.

Two years later, although a compromise had been reached between
the two bodies on certification, fundamental training policy had
become a matter of bitter dispute. The issues are complex. Most
climbers place a high value on the traditions of their chosen leisure
pastime, and desire to ensure that they are truly reflected in the basic

training of young people who are brought to the mountain areas to learn mountaincraft. Trainers and educationists are rightly concerned that all young people who are attracted to the mountains should have the opportunity to acquire the essential knowledge and skills; at the same time, they are responsible to anxious parents for the children's safety.

Relations deteriorated to the point where the BMC took the unilateral step of setting up a training board of its own, which purported to supplant the MLTB. The ensuing crisis threatened to engulf not only those who train and teach, but the whole body of people who climb as a leisure pastime. Even more serious was the harm which this schism could do to the interests of the young people whose enthusiasm for adventure needs to be wisely and competently guided by adults. Happily, strenuous efforts are being made, at the initiative of the Alpine Club and with the agreement of the Sports Council, to mediate between the two bodies in order to find a solution acceptable to both. It is greatly to be hoped that this unfortunate affair will not be protracted, for it is in everyone's interest that our hills should be enjoyed by all and that our young people should be shown the way.

10

Welcome to the English Alpinists

1958

THIS LEGEND, PROMINENTLY DISPLAYED ABOVE THE ENTRANCE
to the headquarters of the SPARTAK (Union of Distributive Workers)
training camp in the Caucasus in 1958, was the 'Open Sesame' whose
key I had been seeking for the previous four years. In 1954 Joy and I
had travelled to Moscow under the auspices of the Foreign Office.
By a pleasant coincidence we were formally seen off by George
Jellicoe, whose landing at the head of his Commandos in Patras had
paved the way for the arrival of my Brigade in 1944. The purpose of
the invitation was to lecture on the first ascent of Everest before an
audience which included Soviet mountaineers; there had, I gathered,
been some scepticism in the Mountaineering Section of the USSR
about our claim to have climbed the mountain. But at the end of my
talk I was surrounded by a group of eager young men, whose doubts
had been set aside. They were Russian climbers and there was a
spontaneous *rapport* between us. I spoke with them through the
interpretership of one of their number whose English was excellent
and idiomatic. His name was Yevgeni (Eugene) Gippenreiter. We
discussed the possibility of arranging that British and Soviet climbers
might join forces in the mountains, even though such informal
contacts between ordinary citizens of our two countries did not exist
at that time.

The wheels of officialdom moved slowly, but it proved possible to
take some preliminary initiatives which were not without their value
in building relationships between individuals on both sides. Among
these, the most important was the friendship which developed between
Eugene and myself; it was, I believe, without the usual connotation, a
case of love at first sight. Everyone who knows him would agree that
Eugene is an easy person to love. Tall and slim, he has one of those
unforgettable faces. Among mountaineers I can compare it only with
that of another close friend, the great French mountain guide Gaston
Rébuffat—a rather small, narrow head with a shock of unruly black

hair, sallow complexion and (unlike Gaston) a black moustache. The unforgettable part is less easy to define, coming from the infectiously good-humoured gleam in his dark eyes. Eugene, with his responsibilities for developing international contacts within the ambit of the Soviet Central Sports Council, has become an indispensable link with sportsmen the world over.

The opening moves were to arrange an exchange of lecturers. Charles Evans went to the Soviet Union to tell the story of the first ascent of Kangchenjunga in 1955; Master of Sport Yevgeni Beletski, accompanied by Gippenreiter, lectured before the Alpine Club and other mountaineering audiences about the philosophy and achievements of Soviet mountaineers. The question of British climbers visiting some of the mountains in Russia was raised at every opportunity. John Neill, a member of the Climbers' Club, had discussed with a few friends the possibility of an expedition to the Caucasus. The theme, according to Ralph Jones, who took part in the discussions was, 'What on earth was there left after Everest?' In 1957 Chris Brasher asked me to join him in making a formal application to take an expedition to the Caucasus and I jumped at the chance. As the year drew towards its close we were waiting anxiously for a reply to the letter I had sent to my contacts in Moscow. Just after Christmas I received the following reply from the Mountaineering Section of the USSR:

> Dear Sir John,
> As for the prospects of your application with Christopher Brasher to climb in the Caucasus next summer in the area of the Bezingi Glacier and Mount Ushba, I am glad to advise you that eventually the Mountaineering Section has received in principle the consent of VAO 'Intourist' to organise this trip.

It was signed by Eugene Gippenreiter. It was a very exciting moment and we immediately went ahead with inviting others to join us, and with the preparations for our journey.

Our interest in the Caucasus range, which runs for about 800 miles between the Caspian and Black seas, derived partly from the fact that British climbers had been among the first to explore and make ascents in these mountains in the early days of the sport. In 1868 Douglas Freshfield had headed a group of mountaineers which visited the central part of the range. Other members of the Alpine Club followed in their footsteps and by the following twenty years all the highest peaks, including Elbrus, an 18,500-feet extinct volcano and the much more difficult Ushba had been climbed for the first time by men from Britain. Between the wars Austrian and German climbers began

10

to fill in the details with some bold and imaginative routes. A party of undergraduates from Oxford set a new standard of difficulty by forcing a way to the summit of Ushba from the south; they were the last British climbers to visit the Caucasus before ourselves. Indeed, we were the first among mountaineers from the Western democracies to receive permission for twenty years.

The party which gathered in the forecourt of the Royal Geographical Society on 25th June 1958 consisted of George Band, the youngest member of the Everest expedition, who had since achieved great distinction by being the first man, with Joe Brown, to climb Kangchenjunga, and to make the first ascent of Huagaruncho in the Andes; John Neill, an industrial chemist and Michael Harris, an engineer, who both hailed from Wolverhampton; Derek Bull was a London insurance agent; Alan Blackshaw a civil servant; Dave Thomas, a geologist and Ralph Jones, a business man, both came from Manchester. Chris Brasher, one of the moving spirits in the enterprise, had achieved lasting fame by winning a Gold Medal in the steeplechase event at the Melbourne Olympic Games two years beforehand and was already established as a journalist. Common to all of us was our membership of the Climbers' Club, whose main base of activity is in North Wales.

With the coincidence of three experienced rally drivers in the party we agreed to travel to Moscow by road. At this distance in time I have no regrets about that decision, but I confess to having harboured considerable misgivings at the time. One of the three cars in our convoy collided with a tram in Mühlheim, it eventually caught up with the rest of us late at night as we camped beside the empty autobahn near Helmstedt, at the end of a breakneck journey of 700 miles across Europe. On the return journey one of the less ambitious motorists in the party, striving to keep pace with a Monte Carlo fiend ahead of him, overturned his car at high speed on a cobbled road in Czechoslovakia and collided with a tree. But aside from these incidents, the journey out also had an historical interest which, if we had travelled by other means, we would not have experienced. Our arrival at the River Bug, post-war frontier between Poland and the Soviet Union, coincided with a crisis between those countries, which had been sparked off by the assassination of the former Hungarian leader Imre Nagy. Gomulka had made a critical and courageous speech, to which the rulers in the Kremlin had taken strong exception. We had been warned by our Ambassador in Warsaw of possible difficulties in crossing the frontier, but we were not aware of the fact that the decks were being cleared for eventual action by the Russians against their satellite State. The railway station of Brest was teeming with Russian officers and their

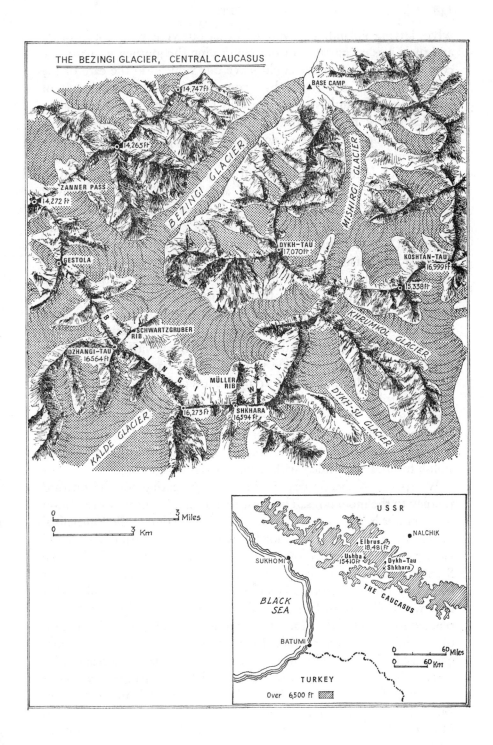

THE BEZINGI GLACIER, CENTRAL CAUCASUS

▲ BASE CAMP

○14,747ft

○14,265ft

ZANNER PASS
○14,272 Ft

GESTOLA○

BEZINGI GLACIER

MISHIRGI GLACIER

DYKH-TAU
○17,070ft

KOSHTAN-TAU
○16,999ft

○15,338ft

B E Z I N G I

SCHWARTZGRUBER
RIB

KHRUMKOL GLACIER

DZHANGI-TAU
16,564ft○

MÜLLER
RIB

W A L L

DYKH-SU GLACIER

○16,273ft

SHKHARA
16,594ft○

KALDE GLACIER

0 ——————— 3 Miles

0 ——————— 3 Km

USSR

● NALCHIK

Elbrus▲
18,481ft

Ushba▲
15,410ft

Dykh-Tau
Shkhara

THE CAUCASUS

SUKHOMI●

BLACK
SEA

BATUMI●

0 ——— 60 Miles

0 ——— 60 Km

TURKEY

Over 6,500 ft ▨

wives leaving Poland. We were told that our visas were not in order
and there was no question of our continuing the journey by road; we
could return home, or we could leave our vehicles in the care of the
frontier officials and travel by train. After twenty-four hours of
frustrating and fruitless telephone calls to Moscow and Warsaw we
decided to opt for the latter alternative and a very jaded and disgruntled group of Britishers piled into two compartments of the Brest
to Moscow express, together with our bulky luggage. To save our
roubles we elected to travel 'Hard' rather than 'Soft', the Russian
euphemism for the bourgeois 'First' and 'Second' class, and arrived
in the capital after a journey of twenty-four hours, travelling at a speed
which barely exceeded twenty-five miles per hour. But far from being
tedious, it was an interlude full of interest. There was the kindness of
the matronly person in charge of our coach, who plied us with tea at
intervals from her samovar and hoovered what little was visible of the
floor of our compartments, between the mountains of men and
baggage. Friendly Russian officers came in to pay social calls; one of
them, the worse for drink, repeatedly expressed his astonishment that
we should have been allowed to travel. 'But the frontier is closed,' he
said again and again. Later, he was removed by police who boarded
the train at Smolensk. Next morning we listened to another speech by
Gomulka while we ate our breakfast in the restaurant car; he was
retracting what he had said earlier; the crisis was over. We then
surmised, I believe correctly, that our train journey had been made
necessary by the fact that the roads leading westwards towards the
Polish frontier were filled with troop movements.

We spent two hectic days in Moscow, preparing for the onward
journey to the mountains. The most memorable event was a reception
given in our honour by the Mountaineering Section at the Journalists'
Club. We sat around a table loaded with caviar and fruit, vodka and
Georgian wines, presided over by Nikolai Romanov, President of the
Section. On my right sat Russia's leading mountaineer, the almost
legendary Vitali Abalakov, Honoured Master of Sport. Vitali at that
time was well into his fifties; small, lean and completely bald, he was
reputed to be still at the peak of his stamina and skill, achieving climbs
of the highest standard of difficulty. On my left was Boris Garf, quiet,
gentle and scholarly, with whom I was soon to strike up a friendship;
communication between us was the easier for the fact that we both
spoke French fluently. Alex Baldin had been an exchange student in
Birmingham, with whom some of us had climbed in North Wales.
Michael Anuvrikov I had met at a film festival in Trento the previous
year.

After speeches and a great deal of *bonhomie*, assisted by the excellent wine, I was invited to be a co-signatory with Abalakov of a *procès-verbal* of the meeting; I was unaware that we had discussed an agenda, but on reading the English translation I found no difficulty in agreeing the terms of the proceedings which were said to have taken place. We had been granted the unique privilege of climbing in the Caucasus, in such areas as we chose, upon any mountains and by any routes we desired. At least, it was unique for foreigners and, within the circle of Russian climbers, only an Abalakov could expect such freedom.

Mountaineering in Russia is a highly organised, closely controlled, and competitive affair. Anyone who expresses an interest in climbing must attend a course, earn a certificate of competence and then, if he desires, to gain further experience, proceed through three standards towards the coveted title of Honoured Master of Sport. Only particular climbs on particular mountains within his certified competence are open to him, under the supervision of instructors, themselves Masters of Sport in mountaineering, at one of the established mountain camps. There is something to be said for this system, which is designed to limit accidents and the consequent searches and rescues. Much of the argument among our own climbing fraternity today stems not so much from a difference of principle as a difference in emphasis when it comes to developing the skills and experience necessary to cope with the risks which are an essential attraction of the sport. How far to carry the application of the principle: that is the question.

We had plenty of opportunity to observe the Soviet system in the sport of mountaineering during our stay at Spartak Camp and to discuss many climbing matters with its instructors and students. We noted the blend of discipline and freedom which governs the camp routine. It begins with a cheerful Доброе утро (Good Morning') followed by a peremptory 'Get Up!' at 7 a.m. on the camp loud-speaker. Ten minutes later we were surprised to observe the students engaging in energetic exercises on the playground in front of the main building; others were running off in disciplined groups into the sur-rounding woods; some were swinging from ropes and parallel bars. One girl, evidently an aspirant speed-skating champion, was going through the movements of her skill as she slowly and repeatedly climbed a flight of steps. Another group were preparing their skis for practice under ski champion Uri Zirianov on the slopes of Elbrus later in the day. I recall with some shame that the contribution of the decadent British climbers to all this purposeful activity was to wander round in our pyjamas taking photographs of the scene.

The morning physical training session was followed by cold showers and a gargantuan breakfast. I can almost feel the post-prandial discomfort I experienced after consuming a heavy sweet pudding, steaks with rice and vegetables, yoghurt and sour milk; *kvass* (a sweet drink made, I was told, of fermented milk and bread crusts); and tea. Then classes set off for the programme of instruction laid down, within the framework of a course lasting three weeks. It culminates in a three-day expedition, the climax of one such we were fortunate to witness. The group, consisting of twenty-five to thirty people, is returning from their excursions into the mountains, marching in step under the leadership of their instructors. They enter the exercise ground and come to a halt in front of Comrade Shevilov, commandant of the camp. The chief instructor reports that they have crossed this pass and climbed that mountain and the commandant says a few words of congratulation. The audience of camp staff, and onlookers like ourselves, applaud and the heroes, weary but delighted, break ranks. The audience moves forward and there are heart-felt handshakes and embraces; garlands and bouquets of flowers are presented. It is easy to be cynical, but I found this little ceremony rather touching, stemming as it did from the unaffected pleasure of everyone concerned. I was even more moved shortly afterwards when a teacher in electronics from a Siberian University—her name was Soya—came forward and presented me with a bunch of flowers which I had done nothing to deserve.

For our first climb in the Caucasus we chose a nearby summit, Pik Kavkaza, of approximately 12,795 feet. Being our first venture in these parts we decided that all our group of nine climbers should undertake the ascent and that we would invite some of the Russian instructors to accompany us. Commandant Shevilov deputed two swarthy Svanetians, stocky and black-moustachioed, Josef Kachiani and Misha Khergiani. We immediately warmed to these beaming, solid characters from one of the valleys on the far side of the Caucasus range. Both were highly skilled climbers, Josef being, at that time, champion rock-climber of the USSR. Later, we were to learn more of the organised competitions in mountaineering prowess which were so alien to Western European tradition. That night the whole party bivouacked on a ledge above the glacier by which we had approached and I shared a tent with Josef and Misha. Sandwiched together with Eugene Gippenreiter in the middle, acting as interpreter, we talked late into the night about mountains and mountain folk; they told me about their homes in the green pastures of Svanetia, surrounded by the dark forest; of their cattle and women folk, and the good red wine. From the voluminous depths of Josef's rucksack emerged quantities of dried, salted fish from the Caspian Sea. So we ate, and talked.

In the dim light of 5th July we climbed up to the west ridge of our mountain and, as a beautiful day dawned, reached the summit. It made a magnificent start to the expedition, for we had clear views the length and breadth of the range. Eastwards we could see the big peaks of the central Caucasus, surrounding the Bezingi glacier which was to be our next destination. Nearby in the east rose the gentle pyramid of Elbrus, monarch of the massif, looking just like the pictures I had seen of Fujiyama in Japan. And immediately opposite, in the south, stood the double-headed Ushba with its satellite, Pik Shchurovskiy, Himalayan in architecture if not in altitude. I marvelled at the daring of our compatriot Cockin who, with a Swiss guide Ulrich Almer from Grindelwald as companion, had reached its northern summit in 1888.

We were lucky to descend the mountain without mishap. The technical difficulties are not great, but the rock was appallingly loose and three of our party were struck by falling boulders; I myself had a narrow escape while abseiling off a rock step when two rocks were dislodged from above, whirring down noisily within inches on either side of me. Mercifully intact, a very happy band of brothers returned to camp that evening in martial order, to be greeted by our hosts with flowers and fruit drinks. This simple but heart-warming little ceremony was so different from our experience of returning anonymously to the valley at the end of an alpine climb. At a reception later in the evening, to which Yevgeni Beletski and the inmates of neighbouring camps had been invited, we were the objects of friendly curiosity as we endeavoured to answer a battery of questions from people who had no previous contacts with the bourgeois Western world. 'What is the highest mountain in Europe? It sounded like a question in a preliminary round for 'Mastermind', and provided an insight into the desire of our Soviet friends to be perceived as Westerners themselves, rather than to be associated in Western minds with the East. 'Elbrus,' I replied diplomatically. Among the many friendly people we met was a large group of Czechoslovakians who invited us to visit their mountains. It started a train of thought which was to bear fruit several years later.

The following day, staggering under loads weighing over sixty pounds, our party started up the Shkhel'da glacier for an eight-day expedition to climb Ushba. Our Russian companions this time were Anatoli Sisoyev, an artist, and a Kiev engineer, Anatoli Kustovski. This was a more serious undertaking, and our plans made it even more so, for we hoped to divide into two groups, and to make a double traverse of the mountain, one climbing from the north, the other repeating the route first climbed by the Oxford expedition in 1937. First, we had to negotiate a steep and heavily crevassed icefall to reach a snow shelf at 13,500 feet below the northern summit. The beginning of the climb was inauspicious; we set off in thick mist and drizzle, which turned to heavy snowfall as we climbed up through the crevasses. So bad were the conditions that we were forced to pitch our tents rather lower on the snow shelf (known as the 'pillow' of Ushba) than we had intended, about 1,500 feet below the summit. By next morning the tents were half buried by the new snow and bad weather persisted; but most members of the party, determined not be to defeated, succeeded in climbing the elegant pinnacle of Pik Shchurovskiy, which rises from the 'Pillow' opposite the north peak of Ushba, before settling down to a siege of that mountain. A Soviet group appeared through the mists and there we remained, nine Britons and eight Russians, prisoners of the elements, for the following three days and nights. Kustovski, the engineer, assisted by Band, Brasher and Black-shaw, put some of the time to good use by excavating an ice cave beneath the surface of the shelf; they whiled away the time with sing-songs and chess. The cave was designed for six, but on the third evening no less than eleven of us crowded into that confined space for the serious business of deciding, not so much whether to acknow-ledge defeat—for Ushba was impregnable under its cloak of heavy snow for days to come—but how to withdraw without catastrophe. Indeed, our descent of the icefall next day, with the snow still falling and avalanches thundering down on both flanks from the unseen mountainsides surrounding us, is one of my more unpleasant recol-lections. Once more, I experienced the misery, familiar from Hima-layan expeditions in the 'thirtes, of floundering waist-deep in heavy new snow.

There was anxiety in the camp about our safety; an accident had occurred to another party and Comrade Shevilov had mustered an eighty-man rescue group to start off in case we failed to return by the time and date we had undertaken to be back. 'Control Time' as it is termed, is a matter to which the Russians attach great importance as a safeguard against accidents; any party which fails to return within their estimates gives rise to a rescue expedition and it ill behoves them to be both safe and late. Fortunately for our reputations we were just within our time schedule, but it was a wet and bedraggled group of Russians and Britishers which drew itself up, attempting a disciplined entry, marching in step into the camp precincts at 6 p.m. that night. Flowers and fond embraces, and a large hot meal, soon restored our morale.

The weather continued to be abysmally awful. 'An unremittingly terrible day' was my diary entry for the fifth continuous day of this depressing spell. But for me it has a happy memory. I had been asked to pay a call at a camp for Ukrainian schoolchildren a few miles away and, on arrival, was surrounded by a milling crowd of eager youngsters, as uninhibited as any of our own kids at home. After doing my best to answer their questions, I thought it might be worth risking a question on my part, which I have often put in similar circumstances in Britain. I asked the head-teacher if the children might have a day's holiday to mark my visit? Well, he did not need to consider the matter, for the reply was provided by the uproarious response of the assembled young people themselves.

It was now 12th July, and we were due to move further east into the central Caucasus; it was time to bid farewell to our charming hosts. At a moving little ceremony in which speeches were exchanged, we presented gifts: to Shevilov a watch; to our two Anatoli friends an air mattress apiece; to Misha a sleeping bag and to Josef a pair of Italian-made mountain boots, with my good wishes for his part in the attempt on Everest, then being planned as a joint venture with the Chinese. In the event, the Chinese went it alone after receiving much help in training, equipment and general know-how from the Russians; the great idealogical divide broke the partnership in this, and every other enterprise in which the two nations had been engaged together.

So we left Spartak Camp, bumping in a lorry along the rough roads northwards to the plains at Nalchik, then east and later, southward bound for the mountains again, to reach our main objective, the great mountain cirque of the upper Bezingi glacier. Eugene Gippenreiter was, of course, still with us. And to our great delight, so was Anatoli Kustovski, the gay and carefree humorist who could make us laugh even without understanding his many jokes. Towards evening we entered a deep gorge and suffered a hair-raising two hours' drive, sometimes through fast-flowing torrents swollen by the recent rains; sometimes squeezing our way between huge boulders which had been dislodged from the cliffs above, wondering whether more might descend upon us. It was with a sigh of relief that we emerged in the failing light on to the uplands beyond, and came upon a sprawling, half-built village.

Bezingi is the chief village of the Balkari tribe; nearby were the ruins of a former site, reputedly destroyed by order of Stalin in 1942 as an act of retribution for the encouragement given by these independently-minded people to the German armies, when they reached the Caucasus and hoisted the Swastika flag on the summit of Elbrus. Stalin banished the entire tribe to Kazakstan in Central Asia. Earlier in 1958 Khrushchev had made the second of his famous speeches condemning Stalin's many brutalities, including his actions against the Balkaris and a neighbouring tribe, the Chechen-Inguzes. He had ordered that they should be allowed to return to their homelands after an absence of fourteen years, and be given every assistance in rebuilding their lives. Our arrival coincided with this return. We motored on a few miles to the end of the road, and set up our tents in a meadow, dog-tired.

Very early next day I awoke to the sound of a querulous voice outside my tent. Peering out, I saw an elderly bearded person seated outside Eugene's tent. He had brought some donkeys to carry our loads to the snout of the Bezingi glacier, but he was clearly displeased with these intruders. Who were we? Why were we spoiling his hay? But his mood changed, his aquiline features broadened into a wide smile when he learned that we were British mountaineers. His father had told him of two other Englishmen (they were Donkin and Fox) who had disappeared on Koshtan-tau, one of the big peaks above us, in the last century. He himself remembered the German expeditions in the 'thirties. He had returned from exile the previous year, but many others, especially the younger Balkaris, had preferred to stay in Kazakstan; some had run away after arriving in Bezingi. He invited us to his dwelling, or *kosh*, where we drank milk. We were his honoured guests.

The last lap of the journey to the glacier was unbelievably beautiful. After reading Freshfield's account of his journey in these parts, I had expected to find a barren waste; but the huge herds of goats of his day, and the human beings who owned them, had been absent for fourteen years. Nothing could have been more strikingly different from his description of 'ugliness' and 'treeless turf'. We wandered through lush meadows, knee deep in alpine flowers; And in the distance, dazzling white against a clear blue sky, was the huge rampart of the Bezingi Wall, its crest at over 16,000 feet; it was worth travelling all this way simply to see, let alone to attempt the climbs on this great barrier. That night we camped on grass-covered moraine slopes beneath Koshtan-tau at the junction of two rivers, and within a few hundred yards of a big Russian camp, occupied by an expedition of the Academy of Sciences. Further away was yet another expedition, of non-academic character: TRUD (the Union of Scientific Workers). We spent the evening with the academicians, who were most helpful in explaining the local topography and advising us on the history of climbing in the area. Boris Garf was there and with him his daughter Marina, a doughty lass who was well on her way to achieving the distinction of being a Master of Sport; as far as I am aware the masculine title includes the feminine in this case. Alex Baldin, our friend from Birmingham University was also in the group. With so much experienced advice it was not difficult to decide on the routes we would attempt on the Bezingi Wall, and to divide ourselves into three parties; it was to be my own good fortune to be with Alan Blackshaw, Ralph Jones and Chris Brasher in tackling the so-called Schwarz-gruber Rib, climbed only once previously, by a pre-war German group, which traces an elegant line up the Wall and leads to the summit of Dzhangi-tau (16,564 feet). Our strongest party was bound for a point further east along the foot of the Wall, to attempt the Müller route, a buttress thrown out by Shkhara, at 17,064 feet, the second highest peak in the Caucasus; it was graded as somewhat more difficult than our climb; Anatoli Kustovski was a member of this group, with George Band, Derek Bull and Michael Harris. Eugene, John Neill and Dave Thomas were to climb Gestola, at the right-hand end of the rampart.

The weather was now fine and looked settled. We were excited by the prospects of these challenging climbs and we lost no time in starting up the moraine of the Bezingi glacier the following morning, 15th July, leaving with the Russians a Control Time of 8 a.m. on 19th for our return. It was a long, weary plod up the valley, carrying four days' food and all our mountain gear. The glacier is T-shaped and we were walking along the stem, heading for a corner where it meets the wide basin, some three miles in length, at the foot of the Wall. Here we stopped for the night, scratching out a platform in a little ablation valley and crawling into our sleeping bags before lighting our Meta stove. In the fading light I looked across the glacier, my eye travelling slowly up the big buttress of rock and the fine ribbon of snow crest, sharply tilted, which would be the focus of all our thoughts and effort during the next three days. It looked formid-able and I stayed tensed and anxious for a while before dropping off to sleep.

It was cold when we stirred ourselves at 2 a.m. Accustomed to alpine starts, we had packed everything overnight and had made a detailed examination of the lower part of the route which we would have to climb in the dark. There was a little icefall, menaced by an impending wall of séracs, but safely frozen at this hour. We swung left, climbing very steep snow slopes and a series of rock bands which led us, our limbs still numb with cold despite the strenuous nature of the climbing, on to the top of the rock buttress. It was 9 a.m. when we stepped out on to a level snow terrasse and began to thaw out in the full sunlight; we had been climbing for six hours. My tensions, sustained throughout that period and culminating in the final stretch of exceedingly steep ice, had gone; I was ready to enjoy the hard climbing ahead.

We were now following the crest of the narrow, sharply inclined snow rib; from time to time there were rock pitches, some of them difficult: a small tower, a rather holdless slab. Then I took the lead, with Ralph on my rope, as a great sweep of ice slope rose above us, about 400 feet in height and angled at 55 degrees. Thus far we had climbed without crampons and, in my concentration on the task ahead, I started up this slope without pausing, cutting steps. But with the increasing angle I stopped and, banging in the first ice peg, asked Ralph to strap my crampons on; it was no place to do the job myself. Ralph is at his best in situations like this; in a social setting he contrives to give the impression of light-hearted frivolity; he is a great yarner and a puller of other people's legs. In an awkward moment on a mountain he radiates calmness and patience; it was this latter quality which was called for as we stood in those ice steps while he fiddled with my crampon straps, refraining from the merited suggestion that I should have thought to put them on sooner.

On we went, for the next hour, up this big slope, I hammering in pegs at intervals to safeguard our progress. As we rose higher, avalanches peeled off the precipices on either hand, but we were safe on the rib and, utterly absorbed in the work, we were scarcely aware of them. As the day wore on I began to feel the altitude; we were impressed by the scale of the mountain, the Wall seemed endlessly high. It was 6 p.m. and we had been climbing for fifteen hours, yet still there was no relenting in the steepness; the rib became rather more ice than snow and more steps were needed; the light began to fail. And then, at long last, we stepped out on to easier ground. The rib was below us and the top of Dzhangi-tau appeared to be no great distance above. The technical difficulties were over. It was time to scrape a platform in the snow, crawl into our Zardski sack and get some food inside us, for we had been on the move for eighteen hours with very few pauses to eat.

I think we all slept reasonably well, despite the cold and the clatter of falling stones. Ralph and I snuggled close together, lying uncomfortably on our climbing rope, our feet in our rucksacks; such bivouacs are long remembered. As the light grew stronger we could appreciate the striking position of the little balcony we had chosen, jutting out over the plunging precipice we had toiled up, the glacier seemed to be vertically underneath us, 6,000 feet below, its surface creased with crevasses. Over the way was the great rock tower of Dykh-tau, first climbed by Alfred Mummery with the Swiss guide Zurfluh in 1888, on which we too, had designs. Thawing out gradually we got ourselves ready in leisurely fashion, confident that our peak was 'in the bag'.

How wrong we were! As soon as we set off it was obvious that we were in trouble. We slanted up towards the summit ridge on snow with a nasty, breakable crust into which we sank to our knees; it was back-breaking work, calling for a change in the lead every 50 yards or so. We came to a big crevasse, its far side defended by a snow wall 25 feet high; there was only one place where it could be crossed. Alan Blackshaw spent more than an hour surmounting the obstacle, ramming in two ice-axes near the top, as make-shift hand- and foot-holds; it was a fine lead. Above, we were on steeper ground which had been swept by an avalanche and the going was easier; but beyond was an area where fresh snow still lay on the hard underlying surface and it was obvious that it was only a matter of time, the effect of the sun's rays and a little human encouragement, to start it sliding down the mountain. I was with Brasher that morning and he led up this deep, treacherous stuff. We came to another big crevasse, bridged precariously by the new snow. Chris crawled across; there was an ominous creaking noise, but he was safely on the upper side of the monster and secured the rope for me to follow. Halfway over the snow collapsed and I was falling into the abyss. But only for about 25 feet, for to my relief and surprise I landed on a secondary snow bridge beneath the upper surface, frail and 'see-through', providing suggestive glimpses of the blue depths beneath, but enough to arrest my progress. This was just as well, for Brasher, placed as he was on the loose incoherent surface above, would inevitably have been dragged in too, and the others would have had a tragedy on their hands. I was hauled out, none the worse for the incident.

It was a moment for decision-making and for mountaineering judgment. There was the crest of the summit ridge, 300 feet above us; the top of Dzhangi-tau was further along the ridge to our right and perhaps we were 600 feet beneath it. But our progress in this awful stuff was terribly slow, the snow was dangerous and, if it held us while we reached the ridge, would surely peel off later, when the sun had warmed it. The unanimous conclusion was negative, we must turn back. It was, of course, disappointing, but we could comfort ourselves that we had climbed the Schwarzgruber Rib and had surmounted the difficult part of the climb, all of which would now have to be reversed; there were many hours of absorbing and taxing work before us. I have often felt sharp unhappiness about giving up a mountain, but this was a moment when I felt quite sure our decision was right.

Descending the snow wall above the lower crevasse, I was last on the rope. One of the two axes which Alan had placed as holds was dislodged by my weight and for the second time that day I was air-borne, doing a neat somersault to land head downwards in the soft, deep snow 25 feet below. This time we were able to laugh—or rather, the others did—at the ridiculous spectacle. Below the bivouac site we found the ice rib a much more difficult proposition than on the way up; the ice was rotting and we took more than three hours to descend the first section, taking great precautions to avoid a slip. Again we bivouacked, less comfortably and in our weariness, slept little. The weather broke that night and the climb down to the distant glacier was something of a nightmare in falling snow and thick mist. It was quite dark when we pulled in our abseil rope for the last time at the foot of the lower rock buttress; in all, we had used this technique on ten occasions, sliding down the doubled length of rope 100 feet at a time. As it grew darker, Chris waxed vociferous, swinging wildly at the end of the rope, more or less blinded by the specially darkened snow goggles which he was still wearing and which added to his short-sightedness. I have seldom felt so weary as when we groped our way across the level surface of the glacier, arriving after 10 p.m. to spend our fourth night out beside the moraine. But for me it had been one of those great climbs and, summit or no summit, I felt deeply content with my companions and the world in general.

The only remaining anxiety was the matter of our 'Control Time'; we were several hours' fast walking away from Base Camp and must report there by 8 a.m. next morning. Chris Brasher, our Olympic hero, was the obvious man for the job. I stirred the reluctant runner at 3 a.m. and for twenty minutes, did my best to keep pace with him while the others packed up more slowly. Then he was away, and saved British honour by redeeming our pledge to be back on time.

The Gestola group were already back when we reached camp, triumphant from their climb; fortunately for them, it was much shorter than ours and they had escaped in time to avoid the bad weather. But we still waited for the return of the Shkhara party, whose 'Control Time' was set for the 20th July. Sure enough, within minutes of their dead-line, there they were on the edge of the moraine, half a mile away, in line and getting their clumsy booted feet into step for the final approach. There was no lack of flowers in the meadow all around us and we scurried about to produce the traditional bouquets for our friends. Indeed, they had earned the accolade. Like ourselves, they had been caught in the mist and snowfall which began before they arrived on their summit, after achieving a climb of considerable character and difficulty. Notwithstanding this they had made an impressive return by a different route, down the North-East Ridge, thus completing a traverse of Shkhara.

It was pleasant to relax after all these adventures. The rain was almost an asset to our social contacts, for we huddled into the larger tents of our friends of the Academy of Sciences and the Union of

Scientific Workers to tell our stories and listen to their singing. For the Russians, impromptu concerts are very much part of the mountain holiday; they had a large repertoire and they sang well. In our honour they had come prepared with a song about British sailors running the gauntlet of the weather and German submarines in the Arctic convoys to Archangel, to which there was a sentimental encore about a British sailor and a Russian girl.

When I recounted our climb on Dzhangi-tau, and our decision to turn back within shouting distance of the top, our hosts were plainly incredulous. Even if this were the case, they seemed to imply, it was not customary to admit the fact. I was intrigued that our confession had unwittingly exposed a wide divergence in our approaches to mountaineering, with deeper philosophical overtones. Not less interesting was a conversation we had at that time, when news reached us over the Russian transmitter and receiver station which is part and parcel of these major expeditions in the mountains. There was trouble in the Near East; marines from the American Sixth Fleet in the Mediterranean had landed in the Lebanon and British forces had re-entered Jordan. Soviet propaganda was making the most of the crisis. What should we do, isolated from our own people in this remote spot? Most helpfully, the Russians transmitted the question I put to our Ambassador in Moscow, Sir Patrick Reilly. They enjoyed the humour of the situation, too. Sitting round a table in their mess tent for our evening gossip, someone suggested that they might help us get over the frontier into Turkey. Someone else thought this might involve our friends in considerable risk to themselves, but he said, 'Never mind. You British can enjoy some splendid climbing for the next twenty-five years or so, in Siberia.'

And we made social calls of a different kind. Two Balkari shepherds were minding a large mixed flock of sheep and goats on the meadow. They told us that wolves had become a menace to the flock, emboldened after the long absence of human beings from the valley. I was impressed by the enormous size of some wolf paw-prints I had seen in the mud beside the glacier. The younger shepherd was especially friendly; they regarded us as their personal guests in Balkaria. Every morning they placed a can of milk outside our tents, from their only cow. Askerbi took his ancient gun, dated 1850, up the hillside and shot a fine ibex, of which we had seen large herds in the valley, tame from many years without threat from human beings. The choicest meat was for us. 'But,' he begged us, 'don't say a word about this to my father in the village. He does not approve of hunting and has forbidden me to shoot.' Askerbi was a man in his late forties, his father had reached a ripe old age, common in those parts, of 107. 'And what,' he asked.

'was the hunting like in England?' We tried to conjure up the familiar scene of red-coated huntsmen, stirrup cups and the like. 'And what did a man have to pay for a wife?' We explained that expenses began after marriage, not before. 'Why (pointing to our packets of Weetabix which, with a kit inspection of our clothing, equipment and special food, we had laid out at the request of the inquisitive Soviet climbers) do you like these dried foods?' We explained the merits of lightening the climbers' burdens (the Russians like carrying heavy tins of fruit, meat, caviar and so on). We added that Vitawheat was especially popular with our women folk, as it helped them to keep slim. 'But why should they want to be slim?' We did our best to speak up for the girls, but our answer will be seen as chauvinistic to some: 'Because it makes them attractive to men.' 'Nonsense,' retorted Askerbi scornfully. 'They are far more cuddly when they are fat.' Of course he was right: love in a cold climate.

There was still time for one more big climb and the choice had to be Dykh-tau. There were casualties in our ranks, but we managed to muster two strong groups: one to repeat the Mummery route on the south buttress, the other comprising our two best rock-climbers, Mike Harris and George Band, who wanted to attempt a formidable pillar supporting the east peak of the mountain, which ran parallel to the Mummery line. I was with Blackshaw, Eugene and Chris Brasher on the latter climb. Ours was a most disappointing story, for I had set my heart on climbing Dykh-tau, having stored up memories of Mummery's description in his book *My Climbs in the Alps and the Caucasus* from boyhood days. Our start was unpropitious; Chris had to send a report to the *Daily Express*, which had helped us with funds. We began to climb two and a half hours later than intended, making it impossible to reach the relatively high bivouac which I considered essential to success. Then he had the great misfortune to be stricken by gastric trouble as we made height next morning. So serious was it that, within 1,500 feet of the summit, we had to settle him in a safe nook among the rocks while we made a half-hearted attempt to reach the summit and return to him within the day. But it was not possible and, about 500 feet higher, we came back and escorted our casualty down to the glacier. I shall always regret that missed opportunity, but I am glad to say that Chris recovered shortly afterwards; and the *Daily Express* had their headline: 'Hunt falls down crevasse'.

At the foot of Dykh-tau on the evening of 23rd July we found Boris Garf, with Marina and two other Russians, preparing to follow Band's and Harris's route. Another Russian party was coming across the Bezingi glacier, after giving up an attempt on the Müller route on Shkhara, recently climbed by our own group. This looked to me like an intentional policy to establish Soviet prowess. The impression was reinforced when, months later, I found that the record of the first ascent of the route eventually forced up the east peak of Dykh-tau by its south pillar, was entered in the name of our Russian friends. Later I was told by Eugene Gippenreiter that the British achievement was recognised by Soviet mountaineers, but that the reason for its omission from the official annals was because no formal report had been submitted by our climbers. I have no reason to doubt the report, sent me by Boris himself after their climb, that his party did succeed; I applaud the many fine achievements of Soviet mountaineers in the Caucasus and elsewhere; but it is most regrettable that the prior achievement of Band and Harris was ignored. I learned later that a second attempt to follow our party on Shkhara ended in tragedy when two Russian climbers fell to their deaths fairly low down on the Müller Rib.

Back at Base Camp, we waited anxiously for the return of Mike and George. It was 27th July and we were due to leave for home; the donkeys were waiting on the far side of the Bezingi torrent. Some of us were going to cross the range at the head of the glacier and descend through Svanetia to Sukhumi on the Black Sea, while others would escort our baggage to Moscow. But there was still no sign of our friends; their 'Control Time' was midday. A few minutes after 12 noon Boris Garf came over from his camp. 'We must organise a search party,' he said. Indeed, there was no alternative; we unpacked our mountain gear and, filled with forebodings, followed one of the Russian girls, Ulla, who volunteered to act as our guide to the northern approaches to Dykh-tau. It was raining hard and the mists were low on the mountains. As we climbed up the screes, I turned over in my mind all the sad and difficult things which might have to be done. Suddenly John Neill, just in front of me, stopped in his tracks: 'There are two figures ahead,' he said. Ralph's binoculars helped us identify them. There was a cheer, we waved our ice-axes and ran forward. They were late, but they had made a great climb; their success and their safety were the only things which mattered.

The rain continued the next day as we walked down the valley; we were dripping wet, but it mattered not at all. We had climbed in 'the frosty Caucasus'; we had been shown courtesy and kindness by everyone we met; the door was ajar for others to pass that way.

Daylight at Midnight

1960

ARCTIC RIVIERA: IT SOUNDED IMPROBABLE, EVEN A CONTRADICTION in terms. Yet the pictures in that book by Andreas Hofer about the Staunings Alper in Scoresbyland, at about 73 degrees north on the east coast of Greenland, enticed me to go and see for myself; I had long wanted to travel in polar regions. Up till the late 1950s, only four or five expeditions had explored that area, but a Scottish party led by Dr Malcolm Slesser had been there in 1958 and he was preparing to make a second visit in 1960. It seemed worth suggesting that we join forces and before long we were beginning to put together a joint party for the summer of that year.

George Lowe had been a member of the Everest expedition; he had also crossed the Antarctic continent with Sir Vivian Fuchs; Tony Streather had made the first ascent of Kangchenjunga in 1955; Alan Blackshaw had been with me in the Caucasus; Ian McNaught-Davis had climbed the Muztagh Tower in the Karakoram; John Jackson, one of the 'reserves' for the Everest expedition, was Director of the National Mountaineering Centre in North Wales; Dr David Jones had just returned from eighteen months' secondment to the Falkland Dependencies Survey. John Sugden was one of Her Majesty's Inspectors of Schools and a geographer with two previous Greenland expeditions to his credit; they were my choices. As for Slesser's, Iain Smart had been with him in the previous expedition to East Greenland; Tom Weir was a noted climber, ornithologist and photographer. And we later added a marine engineer, Roddy Cameron, having been offered the loan of a motor boat by the Greenland Department of the Danish government.

At about that time I was discussing with youth leaders the value of encouraging young men who had gained the Gold Award to extend their experience of adventurous journeys beyond the shores of Britain. Among them was Dick Allcock who was at that time Field Officer to the National Association of Youth Clubs, of which I was President.

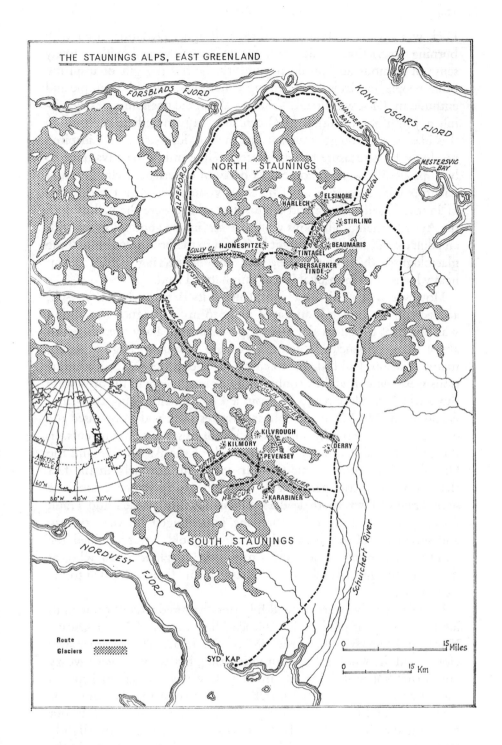

THE STAUNINGS ALPS, EAST GREENLAND

FORSBLADS FJORD

KONG OSCARS FJORD

MENANDERS BAY

MESTERSVIG BAY

NORTH STAUNINGS

ELSINORE

HARLECH

STIRLING

SKEL GA

ALPEFJORD

GULLY GL.

HJONESPITZE

BEAUMARIS

TINTAGEL

BERSAERKER TINDE

WEST POINT GL.

SPAERRE GL.

SEBJØRNE CRAG

70°N

ARCTIC CIRCLE

60°N

50°W 40°W 30°W 20°

KILVROUGH

KILMORY

DERRY

JUPITER GL.

PEVENSEY

DON GLACIER

KARABINER

MERCURY GL.

Schuichert River

SOUTH STAUNINGS

NORDVEST FJORD

Route

Glaciers

0   15 Miles

0   15 Km

SYD KAP

Dick was already a close and valued colleague. Dynamic, fired with burning convictions which are, fortunately, leavened with a lively sense of humour and by deep humility, he has the gift of inspiring other people, particularly the young generation, with his example and enthusiasm. Dick was already thinking about the possibility of organising a youthful expedition to Greenland. My immediate reaction to this idea was to counsel caution; but then an idea struck me, inspired no doubt by a measure of self-interest. There might be advantage to both parties if I were to combine a party of experienced climbers and scientists with a contingent of fit, keen youngsters, with the qualities of initiative, self-reliance and team spirit which were the hallmark of the Award Scheme. The boys would be serving an apprenticeship with an adult expedition. They might be useful to the ornithologists and the glaciologists; they would help the mountaineering parties hump heavy loads in an inhospitable and uninhabited land.

However much this idea commended itself to Dick and myself, and acceptable though it appeared to be to my colleagues, the notion was not easy to sell to the Danish government. They were anxious about the emergencies which might arise among so large a group, many of whom had little or no comparable experience. Communications were tenuous and the only rescue arrangements in the area were those which would have to be provided by a small mining company. At home the NAYC, under whose auspices Dick and I organised the expedition, was naturally anxious on behalf of some of the parents. In the end I was able to allay the fears both of the Association and the Greenland Department; our strength would lie precisely in the fact that we were a large party, with a wealth of experience among the senior ranks. Two youth leaders, David (Bunny) Roach and Frank Gwatkin and a group of twenty-one juniors aged between twenty and seventeen, all of them holders of the Gold Award, joined the climbers and scientists; Joy and my second daughter Susan who, at that time, had just left school, added a welcome feminine touch to the expedition.

In the dim early hours of 22nd July our chartered aircraft came in to land on a strip of sand beside the ice-filled waters of Kong Oscar's Fjord, at Mestersvig Bay, the site of the mine. The weather was cloudy and the whole scene most uninviting, but we were very weary after many hours of flying. By midday, however, the sun had turned the sea deep blue, flecked with icefloes and small bergs. The dramatic skyline of Traill Island was clearly visible on the horizon, and in our camp on the shores of the fjord, spirits were soaring, only slightly tempered by the midges, which came out of their hiding places in the tundra whenever the temperature rose.

There was much to do. First we had to move ourselves, with the bulk of our equipment and food to a base camp twelve miles west along the coast, on the shores of Menanders Bay. Here a valley, the Skeldal, leads southwards towards the mountains we were going to explore. While a group of off-shore islands was the focus of interest for our two ornithologists, Tom Weir and Iain Smart, with a group of boys to assist their work; in particular, Iain planned to make a complete study of the breeding and nesting habits of the Arctic tern, which annually produces its young in the Arctic summer, then flies some 11,000 miles to the coast of Antarctica for the summer season there. In a very real sense, this little bird, at the expense of much travel, has the best of both worlds.

We had hoped that most of the loads would be transferred from Mestersvig to Menanders Bay by the borrowed motor boat, the *Polypen*; Roddy Cameron had now made her reasonably shipshape, but was having teething troubles with her engine. Rather than wait around, I organised two large carrying groups to travel overland along the coast as far as the Skel. This was a back-breaking job, for we were carrying each at least sixty pounds to save journeys; after one shift, we all began to slow down. Rested though most of us had been on that first fine sunny day, after a good night's sleep, one difficulty was to control our working hours irrespective of, rather than according to, the time of day. At midnight we were still at it, in full sunshine, wondering why we were beginning to feel jaded; for few of the party were regular night workers, accustomed to going to bed in broad daylight.

By a great stroke of fortune an ice survey vessel, the *Noona Dan*, sailed into Mestersvig that evening, after being held up by shifting sea ice. Joy made friends with the skipper; George Lowe discovered that the engineer had sailed in the *Magga Dan*, a ship of the Lauritzen company, which had carried him with Fuchs' party to the Antarctic in 1956. The result was that *Noona Dan* made a quick and painless job of helping us settle into our Base Camp, with *Polypen*, now in working order for the time being, ferrying loads ashore from the ship.

Here there was a parting of the ways within our large group, whose members were about to pursue a number of different tasks. John Sugden, with Joy and Susan as well as six boys, sailed on in *Polypen* another 100 miles westwards into a tributary fjord, the Alpefjord. Near its head was the snout of a large glacier, the Sefströms, whose movement into the waters of the fjord caused enormous masses of ice to break off, or calve, from time to time; these were some of the icebergs which sailed out into the Arctic Ocean. The Sefströms glacier was the ice-stream chosen by John to make a number of glaciological observations in the course of the following month. He was also interested in recording the local geomorphology; in particular, the beach levels along the flanks of the Alpefjord which showed the changing height of the sea, dictated by the advance and recession of ice southwards into Europe through the ages. While the bird-watching party prepared their canoes for visits to the islands, the main party, in two groups led by Malcolm and myself, started moving loads further up the Skeldal.

It was a severe test of guts and stamina for the boys. The loads continued to weigh well over sixty pounds to reduce ferrying – some were more than seventy pounds. The ground was boggy, traversed by torrents which required a steadying rope; and, to add to our difficulties, the clouds hung low on the hillsides – and it rained and rained. The rain fell, with only occasional intermissions, dank and chilly, for five continuous days during the last week of July. We walked, ate and slept in sodden clothes; our tents leaked, subjected as they were to the endless drumming of rain on the canvas without and the movement of crowded bodies within; the ground-sheets were awash. On 1st August my group at last pitched our tents some way up the glacier whose surroundings we intended to explore, the Bersaerker Brae. With the rain still teeming down, I wrote in my diary: 'More than one inch of rain in the saucepan last night. I feel near to despair.' But it kept the midges at bay; and the Arctic foxes did their best to entertain us. Marvellously tame and very hungry, they came to pay social calls, and were not averse to sharing our supper. One fox evidently favoured Scottish nationalism, insisting on taking his seat on their national flag, before he accepted biscuits from the boys. Another came into the tent occupied by Tony Streather and myself one evening as we lay in our sleeping bags. He made it abundantly clear that he would appreciate a helping of our cheese.

Then our misfortunes were magically dispelled by one of those sudden transformation scenes which mountains are wont to produce. I woke on 2nd August to find the sun shining through the tent wall; for the first time we could look upon our environment. Opposite was a fine rampart of snow mountains; four miles up the glacier the head wall with the highest mountain, the Bersaerker Tinde, rose a sheer 2,000 feet of red granite buttress and steep ice couloirs. Somewhere up there Malcolm Slesser's group was camped, in an area where there was evidently some excellent climbing to be done. Some way down the glacier, where another tributary ice-stream joined it, stood a fine-looking snow mountain topped by an impressive needle of rock. Without further ado, we decided to climb our first mountain. Tony Streather, Alan Blackshaw, David Jones and I got ready; we invited two boys who had rock-climbing experience in Derbyshire to join us. Seven hours later we stood at about 7,500 feet on the narrow shelf on top of that needle; or rather, we went up one at a time, Brian Mills in the lead, for it was too small to accommodate more than one. We named our peak 'Harlech' as a mark of respect for the Welshman in the party, David, who chose to climb all that day wearing pyjamas; it was the first of a series of place-names commemorating British fortresses which we, perhaps with some presumption, imposed on Greenland's icy mountains, and which an understanding Danish government later confirmed.

More rain did its best to take the edge off our high spirits after that success. Then we set off again. We had admired another and higher peak, further up the side glacier (we named it 'Harlech Glacier') and apparently a tougher proposition. We took skis, a tent and a bivouac sack but, anticipating serious climbing problems, decided that the boys should not come with us. At the foot of a couloir running down from the mountain's East Ridge we left all our overnight gear and climbed up the avalanche-swept slope to a little col. We noted that, as a result of the bad weather, a number of avalanches had recently swept the South Face. There was a stupendous view northwards, to Kong Oscar's Fjord.

We started carefully along the ridge, over shattered rocks which led to a narrow snow crest; the summit was now only about 250 feet higher and perhaps 400 yards distant. But it was obvious that it would not be easy. On the right, a convex slope of snow dropped sharply away to the glacier, some 1,500 feet below us. The texture of the surface was slabby; from much experience of windslab avalanches I was sure it was not safe. On the left the crest hung over the very steep south face in huge cornices; at one place the overhang may have been as much as 25 feet. Clearly, we must be careful. I asked Tony and David, on the second rope, to remain at the end of the rocks while Alan and I went ahead; he and I started along the ridge, moving one at a time. After running out all our 250 feet of rope, Alan moved along and passed me at my stance, while I belayed his rope round my axe. I had a nasty premonition of disaster, fearing that in my anxiety to avoid disturbing the slabby layer of snow, I was positioned too near to the cornice. Hardly had I called back to Tony for a second opinion when, with a resounding 'woompf' the whole cornice broke away, some 15 feet from where I was standing, and over a distance of 10 yards. I went with it, falling head downwards on my back at tremendous speed on the board-hard snow in the wake of the cornice; above me I looked at the gap through which I had been projected, framing a patch of blue sky. I waited for the tug, expecting to see Alan caterpulted over the precipice towards me. Instead, when it came I was brought up short with a violent jerk, winded by the sudden pull on my waist. My axe, threaded through a loop of rope on which I had anchored it to safeguard Alan, was still dangling, and within reach. Thanks to this I was able to cut steps up the slope, surmount the final eight-foot vertical snow wall where the cornice had once adhered, and rejoin Alan. His action, by rolling promptly down the other side of the mountain as soon as he heard the tell-tale sound of the collapse of cornice, had been our salvation.

So near, and yet so far. 300 yards to go, 200 feet to climb. But more heavy cornicing, more windslab, no security. It would have been folly and we turned back to our companions. They at least had enjoyed a grandstand view of the drama.

Several days later, we divided again. Tony took our group back to Base, which was now to be moved up to John Sugden's camp above the Alpefjord. I went up to join Malcolm's party, changing places with George Lowe. Among our climbing plans was the ambitious project of making a first traverse of the whole northern range from east to west. The weather smiled upon us for a whole week while Malcolm, Ian McNaught-David, John Jackson and I carried out this epic journey, in the course of which we made, between the four of us, four more first ascents and the crossing of a high col, the Col Major, up which we carried our monstrous loads, skis and all, seventy-five pounds a piece. Or rather, this was the task which Jacko and I elected to do, no less than three times in 24 hours up and down a 1,700-foot ice slope, angled at 50 degrees, to enable the others to climb Greenland's second highest mountain, the 9,449 feet high Hjonespitze. If Jacko and I were feeling exhaustedly virtuous the heroes, Malcolm and Mac, could register justifiable triumph after a difficult rock climb lasting nearly thirty hours, during which they had been almost continuously on the move. In all, it was a most satisfactory combined operation. Satisfying, too, in a different area of my mind, was the midnight sunlight, touching the peaks above the col and bathing them rose and gold, picking out the icefloes far away to the north on the smooth waters of Kong Oscar's Fjord.

Then down we went, on skis, through a maze of monster crevasses, to a point when we had become so encumbered and tired by the weight of our loads that we resorted to the desperate measure of abandoning the skis beside the glacier; for all I know, they may still be there. They had served their purpose, for we were now on dry ice, well on our way towards the Alpefjord. There remained some climbing problems and the skis might make things awkward. None the less, I looked wistfully back at the four pairs of boards which had served us so well, even though it is only a pleasant illusion to think that one's tools, be they ice-axe, boots or even a favourite rock peg, have enjoyed the experience. It was a great moment when, on the fifth day, our anxieties behind us, we stood on the edge of the Gully glacier down which we had been travelling, and looked upon the milky waters of the fjord 2,000 feet below, where the little *Polypen* was cruising up towards our own destination. Across the great divide of the Alpefjord was a high, ice-covered tableland: the rim of the Greenland icecap.

On 14th August we began the second phase of our programme which, as far as the mountain explorers were concerned, was to take us into the southern part of the Staunings. The weather broke again as, with the help of John Sugden's amateur glaciologists, from whom Joy and Susan had detached themselves to join the southern party, we groped our way up the Spaerre glacier, heavily crevassed, heading for a high pass somewhere in the enveloping mists ahead of us. Our destination was the Schuichert valley which runs southwards towards the shores of Nordvest Fjord, and which I had originally intended to reach from Menanders Bay.

The ensuing programme hinged on one essential condition which, had we still been based at Menanders, would have presented no problem: food and fuel had to be air-lifted, by an Auster aircraft belonging to the mine, to the area where we expected to arrive after making the crossing. I still quake a little when I think of the risk I then accepted on behalf of us all. Just before we set off, a message arrived from Iain Smart that the Auster had crashed at Mestersvig; to make things worse, a relief aircraft had also come to grief, while on its way, somewhere in Scotland. Iain reported that our good friend Mr Brinch, the mine manager, had promised to do his best to get our stores across the intervening pass into the Schuichert valley by a tractor and sledge; this was an easy journey in winter when the ground was covered with snow, but the traverse had never been attempted over the boulder-strewn terrain in summer. Aside from the severe misfortune for the mining company and the individuals involved in the plane accidents, this set us a difficult problem. Should I risk it? We could, by humping fairly heavy loads, carry only four days' food. If the new supply plan failed, we would be in difficulties, but I knew that the company had an advanced base somewhere near the head of the Schuichert for mining molybdenum which, if we could locate it, might help in an emergency. I decided that we would go.

Three days later, walking happily down the dry ice of the Roslin glacier in glorious sunshine, with the wide expanse of the Schuichert valley spread before us, we were still confident that we would find a dump of stores awaiting us. As we stepped off the ice and dodged through the huge boulders of the moraine and on to a beautiful, grassy meadow on which musk oxen were grazing, it was still difficult to start worrying. The strange creatures looked at us with lazy unconcern, then went on eating; they may, or may not have seen humans before, but evidently had been given no cause for alarm. It was such a peaceful, pastoral scene.

But there was no sign of a dump and a sense of weighty responsibility clouded my happiness. Search as we might through our binoculars, there was still no sign. Far up the valley, beneath a big rock bluff beside the Schuichert glacier we fancied that we could see some huts. Nearer by, across the river, there were faint traces of a track leading westwards. With only twenty-four hours' food left, there was no time to lose. If we failed to find a dump we would have to beat a hasty retreat on starvation rations to Mestersvig, some three days' journey to the north. I divided the party into pairs and we set off in various directions, with instructions to be back by midnight. By that time all had returned, with the exception of one pair: George Lowe and John Jackson had last been seen earlier in the evening, crossing the swollen waters of the Schuichert, apparently making for that faint track. A possible tragedy loomed large.

The anxieties of that night were eased for us by the cheerful optimism of one boy. Eighteen-year-old Colin Williams, a tally clerk at a South Wales coal mine, refused to allow the rest of us to sink into morbid imaginings and his example was an inspiration to everyone. His faith was rewarded next morning when we resumed our search, not now so much for the food as for our missing companions. At least we found them. They had safely negotiated the river crossing and followed the track to a hut about a mile away, found it stocked with food, and happily settled down there for the night. And here they were, back on our side of the river, feeling very pleased with themselves. It was such a relief to us all that we could feel pleased too, despite the fact that they had not thought to bring across some of the food. If necessary, we could risk the river crossing again.

But we continued our search for the rations dump all through that day. Alan Blackshaw, John Jackson and I waded through the river, less turbulent at this early hour, and plodded on up towards the head of the main valley. We were getting a little weary when an event occurred to banish all our tiredness and anxiety. We heard the engine of a light aircraft approaching over the mountains. A moment later it skimmed across the pass ahead of us and flew low down the valley, making straight for our camp. We watched it land, take off and start back again. Then it reappeared and, to our mounting excitement, made straight towards us. Dancing with joy, Alan and I stripped off our shirts so as to make ourselves more visible, while Jacko flashed the lid of a cigarette tin. As the pilot zoomed over our heads a small package was dropped; it contained a message from Joy, who was on board, saying that the stores had come. For me that moment ranks almost with that other time, when Ed Hillary and Tenzing broke the news to us in the Western Cwm that they had climbed Everest.

In the week which followed, George Lowe led one group, with Joy and Susan and several of the boys, to the shores of Nordvest Fjord, filled with enormous icebergs like the battle fleets of the world riding at anchor. They hoped to pay a call on a party of Eskimoes who were reported often to visit Syd Cap to hunt the narwhal. Instead, they found the hut the Eskimoes had built there as a base deserted, and badly damaged by maurauding polar bears. It was doubly disappointing, for we had also hoped to make the acquaintance, at a safe distance, of some bears during our stay in the Arctic. Indeed, we had brought three revolvers to protect ourselves in case the encounter turned out to be rough. The nearest we came to seeing one, however, was a fresh skin hanging on a line at the mine.

My party spent six unforgettable days as the first explorers to penetrate into the South Staunings Alps. We climbed four mountains and traversed several glaciers, making rough survey observations and supplying both peaks and glaciers with names. There were more castles on the map; a Manchester climbing club, the Karabiner, of which I was president at the time, was also commemorated. For the rest I chose a less nationalistic, or parochial nomenclature, calling on the universe for inspiration: Orion, Jupiter, Mars, Neptune and so on. Looking back on that experience, I see it as the opportunity of a life-time which we only partly seized; time, that exacting task-master, dictated otherwise. Happily for succeeding explorers, we left them plenty to find out for themselves.

On 1st September we were standing on the shore at Mestersvig Bay, awaiting the arrival of our charter plane to take us home. My worries were over, for all the scattered groups: ornithologists, glaciologists, Malcolm's climbing group which had stayed on at the Sefströms camp, as well as our two Schuichert parties, were safely back. The groups at Alpefjord had had their own crisis, when the *Polypen* about whose adventures with her Scottish skipper much else could be told, again broke down. This was a problem which occurred several times during our expedition. I have a note scribbled by Susan during the first part of the programme, addressed to the skipper of the *Polypen* and left on the beach of the inner fjord, called Dammen, where the boat made its landfalls: 'Welcome to Starvation Camp! We certainly will be glad to see you. The idea of a survival diet and retreat down the fjord is uncomfortably close.' To ease the dearth of rations, Malcolm and two boys had elected to return on foot along ninety miles of difficult and largely untraversed coastline, but there were no casualties. Dr David Jones was extracting his final samples of bristles from our chins for his study of beard growth; we had listened for the last time to the soft voice of Roddy as he led our songs to the accompaniment of his guitar: 'Sorry to say, we are on our way, won't be back for many a day . . .' Affectionate farewells were being exchanged with our good friends at the mine and with an American geomorphologist, Brad Washburn and his family, who had provided a touch of home comfort for some of us in that far country. The big plane swooped in.

But Mr Brinch was a worried man. His assistant manager and another colleague had been missing for six days while on a reconnaissance in a small motor boat down the coast; in those ice-infested waters the chances of survival could not be rated high. He asked if the pilot might fly close along the Liverpool coast for some miles on our way south. Half an hour later we were over the Nordvest Fjord, looking down upon that great array of icebergs. Suddenly, the plane started a steep descent towards the sea. As it banked, we could see a tiny spot of red on the blue water: a motorboat with a red sail. A moment later we could make out two figures, clad in red anoraks, waving wildly. The pilot radioed their location and for some time we circled round, waiting for a float plane to arrive from an American ice-breaker which was in the vicinity. It made a grand finale to our stay in the land of the midnight sun.

12

Concord and Discord

1962

BEFORE LEAVING MOSCOW IN 1958, I INVITED OUR RUSSIAN friends to come and climb with us in Britain. They were enthusiastic, but official response to my overtures was slow in coming. In a conversation with the Soviet Minister for Culture during his visit to London towards the end of 1960, I mentioned the application which I had sent through official channels; he was aware of it. 'But,' he asked, 'what mountains are there in your country?' In relative terms it was a fair point, but the inference appeared to be that our crags and cliffs would not provide opportunities for Soviet sportsmen to demonstrate their prowess. Yet in the end, they came: Eugene Gippenreiter, Misha Khergiani and Eugene Tur were old acquaintants; who had climbed with us in the Caucasus; Michael Borushko was their genial leader. Among the others, Anatoli Ovchinnikov was one of the leading Russian climbers at that time; short, sparely built, with open, friendly features and deep-set eyes, he was an easy person to like at first sight. Later, he was to impress us with his sterling qualities under stress.

We had arranged a programme which, apart from lectures at a number of centres on mountaineering in the Soviet Union, would enable our guests to meet and climb with many of our own people in North Wales, the Lake District and Scotland; there was much interest among the local climbing clubs. At the level of personal relationships the visit was a great success. Many new contacts were made, some fine climbs were shared and much mutual respect generated. Rivalry and prestige inevitably obtruded a little during the first week. Some of our people were intent on demonstrating to the Russians the very high standards of performance among British climbers. Competition, although not organised as it is in Russia, is strongly implicit on the crags in the pass of Llanberis and on the cliffs of Clogwyn Du'r Arddu. The Russians were, of course, on their mettle to meet the challenge. In the first few days two accidents occurred: Eugene Gippenreiter suffered a slight skull fracture after a fall on 'Cloggy', while one of our men came off while climbing in the pass and broke a leg. With honours even, I nearly tipped the balance by becoming a victim myself, for which the competitive instinct, never my strong point, was in no wise responsible.

After climbing with Misha, Anatoli and Eugene Tur on the Direct Route on the Nose of Dinas Mot and the Main Wall climb on Cyrn Las, I joined Alf Gregory, one of my companions on Everest, and a friend of his on the Central Route on the latter crag. At the top of the final pitch I belayed and took in the rope for Greg's friend. I was securely anchored, or so I thought, to a huge block on the finishing ledge. Suddenly, and without warning he fell from the chimney he was climbing; the immediate and violent jerk on the rope dragged me to the edge on the ledge; the rock to which I was belayed was dislodged by the strain and I sailed out into space.

Two miracles intervened to save an event which would have been fatal to all three of us. First, instead of continuing to fall, my second landed in the base of the chimney; he was in a state of shock and would not have been able to check my own fall, but at least there was no pull on the rope connecting us. Then, by an even greater stroke of fortune, the slack rope which I had been gathering as my companion was climbing, caught on a small excrescence on the ledge; it stopped my precipitous progress towards the screes. Within seconds, pulled up sharply, I was hanging suspended, some thirty feet below the place where I had been standing. With a push against the rock I was able to swing in a pendulum movement into the foot of the chimney where the second man was lying. Gregory, who had been happily engaged in photography at the moment of the accident, but now thoroughly alerted, climbed up past us, released the snagged rope, and we resumed the climb. Away across the intervening gully Joy, Mike Ward and George Lowe were climbing Main Wall, blissfully unaware of the drama which was being enacted barely a hundred yards from them.

The Russians greatly enjoyed the casual informality with which they were treated during their visits to our climbing clubs; the earnest sense of purpose which had prevailed in London, where they lectured and went for runs and physical training in Hyde Park – 'In London only the dogs do this,' remarked Eugene – wore off. Towards the end of the programme, in a Scottish hut on the island of Skye, they were glad to have mugs of tea brought to their bunks by their Scottish friends before getting up. The zest for physical training and deeds of daring had waned and there was more enthusiasm for chess, card games and sing-songs than climbing on slippery rock in the mist and rain.

During their stay a number of British climbers enquired about the possibility of further visits to the mountains of the Soviet Union. It was made clear to us that applications should be made at the level of some national body. I was keen that the British Mountaineering Council should sponsor such an important event, but the BMC's advice was that the clubs with some claim to national status should take their own initiatives. So, independently of one another, both Malcolm Slesser and I wrote formally to them for permission, he in the name of the Scottish Mountaineering Club, I on behalf of the Alpine Club, to bring expeditions to the Pamirs. There was friendly rivalry between us as we began to form two separate groups, and waited eagerly for the response from Moscow; we anticipated that only one request would be favoured. The issue of nationalities within the United Kingdom was neatly solved by the Soviet authorities. I have since wondered whether their underlying purpose might have been to divide, rather than strengthen the Act of Union of 1707. Both our parties received identical telegrams dated 23rd May 1961, as follows:

> Agree to visits of united groups of Scottish Mountaineering Club and Alpine Club total 12 members July August 1962 Pamir Pik Stalina region for 65 days letter follows regards.
> USSR Mountaineering Federation.

So Malcolm and I, for the second time, combined our parties and co-ordinated our plans; the Scots generously invited me to lead this British group. For a start, we agreed to accept that those whom we had separately invited should be members of the joint expedition. Malcolm's party comprised George Lowe and Ian McNaught-Davis, both of whom had been with me in Greenland and George also on Everest; Dr Graeme Nicol, an Aberdonian with some Alpine experience and a high reputation for his climbing in Scotland; Ken Bryan, who had been a member of Malcolm's Scottish expedition to the Staunings Alper in 1959; and Robin Smith, who had just acquired a first class honours degree and was probably the foremost Scottish climber of his generation. I had invited Wilf Noyce, Derek Bull and Ralph Jones to come with me. Ted Wrangham, a fellow member of the Alpine Club and the Climbers' Club had taken a lead in our efforts to obtain permission for a British party to visit the Pamirs, so he was added to the list. To give further strength to the Anglo-Scottish group we then invited Joe Brown, who had climbed Kangchenjunga with George Band and was, in the early 'sixties, at the height of his climbing career. It was a party which seemed to combine exceptional all-round experience and skill within a fairly wide age-bracket.

We were delighted that our expedition area should be in the vicinity of Russia's highest mountain; soon afterwards its name was purged along with all other similar place-names in the Soviet Union. It was only shortly before we departed for Russia that we were told its new title: Pik Kommunizma. There was a difference of view regarding particular objectives. The Russians named three peaks: Pik Moscowa, Pik Garmo and Pik Kommunizma as being mountains they would like us to climb, they expressed the hope that the two former peaks might offer the prospect of hitherto unclimbed routes. We preferred a two-stage programme, the first period being primarily designed to enable us to get fit and closely acquainted, in preparation for the climax on Pik Kommunizma. The matter appeared to be mainly a question of emphasis rather than principle, or so we hoped. It was left over for later discussion, as was the important question of whether there should be one leader of a combined British-Soviet expedition, or two groups working as closely together as possible. This planning by correspondence was not an entirely satisfactory basis for setting up an ambitious and complex venture such as this. Malcolm made a helpful visit to Moscow at the turn of the year to iron out some details; but from my experience of Everest, I was convinced of the need to involve everyone in the planning and to undertake some preliminary training together. The English and Scottish members did, in fact, spend an enjoyable weekend on Ben Nevis, based on the Charles Inglis Clarke hut, the weather obliged us by providing testing conditions: snow and mist, with a strong wind. It was pleasant to be on the rope with Malcolm again as we climbed the North-East Buttress of the Ben which, under those conditions, assumed the character of a fine Alpine route. Our foremost performers, Joe Brown, Robin Smith and Wilf Noyce, were able to measure and gain respect for each others' skills on some harder routes. For me, the occasion was a useful opportunity to observe the different personalities among this group of highly individualistic men. There might, I foresaw, be some problems, not least on account of the age gaps between us. But on the whole, I felt we had the makings of an effective and happy team. We had yet to meet our Russian colleagues.

We met them in darkness and stuffy heat at the airport of Dushanbe, capital of the Soviet Republic of Tadjhikistan, after a flight from Moscow lasting five and a half hours which had made us as remote from the Russian metropolis as that city was from London. Friendly faces and warm, welcoming handshakes; a few words in Russian from our side—like some of my companions, I had been struggling with a grammar book for several months—and much more accomplished English from their leader Anatoli Ovchinnikov; here was one firm

Climbing friends from the Caucasus. Josef Kachiani, above left, and Eugene Gippenreiter, left, with, above, Misha Khergiani on Dinas Mot during a return visit to Britain.

Beaumaris summit in the Staunings Alps, John Jackson tracing our route westwards.

On the Bersaeker Brae glacier looking towards the Bersaerker Tinde.

friend, whose understanding had been sealed by those climbs in the pass of Llanberis. He introduced another 'Tolia', Anatoli Sevastianov, quiet, serious, self-effacing. The two Anatolis were already an effective climbing partnership and inseparable companions; in the interval of fifteen years I have received annually a New Year greeting card signed by them both. Nikolai Shalaev was an older man, a solid and undemonstrative citizen, who was employed by the Moscow Post Office as a carpenter. Kolia had no English and it was only later, in the mountains, that I was able to appreciate the fine mountaineering qualities and hidden depths of this endearing companion. Vladmir Malakhov and Nikolai Alkhutov were still teenagers, full of promise as mountaineers, but as yet undecorated with sporting medals and intent on gaining the accolade of a Mastership of Sport. On first impression in the shining sincerity of their welcome, I liked them all.

On the maps we had brought with us Dushanbe was still called Stalinabad. The change in nomenclature may have been agreeable to the peasantry in this far Republic of the Union who had resisted Stalin's harsh enforcement of his collective farming policy to their cost. Dushanbe is a Tadjhik word for Second Day in the Muslim week, which is Monday. It was also market day in those parts. The town had grown rapidly in recent years, from a collection of three small villages with a few hundred inhabitants, to a flourishing trade centre comprising a quarter of a million people of several races. At the time of our visit nearly half of these were Western or White Russians, the remainder Tadjhiks, with a smattering of other tribesmen – Uzbeks, Kazaks, Kirghizis.

During our first days in the capital we paid visits to an all-age school and a collective farm, swam in the local lido, sorted out our equipment which had arrived by rail from Archangel, and discussed our plans for departure to the mountains with Ivan Nikolaivich Jakovlev, head of the Intourist bureau. Ivan had been one of the fortunate few to have survived, after being picked up by General Horrocks' 30th Corps during the advance of the Allied armies through Germany and forcibly repatriated to Russia. We were also able to spend some time observing the gathering of the different peoples of the region at the weekly market. There were the tall, handsome mountain Tadjhiks, aquiline of countenance and similar to the Pathan and Afridi tribesmen with whom the British used to wage intermittent warfare on the former North-West Frontier of India. Their elders, with flowing beards, gorgeous striped coats of many colours, cummerbunds and long leather boots, seemed to have walked straight out of the pages of the *Arabian Nights*. Their women folk were just as colourful: rosy cheeked, wearing bright

12

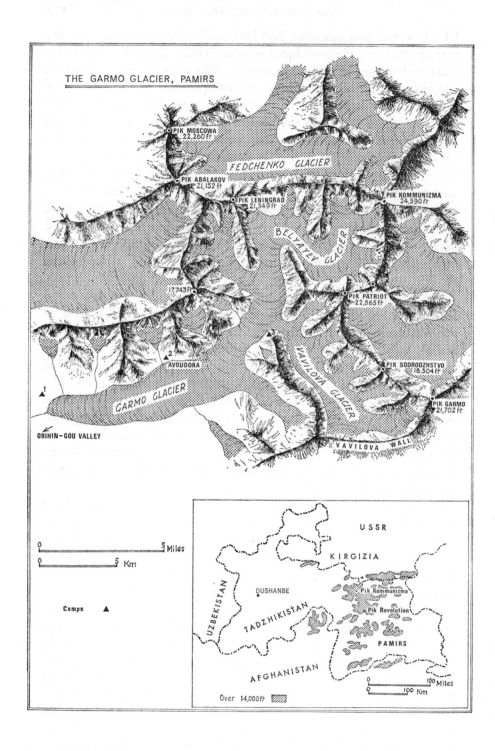

THE GARMO GLACIER, PAMIRS

PIK MOSCOWA
22,260 ft

FEDCHENKO GLACIER

PIK ABALAKOV
21,152 ft

PIK LENINGRAD
21,349 ft

PIK KOMMUNIZMA
24,590 ft

BELYAYEV GLACIER

17,743 ft

PIK PATRIOT
22,565 ft

3

2
AVOUDORA

VAVILOVA GLACIER

PIK SODROOZHSTVO
18,504 ft

1

GARMO GLACIER

PIK GARMO
21,702 ft

OBIHIN-GOU VALLEY

VAVILOVA WALL

0 _____ 5 Miles
0 _____ 5 Km

Camps ▲

USSR

KIRGIZIA

UZBEKISTAN

DUSHANBE

Pik Kommunizma

TADZHIKISTAN

Pik Revolution

PAMIRS

AFGHANISTAN

Over 14,000 ft

0 _____ 100 Miles
0 _____ 100 Km

smocks and baggy trousers, their hair dressed in many plaits. It was, perhaps, not without significance that the headman of the village collective farm we had visited told us: 'Alexander Macedonski was here'. The plainsmen were contrastingly drab, mongoloid in feature, more stocky; the stamp of the invasions of Ghengiz Khan was plainly upon them. All were there doing their weekly shopping, rubbing shoulders with men and women from the West; though I gathered from Ivan that there was as yet little social intercourse between Easterners and Westerners. I noticed that the Tadjhik old-style dwellings were separate from the new Western-style apartments. For eager photographers the scene was irresistible. So much so that George Lowe and I received a menacing warning to desist, and Derek Bull, who disguised his singularly sweet disposition behind a vagabond appearance, was arrested and thrown into the local gaol for a few hours.

For English-speaking visitors to a remote Soviet republic, Ivan was a most congenial companion. Taken prisoner by the Germans on the Russian front, he escaped when the Allies advanced towards Berlin and fell into the hands of our 30th Corps—I believe he became a guest of the 52nd Highland Division, which had been trained for a mountain rôle, but was committed into the flatlands of northern Europe. He was only one of thousands of captured Russian soldiers whom the Allies sent back to the Soviet Union at the end of the war in response to a Russian demand, despite the expectation that they would be executed as traitors; Ivan was one of the lucky ones. He described the presence of White Russians in Tadjhikistan as comparable with the Roman occupation of Britain. There was no evidence of this in the market place and my impression was that many young Tadjhiks were adopting the Western dress and culture; but there was a striking difference between the apartments occupied by the Russians and the humble, mud-built dwellings in which the Tadjhiks lived.

The city was immaculately clean, Ivan even carried in his pocket an envelope into which he tapped the ash from his cigarette. There was also an impressively purposeful busy-ness among the citizens. In a Univermag windowfront we observed two separate lists of employees posted: on one side were those who had earned the gratitude of the community for exceeding their allotted norms; on the other, identified by most unflattering photographs, were others who had done less than their share. I gathered that if this kind of pillory, together with exhortation, failed, forced labour would follow.

One evening we were entertained by the Tadjhik Federation of Mountaineers in a local *Chae-Khana*. It was a wholly delightful, if gastromically exacting occasion. After consuming great quantities of *shashlik*, curries and flat bread, we repaired to recover in an upper

chamber, normally reserved for the elders, for quiet conversation over
cups of green tea. The tradition was as civilised as that in any Oxford
college, notwithstanding the fact that we sat shoe-less and cross-legged
on the floor. The director of the establishment told us something of
local customs and added a plug for his restaurant; he claimed that some
2,500 people patronised the place every day. One of the waitresses, a
motherly character, took a fancy to me; to my embarrassment, but to
the amusement of everyone else, she addressed me with unmistakable
meaning in her voice. 'What do you want to have to do with all these
immature young men?' she enquired. 'Why not let them go off to the
mountains and have their fun, and you and I will enjoy each other's
company here in Dushanbe?' Not sure whether to be flattered or
dismayed by this revelation of her feelings and my age, I compromised
by accepting an extra cup of tea.

It was while we were in Dushanbe that the first cloud shadowed the
sun of our good relations. The Russians informed us of a change in the
plans outlined in correspondence with myself and during Malcolm's
discussions in Moscow the previous winter. Instead of travelling by
air to a small township named Tavil Dara and thence by lorry and on
foot, with horses to carry our baggage, up the Obihin-Gou valley to
reach the Garmo glacier, we would have to fly to Jirgatal, in the valley
of the Muk Su river, whence two helicopters, which had been ordered
from the military academy of Frunze, would convey us to our
destination. Apparently Tavil Dara and the approach valley had been
declared an area prohibited to foreigners. This was a serious blow. It
would have implications for our limited financial resources in more
ways than one. There were the unbudgeted plane fares, of course, but
as well as that Malcolm and Mac were worried lest they might not be
able to provide a photographic record for the *National Geographic
Magazine* of America, with whom we had negotiated a contract. Once
again the demands of the media had to be taken into consideration and,
for me, roused sour memories of the delayed start for Dykh-tau back
in 1958. There was, however, one thing about which we all agreed
strongly. We disliked the notion of dropping in on the mountains,
rather than approaching them on foot. There was the physical handicap
of arriving, unfit and unacclimatised, at the start of the strenuous part
of our programme; there was a psychological need for a period of
mental, as well as mutual adjustment, which an approach march
provides, before undertaking big climbs. There was also an aesthetic
point. By walking towards the high mountains from the valleys, it is
possible to appreciate the whole area, of which the higher reaches are
only a part; to enjoy the living foreground of forests and flowers and,
perhaps see some wild life; to meet people whose homes and liveli-

hoods are among those mountains. All these things we would be missing. Years later, as Joy and I were flying by helicopter to the Base Camp of the Alpine Club of Canada beside the Steele glacier, to join their Centennial Expedition in the Saint Elias mountains of the North-West Yukon, I had this same feeling of being denied the enjoyment of the forests and living creatures below us.

There was a sharp difference of opinion between us as what should be done. Malcolm had signed an agreement on behalf of our party during his visit to Moscow, which only outlined in general terms an undertaking on the part of the Russians to bring us into the area of the Garmo glacier. But the formal letter of invitation which had been sent both to the Scottish Mountaineering Club and myself, though couched in cautious language, had been more specific:

> I can inform you in a preliminary way that a tentative region for the operations of the expedition will be Garmo glacier . . . the route is as follows: Moscow–Stalinabad by regular flight; Stalinabad–Tavil-Dara by local plane, Tavil-Dara–Saed farm by lorry and further by caravan to the upper reaches of the Obihin-Gou river . . .

It was on this basis that our contracts and our budgeting had been drawn up. Malcolm was incensed by this change in plan and he demanded that I should call what he believed to be the Russians' bluff. He even suggested that we should pack our bags, depart for the Afghan frontier, and climb in the Hindu Kush instead. I disagreed. We had no permission for that area, we had no maps or essential contacts. It was very doubtful if we could carry out such a threat without cutting off our noses to spite our faces; it would merely be a counter-bluff. However much we might dislike the decision, the Russian authorities doubtless had reasons which were important to themselves; I did not think they would back down. In any case, as guests in a foreign land, we were in no position to throw our limited weight around. Above all, I was anxious to maintain a happy relationship with our Soviet climbing companions who were not, themselves, responsible for political decisions. A confrontation at this point would have ruined the prospects of unity in the mountains on which the success of our climbs would largely depend and which was, as far as I was concerned, the main purpose of the whole exercise.

The incident passed and we flew in to our destination as the Russians wished. Fortunately there was a solid core of good sense and moderation in our company which helped to smooth over the raw edges. But the incident demonstrated a weakness within the British party of

individuals who had taken separate initiatives towards realising this
privileged journey, and whose thinking on the issues and the objectives had not been fully blended. It left a scar which was never
entirely healed. What were the Russians' reasons? As we flew up the
Obihin-Gou valley we looked down upon the shells of homesteads in
a landscape apparently deserted by human beings. 'Avalanches' was
the explanation given to us. I remembered the ruins of the old Bezingi
village in the Caucasus, from which Stalin had evicted the Balkari
tribesmen. 'Avalanche' was the reason given for that, too. Both
explanations seemed very implausible to me.

Whatever the reasons and despite this set-back, there was one
important matter on which we were all agreed. From now onwards
the whole party, Britishers and Russians, should work as a team; there
should be one leader. It was flattering, if a trifle daunting, to be invited
by the Russians to fill that rôle. Such a union, in contrast with the
co-operation we had enjoyed while climbing as a separate entity in
the Caucasus, put a new complexion on the nature of this enterprise.
It was pleasing to enjoy the confidence of our hosts, but I realised that
it would raise serious problems of management. There was the large
assumption that our mutual relationships and understanding about
mountaineering, both on a technical and philosophical level, had
already progressed to that point over the years since 1954. In the light
of events I am inclined to doubt whether that point had been reached
by all members on either side.

Our arrival at the site chosen for Base Camp was spectacular and
alarming. The heavily laden helicopter, unable either to touch down
lightly from a vertical position in the thin air at 10,000 feet, or to make
a run in along the boulder-strewn ground in the valley, plummeted
down from ten feet or so in the air and gave us a severe shaking; it
appeared to have been a chancy landing. What was more, we found
ourselves dumped, with our mountainous baggage, half a mile below
the snout of the glacier instead — as we had hoped — of on a grassy site
named Avoudara some miles up-glacier and 2,000 feet higher; on foot,
it involved a tedious journey of about four hours. The prospect of
humping thousands of pounds of gear, day after day for about a
week to that higher place was a depressing thought. In our state of
unfitness the daily corvées proved to be as back-breaking a labour as
we had feared. The Russians had the edge on us, for they had trained
assiduously for the expedition and, with the exception of Robin Smith,
were much fitter than we were at that stage. My concern was both
personal and on account of the time which would be needed to shift
our loads, not only to Avoudara but to higher camps; there would be a

serious encroachment on the total time of sixty-five days granted us in our agreement with the Russians.

In the circumstances, something drastic had to be done. I had a chat with the senior of the two pilots, who were now engaged in flying in a large Soviet expedition. He proved amenable to the suggestion that he might attempt an air-drop of our less perishable gear at two or more sites further up the glacier. A bottle of Scotch, while it was in no sense an inducement to undertake this task, was the least we could offer by way of gratitude for his co-operation. The pilot pointed out that he could not operate above the maximum altitude of 13,000 feet at which his machine could safely fly, and even so, it might be a risky affair.

So indeed it seemed to George Lowe and myself when, acting as air despatchers on the first flight, the following morning, we skimmed at 15 feet above the moraine and, travelling at 60 m.p.h. jettisoned the loads. I found the experience quite hair-raising. That evening I wrote to Joy: 'I had a sudden thought that George and I had no business to be doing that sort of thing.' George was to marry my daughter Susan when we returned to England.

The Russians did not avail themselves of the air drops; nor did they appear to have calculated their food requirements exactly, either in terms of a balanced diet or in the quantity to be carried to each of our camps. This is an aspect of expedition planning to which we Britishers pay much attention and which we may tend to make too complicated. Russians' strength and stamina, which made it possible for them to carry large amounts of tinned food—crabmeat, beef strogonov, caviare and fruit—was certainly a surer, if slower means of ensuring that the loads reached their destination intact. When we arrived at our higher camps we found tea, sugar, jam and cereals scattered, most of it irretrievably, over the snow and among the boulders.

During those first days at Base Camp we hammered out our climbing plans, for me it was an interesting exercise in team management. There had already been exchange of proposals by correspondence; now, sitting on packing cases in a rather dreary wood at the edge of the upper Garmo valley, in its setting of barren and featureless mountains, it was time to iron out the differences. I explained our preference for a preliminary programme of joint climbing on some lesser peaks, in preparation for the highlight of the expedition: the ascent of Pik Kommunizma. I explained how we needed this period to get fit and acclimatised, as well as to know one another better. I also suggested that there would be advantages if we chose an area in which the whole expedition could remain in contact, in case there should be any emergency. The Russians had proposed that we should be widely separated during the first part of our stay, with one group climbing Pik Garmo and the other moving out of the Garmo basin to make a climb on Pik Moscowa. To reach that peak some of our party would have to climb over a high pass above Avoudara, separating themselves from the rest of us and carrying all their requirements for at least a week. Instead, I proposed that we should all base ourselves on the Vavilova glacier, at the head of which stands Pik Garmo. There was visible disappointment on the part of our Russian comrades, especially the young pair, Vladimir and Nikolai, with their sights set on their masterships of sport. But apart from Pik Garmo, our sketch maps showed other peaks above the Vavilova which might provide good climbing, and in the end everyone appeared to be reasonably happy. As far as I was concerned, the helicopter trip up the glacier had revealed a scene of beauty and promise. The huge wedge-shaped mass of Pik Kommunizma dominated the panorama; while Pik Garmo, also a noble mountain, stood, without rivals in altitude, far away on the right. There was an imposing ice wall up there at the head of the Vavilova glacier and some fine peaks along the northern flank. Highly excited by all this dazzling display, I pushed my camera through the gun port of the helicopter's perspex window and took one picture after another. By chance I pointed it at a shapely, unnamed peak which I did not note especially at the time, little thinking that, only ten days later, I was to stand on its summit.

Despite the reservations of some big wall enthusiasts in our midst, this revelation, and making the air-drops, brought about a significant change for the better in the expedition's morale. We had been depressed by the daily chore of carrying heavy loads to Avoudara, by the dreary environment of Base Camp and the dust storms and rainfall which occurred every afternoon. Our efforts to mix, eating together and sharing tents, had only been a partial success. Now we could move forward and start climbing together. An air of purpose and expectancy replaced the awkwardness and gloom.

Before we left Base Camp it was, for me, a delight to meet again some old acquaintances among the incoming Russian group. They represented Spartak Camp where we had stayed in the Caucasus; the leader was Vitali Abalakov.

The cinematographer Michael Anuvrikov was there, and Nikolai Romanov, now retired from the post of chairman of the Mountaineering Federation, and his successor Borovikov. It was a special joy for all who had met him, whether in the Caucasus or in Britain, to greet Misha Khergiani, who had now displaced his fellow Svanetian Josef Kakhiani as rock climbing champion of the USSR. This formidable party had come to attempt the first ascent of the South-West Face of

Pik Kommunizma, hoping to win the prize presented annually for the outstanding face climb of the year. I asked Abalakov whether some members of our party might follow his group up their route at a later stage in our expedition; he raised no objection.

By now I was really fit; even carrying those enormous loads was no longer unbearable; it made a tremendous difference to my own outlook on life. In my sleeping bag at Avoudara, on our way up the glacier, I wrote: 'Lying out under the stars, in a half moon, life takes on a new perspective.' Three days later my mood of optimism was even greater. We were at our Camp 3, at 14,000 feet, high above the junction of the Garmo and Vavilova ice-streams; it was a cock-pit position for viewing a panorama of breath-taking splendour. Now we could see beyond the containing ridges of the Garmo glacier, to peaks Moscowa and Leningrad. The former looked a long way away and I was thankful that we had resolved not to divide the expedition by attempting it. Pik Kommunizma towered above us, slightly to our left; immediately across the Vavilova glacier were two high mountains, one behind the other and both impressive. The nearer one was named Patriot. It had been climbed once by its East Ridge, which gave promise of a fine climb. Behind it stood a peak which still bore a forbidden name on our sketches—Molotov. How should we refer to it? 'There is no harm in calling the mountain Pik Former Molotov for the time being,' said Anatoli Ovchinnikov.

In these glorious surroundings, with the call of the big peaks on every hand, plans for the disposition of three climbing groups presented no difficulty. It was easier to discuss differences in tactics, too. At that time we followed Himalayan principles of a progressive advance, first to establish a succession of camps up the chosen route, then stocking and manning them, before a few selected climbers went through to the summit, well supported by their comrades at various points on the mountain. By contrast, it was the Russian practice for a whole large group to move *en masse*, carrying all their gear as a self-contained, but heavily encumbered, unit which could subsist for days, even weeks high on the mountain.

We decided that a strong group should tackle Pik Garmo, if possible by its unclimbed West Face: Wilfrid and Robin, the two Anatolis, with Derek Bull and Ted Wrangham, who were still not fully fit, in support, would comprise this party. The East Ridge of Pik Patriot presented another serious challenge: Malcolm would lead that climb, with Joe Brown, Ian McNaught-Davis and the two young Russians. The latter were now content because success would provide them with a further step in the ladder of sporting promotion. Perhaps through some intuition of coming events, I was concerned that there should, in case of emergency, be eventual means of supporting these two main thrusts. The third group would, therefore choose a peak located somewhere along the ridge on the far side of the Vavilova glacier, between Piks Patriot and Garmo. Fortunately Ralph and Joe, who had climbed 1,500 feet or so above our camp, had seen a fine-looking summit, perhaps 19,000 feet in height, which bore no name; it might make a worthy first ascent and, without the accolade of a Mastership of Sport, be an invisible feather in the expedition's cap. We should take less time to climb this mountain than the others to achieve theirs. So I agreed that after our own attempt we would first visit the Garmo party and then Malcolm's group to enquire whether they needed help.

So Ralph, Graeme Nicol, George Lowe and I, with Eugene Gippenreiter and Nikolai Shalaev, headed diagonally across the Vavilova glacier on the morning of 18th July, after having made a previous journey laden like pack mules, to place an advanced dump of stores on the far moraine. All three groups parted company in good spirits, agreeing to be back at Camp 3 on 27th July to rest and recuperate for the second phase.

On the evening of 20th July we were comfortably ensconced in two tents in a romantic spot, at the end of a level section of snow arête at 16,000 feet on the West Ridge of our peak. From that point the ridge steepened considerably and the climbing was more difficult. Ralph and Kolia had continued for two or three hours, fixed a rope at one awkward place, and reported that the way ahead looked promising. All was ready for an early start next morning. Would we make it? I think we were all a little keyed up. 'My tummy is full of butterflies,' I wrote in my diary that evening, 'with doubts about my own ability to tackle what promises to be a hard and high mountain.' George Lowe was nursing even greater doubts; he felt he should not be courting risks on the eve of his marriage. Sensibly, he elected to stay behind and have a hot meal ready for our return.

We left our camp site in the grey light of dawn on the 21st under a lowering sky. First up a rock step behind the tents, then along an impressive narrow stretch of the ridge on rock and snow to the tower where Ralph and Kolia had left the rope. When we arrived they had already removed it – for they had gone ahead of Graeme, Eugene and myself – intending to fix it on a bigger vertical rise further on; in crampons, on rotten rock, we found this passage quite hard. After more narrow ridge climbing we caught up the leading pair at the foot of the larger obstacle. Here the rock was even worse and Kolia's lead up an ice-filled gully, the ice adhering precariously to the crumbling rocks underneath, was a particularly good effort. Somehow, despite the looseness, Ralph managed to hammer in a piton to provide security for the party on this difficult pitch.

Once again there was a narrow section of ridge, impressively airy and, on the hard frozen snow, especially enjoyable. It led us to a big sweep of steep snow rising about 1,000 feet to the foot of the summit rocks. When we reached it Kolia and Ralph were already well launched upon it and I was much relieved to note that the snow appeared to be in good condition; they were climbing steadily on a hard crusted surface. It was very hard work and, although the angle was not particularly steep—about 45 degrees—we moved one at a time, as much to rest as to provide each other with protection. Moving thus, rope length after rope length, the climb seemed endlessly long. At last we reached an outcrop of rocks which marked a change in gradient; we turned this obstacle on the left, only to find ourselves confronted by an ice wall which barred progress on to the final slopes. This required a long time and much pegging and step-cutting to master; as an ice climbing enthusiast, I remember feeling slightly envious of Ralph as he gave us a particularly good lead up this pitch.

Then there was some more exhausting plodding until, at last, we arrived at the summit rocks. The final 200 yards along the ridge called for all my reserves of physique and will power and I fancy the others were in much the same plight. I was leading at this stage and found I needed two or three breaths to make one forward step, with halts every ten paces or so to gasp in more oxygen. Just below the summit I waited for Eugene and we stepped on to the top hand in hand. Heartfelt hand-clasps and bear hugs for joy! It was 1.35 p.m. and the altimetre registered 5,600 metres (it was later officially computed by the Russian authorities as 5,640 metres, or (18,504 feet) and graded as IV.B—1.

Thick weather had blown up and thunder rumbled in the distance, which gave us cause to worry about the descent, but we spent an hour on top, melting snow on a *Buta* stove and taking pictures; not of the view because there was none, but of ourselves holding aloft two small flags, one of each nation, before depositing them in a box which we left beneath a cairn.

Then we turned to go down. I had never before been so acutely aware of the danger of an accident, for the big snow slope had deteriorated into heavy, slushy snow, lying on top of hard ice. We floundered deeply into it at every step, trying to keep our crampon points cleared from balling so that they could find purchase on the underlying ice; it was an exhausting and nerve-racking business, with a precipitous, plunging view of several thousands of feet to the glacier beneath our feet. The sections of snow ridge were just as bad and we thankfully abseiled down the rock steps, glad at least to feel secure in those places. George saw us as we came down the lower step and it was very good indeed to receive his warm welcome and congratulations. Hot soup was awaiting us, too, when we reached the tents at 7.20 p.m., after a climb of thirteen hours.

Back at our Advanced Base Camp beneath the peak, we rested and prepared to move off to join the group on Pik Garmo. I was filled with a vague sense of urgency, but perhaps it was just as well that we were delayed during 23rd July by a bout of sickness, fortunately only passing, which George suffered that morning. We were all tired and, though we could not know it, we were going to need all our reserves of strength in the days ahead of us. For the present it was a time for talk; of our climb, of other adventures; of our homes and families, our life styles and beliefs. Here in the mountains we could discuss freely the different ideologies which guided, or governed the affairs of our two countries. Kolia, who up till now had stayed in the background, speaking no English and feeling somewhat out of things, brightened up and became loquacious. He told us about his work, his wages, his family who were on holiday on the Black Sea coast. Eugene spoke of his hopes to study in order to write a thesis on high-altitude physiology. Ralph is an incomparable spinner of tall stories and we laughed a lot. All in all, I felt, these were the best summit talks which had taken place up to that time.

Eventually we were able to make a start up the Garmo glacier on the 24th, only to be held up again for the second part of that day when Eugene fell into a crevasse. As is usual on these occasions, it all happened with dramatic suddenness. We had just roped up in two parties of three in view of the appalling state of the soft snow overlying the crevasses. Eugene was in the lead, when I suddenly heard a shout just over an intervening rise. Running forward I saw that the rope ran from George straight into a gaping hole in the snow; George was holding on for dear life. Going forward to the hole I could see Eugene, 20 feet down the crevasse and up to his neck in icy, slushy water. He was amazingly calm, yet thrashing around out of his depth with an enormous rucksack on his back. We sent down a spare rope and hauled out, first the sack and then a soaking, but still smiling Eugene. He was, as soon became apparent, suffering from shock and we made an immediate decision to go back some distance to safer ground and put up our tents. Had we pressed on, the chances were that the incident would have been repeated, possibly with more serious consequences.

That evening we debated whether to push on next morning, or return to Camp 3. We scanned the South Face of Pik Garmo and its

West Ridge in vain looking for signs of Wilf's party; some old tracks nearby seemed to be heading down hill and we wondered whether they had already climbed their peak, or had perhaps even given up the attempt. But I was uneasy; the urge was stronger than ever to get up to the upper corrie of the glacier, underneath the West Face. I noticed a small ice avalanche falling down the rock face at about 6.15 p.m. Something seemed to be wrong, but we could not find a reason for our disquiet. Early on 25th we moved rapidly up the glacier on hard frozen snow; then on up the right edge of a lower icefall to a snow basin where, greatly to our relief, we came upon a Russian tent. A few minutes later our remaining worries seemed to have been dispelled when we spotted two figures high above, on the West Ridge. I was relieved by the thought that they had climbed by that ridge rather than attempting the fearsome looking and unclimbed West Face. We ate a meal, for we had started in haste without breakfasting. Then Graeme and I went up the higher icefall, towards the higher glacier corrie. It was very hot in the sérac area and route finding would have been difficult but for faint tracks, evidently several days old.

We could now see at least two people descending the steep snow slopes from a col on the left-hand end of the ridge, they were going so slowly that we suspected that one of them might have been injured; nor would they respond to our shouts. We would have to wait, so we found shelter in a huge ice grotto beneath a bergschrund at the bottom of the slope they were descending; it provided welcome relief from the glare and fierce heat outside. Then, surprised that they had still not arrived, we started up the slope ourselves, with a vague idea of reaching the ridge and looking down upon the Fedchenko glacier on the far side. Suddenly, they were immediately below us. A few shouted words from Derek broke the awful news that Robin and Wilf were dead. Yet unwilling to believe and cheering each other with unlikely explanations of some mistake, we went carefully down again. Both parties now moved towards one another and, for some reason, I stopped to take a photograph of our friends; the two Anatolis were, I noticed, there as well.

At about the same time on the evening of the 24th as we were discussing what to do, four people were, in fact, descending from the summit of Pik Garmo. Wilf and Anatoli Sevastianov were on one rope, Robin and Ovchinnikov on the other. They had not gone far when both Anatolis stopped to put on their crampons, which they had not used for the ascent. The British climbers had done so and Robin suggested that, to save time, he and Wilf should rope together and continue, leaving the Russians to follow; so a fateful change was made in the climbing order. A little later, the two Russians shouted advice to Wilf not to continue down a certain snow couloir because of the atrocious state of the snow; it was just as we had found it on our peak. But the British climbers descended it without mishap. Beyond it, across some intervening rocks, was a steep snow slope, with underlying ice covered by snow saturated by the sun. Ovchinnikov, leading down on the Russian rope, suddenly saw one of the lower pair slip; they started falling with gathering speed.

From their highest camp some 1,500 feet below on the West Ridge Derek and Ted, who had turned back on that same slope earlier in the day, came out of their tent on hearing a yodel, doubtless intended to announce victory and to suggest that they start cooking supper.

At that very moment they saw Robin and Wilf falling, first into a snow couloir, then down a rock gully, moving now at a terrific pace. Horror-struck, they hoped against hope that their fall might bring the two men out to the right, on to less steep ground; but it was not to be. They fell to the left, over the edge of the ridge and down a huge ice slope which borders the West Face, towards the upper basin of the Garmo glacier, down the precipice, first over an upper bergschrund and then over the edge of an ice cliff which marked the upper lip of an even bigger schrund. To Derek it seemed that the fall was arrested at that place, on a terrasse below that 60 feet high ice cliff. Both thought that they could see one of the bodies lying there; there was no sign of life. The time was 6.20 p.m.

So died two outstanding British climbers.

There was little to say just then; the truth had not fully sunk in. It was suggested that we should go and look for the bodies, but I decided we should all return to the Russian tent where my party had camped. It was too late for safety and we were all tired. A sad and silent party descended through the séracs. Ralph and the others saw us and shouted words of greeting, but we in our turn did not reply. Then I broke the news to them.

What to do? We debated the problems at length. At last all was resolved and preparations were made that night for the sad and difficult job to be done next day. I slept little, thinking of Wilf, and of his wife, Rosemary, who wanted him to give up climbing. Yet a few days later, while going through his gear at Base Camp, I found some notes which Wilf had written on the subject:

When I knew that an expedition was being organised, it did not occur to me that I could or should go with it. And when the chance came I was filled with doubt. . . . To me, brooding, it seemed that mountaineering had hitherto been a private adventure, a self-seeking . . . whether I was alone or with companions. . . . To be with those who thought and spoke differently, yet on common ground and with common aims – this might be a bridge perhaps, even in a small way, of the gap separating East and West over all other fields of thought.

I thought of Wilf and our friendship during twenty years. He had joined my regiment, as a most improbable warrior, in 1942 and we had served together for a while in the 10th battalion. We had run that 'toughening course' together in North Wales and it had provided opportunities to climb at odd moments. I remembered a marvellous day in the Lake District at Easter just after the war, when Wilf had led me and a friend with effortless ease up Savage Gully on Pillar Rock, down over the Nose and again up the crag by the North-West Route, in one continuous climb. We were late for supper as a result—a serious misdemeanour on the part of guests of Professor Pigou at Gatesgarth. But Philip Noel-Baker, who had lain on the turf beneath the Rock to watch us, had gone ahead and reported our performance in such glowing terms that we were forgiven.

Then came Everest, and Wilf's distinguished part in the climb; he it was who first reached the South Col with the Sherpa Annullu, giving his companions a tremendous sense of uplift as we watched their blue anoraks blend with the background of sky behind the rocky edge far above us. During my own descent from the South-East Ridge with Bourdillon and Evans, Wilf was at Camp 6 and, but for his ministrations, especially to Tom, I wondered how, and even whether, we would all have survived that night. There had followed three marvellous Alpine seasons together, in which some of our setbacks, including those on the Frontier and Peuterey Ridges of Mont Blanc, rank in memory almost as highly as our many successes. I remembered a double traverse of Mont Blanc, over the Aiguille de Bionnasay and Mount Maudit to the Torino hut, and back over the great mountain by its Italian face, up the Voie de La Sentinelle and down past the Grands Mulets. I remembered other occasions, amusing or poignant: a bivouac on the Requin; eating our lunch in a severe electrical storm on an exceedingly steep slope of snow; a glorious day on the blade-like sharpness of the Arête de Rochefort; the Grand Diédre on the Aiguille de la Brenva; the integral traverse of the Aiguille du Moine in bad weather. None of those episodes mattered as much as the man with whom I had shared them. To climb with him, on a Welsh crag, an Alpine or a Himalayan peak, was an object lesson in rhythm and balanced movement. Sometimes he seemed oblivious to the limitations of lesser men; after surviving three falls, on one of which I fielded him, I wondered whether he was aware that there were limits even to his own exceptional powers. Wilf was without guile or pretence; he was an easy person to be with. Though we had shared many mountain and social occasions together, I knew that his mind was often away on some far peak.

Should I have persuaded him to join me, this once more? Well, it was too late now.

And Robin, who had shown so much youthful promise, and who, despite his academic honours, lived only for climbing. I remembered my first impressions in the CIC hut under Ben Nevis, as he lay cosily in his sleeping bag watching me, with what I took to be cynical appraisal, as I busied myself with sweeping up the mess on the littered floor. Robin, about whom I had written in my diary at Base Camp, 'is doing his best to be a good member of the party'. And later, at Camp 2; 'Derek, Robin and, of course, Wilf are wonders of selfless labour in the common weal.' Robin had decided to be one of us before his untimely end.

And I thought of the expedition, whether it should go on; and what I should do personally. I told the others that we should come to no hasty conclusions on these matters; but I could not switch them from my mind.

6.00 a.m. on 26th July, and a cold, clear morning. I asked Derek and Ted to stay in camp and prepare for our return. Eight of us started off; in one hour we were back in the upper corrie and moving towards the foot of the great ice slope and the bergschrund where we believed our friends to be. Here George and Eugene stopped, ready to help, collecting the gear which Derek had thrown down from the ridge the day before. Six of us roped up on two ropes; the Anatolis with Graeme, Ralph and I with Kolia Shalaev. The climbing was difficult; it included some really steep ice which we ascended on the points of our crampons. At last we reached a short ice wall below the big schrund; it proved to be less of a problem than we had feared. We stepped on to the terrace, and there they were. Wilf and Robin lay side by side, as though they had lain down there to sleep.

We decided not to bring them down. There was a crevasse at the lip of the terrace and we put them in there. It was a painful act, which proved to be too much for my composure as I helped with Wilf. Ralph recalls that our Russian friends fired a Verey pistol as a last salute. It is a measure of my own emotions that I was quite unaware of it. So down, again, mercifully preoccupied with the technical problems of descending steep ice, fixing pitons, moving one at a time. Lower down, as Ralph and I unroped and went ahead, a big stone—fore-runner of many others—came humming and whining down the cliffs and passed neatly between us. It was a near-miss and a timely warning that the mountain wanted to get rid of us.

Two days later we were back at Camp 3, where we found a note

Pik Sodroozhstvo, the Peak of Concord, in the Pamirs.

Left, Anatoli Ovchinnikov, with Kolia Shalaev behind; and right, Misha Anuvrikov, Vitali Abalakov and Nikolai Romanov.

Sharing experience in the Pindus mountains, above, and below, in the Tatras, looking towards Ganek and Gierlach.

from Malcolm that they were down at their camp beneath Pik Patriot, on the far side of the glacier from ourselves. We were very tired, but it seemed vitally important not to delay in telling them what had happened. After a short rest, Graeme and I started to thread our way through the maze of crevasses to reach their camp. By now Graeme and I were close friends. We had shared both the heights and the depths of mountaineering experience, which had forged a special relationship. Malcolm and his party greeted us warmly, but were silenced for a while, shattered by our news. Later, we spoke of other matters and I was glad to extricate my thoughts from the dark despond into which they had been plunged for the past three days. Joe and Mac began to talk about their experiences on Pik Patriot. They gave us the good news that Vladimir and Nikolai had climbed the peak; but they did not seem to have been a very happy party. Even Joe Brown, with his world-wide reputation for climbs requiring exceptional skill and daring, had found the mountain so dangerous that he felt it unjustifiable to continue beyond a certain point.

I turned the conversation to our future plans. By now I knew the answers to my own questions. I would go back to see Rosemary Noyce and Robin's mother Mary Smith. I wanted to be sure that the story was properly told and that the tragedy should be seen in a true perspective. But the expedition must go on; aside from any personal preferences, we owed this to the Russians. Who would carry on? As I had hoped, all the Britishers in Malcolm's group wanted to do so; they had not been directly involved in the affair as we had. Graeme said he would stay and so, later, after much heart-searching, did Ralph. Derek and Ted, as well as George, would return with me. So six British climbers would continue the programme with the six Russians. I explained this to our Russian team mates, who were both sympathetic with my personal decision and relieved about the expedition's future.

On 25th July we reached Base Camp, where Abalakov's Spartak Party learned the news. On the following morning I received a message from him that he would like to see me, so I walked across to their camp. Abalakov received me with a show of formality and, with three movie cameras operating at point blank range, proceeded to criticise my decision to leave the expedition. I stated my reasons, which seemed to have the approval of some of the Russians surrounding us. But Vitali was adamant in his view that the expedition would not be in safe hands—he used the word 'hotheads'. He claimed that it was not the practice in the Soviet Union to modify or abandon an expedition's programme, when a disaster occurred to one or more of its members. Those who mourned in Britain, he suggested, needed me less than those who were here to tackle the serious climb on Pik Kommunizma.

Anyway, relatives of climbers were prepared for accidents to happen. There was nothing to be said in response to such opinions and I returned to my own friends, considerably upset.

It is only right I should here record that, ever since the accident, our Russian comrades had shown themselves as towers of strength and support to us, sensitive to our sorrow and sharing our sense of loss. I will never forget Anatoli Ovchinnikov's personal consideration for me during that sad climb up 800 feet of steep ice to find Wilf and Robin. Moreover, from the moment the news was sent back to Dushanbe and Moscow the Russian authorities gave us wonderful assistance at every stage of our journey home.

I believe that Abalakov's rebuke was, in fact, intended for an audience other than myself. A record had been made of it and he had probably done no more than his duty. That same evening we entertained him and a number of his party, with all of my expedition members, in our large mess tent, where the mood was convivial and some interesting discussions took place about the contrasting attitudes and practices of climbers in each country. The fare was Ovaltine and biscuits spread with honey; Abalakov firmly declined Scotch as an alternative beverage.

After the four of us had left for home the joint expedition rounded off the programme by unfurling huge banners which displayed the Hammer and Sickle and the Union Jack on the summit of Russia's highest mountain. At Base Camp the Russians built a cairn and draped a banner bearing Wilf and Robin's names across it. Due respect had been paid and the honours, in the contest with the mountains, were divided, even if something had gone out of the spirit of the enterprise. But despite opportunities missed, something had been gained in return for much which was lost. Perhaps the name Содржество [Sodroozhstvo], meaning Concord, bestowed by the Russian authorities on the peak which Eugene and I had climbed with our group, summed it up. It conveyed truly the sense of our endeavours on that peak above the Vavilova glacier. I fancy that Wilf would have felt that Pik Garmo, on which he died, was that 'bridge of a gap' about which he wrote while at Base Camp.

Sharing Experience

1963–67

FOR EVERY GOAL THERE NEEDS TO BE SOME FURTHER HORIZON, some higher peak of achievement towards which the young may direct their endeavours. In 1961 Joy and I went to Greece, where I was invited to undertake a lecture tour by the British Council. I took the opportunity to discuss with our hosts, the Hellenic Alpine Club, some tentative ideas which Dick Allcock and I had been turning over in our minds since we returned from East Greenland. We were sure that the experience of that expedition had been valuable to the boys who took part in it; they had learned the ropes of coping with the business of living under difficulties in an uninhabited and hostile environment; they had met with wild creatures which were tame, unpersecuted by human beings, they had memories of marvellous scenery and behind it, had gleaned an inkling of geological time. Greece could present young people with another and quite different, but perhaps more relevant experience. The Pindus mountains which form the backbone of that country are somewhat less high and precipitous, the climate less rigorous; older people and younger could travel together in a less dependent relationship. What was more, whereas in Greenland we had been an isolated British group in an area beyond the northernmost Eskimo settlements, in Greece we would be able to travel with Greeks and meet the people who lived in those mountains. It was also typical of Dick that he wanted, by way of expressing gratitude for the opportunity of having such an experience, to render some small service, even if only a token, in the course of a journey through the mountains.

I proposed to Nassos Tzartzanos, General Secretary of the Hellenic Alpine Club, that we might co-operate in making a complete traverse of the Pindus range, starting near the shores of the Gulf of Corinth and finishing close to the Albanian frontier. There was considerable enthusiasm among our hosts, who informed me that no such journey had ever been made before. Some of the Greek climbers, they assured

me, would be delighted to travel with us. I also contacted the Anavrita
school near Athens, whose headmaster until shortly before our visit
had been Jocelyn Young, son of Geoffrey Winthrop Young and a
former pupil of Hahn at Gordonstoun, with which the school had close
links. They agreed to send six boys to join our expedition. And later
additions were some officers and other ranks of the Greek Special
Services Brigade, whose traditions were similar to our Army Commandos. I was particularly happy about these links with my own past,
both in Greece and with wartime Commando training.

In planning the journey with the Greek alpinists, I noted their
advice that May would be the best month, but the boys were all in
jobs and Dick assured me that they could not be spared at that time
owing to examinations, and other demands on their working time. In
spite of the vagaries of the weather in the Pindus mountains, and the
certainty that there would be a lot of snow still lying above 4,000 feet
after a severe winter, I decided to attempt the traverse in April, when
the various firms could grant their young employees the necessary
time off. But the available time was short—six weeks in all; allowing a
week on either side of the trek itself for travelling by road through
Italy and back through Jugoslavia, there would be barely three weeks
for the journey itself, scarcely enough to traverse about 250 miles of
rugged mountain country so early in the year.

The group which assembled in London at the headquarters of the
National Association of Youth Clubs on 22nd March 1963 to board a
fleet of four minibuses, with a baggage lorry to complete the convoy,
consisted of twelve seniors and twenty-two boys. As had been the
case in choosing members for the Greenland expedition, the criterion
had been the Gold Standard of the Edinburgh Award, except for two
boys who had completed a two-year course in a comparable scheme
named Endeavour Training which Dick operated under the auspices
of the NAYC. George Lowe and Susan, now married, were in the
senior party; so were Tony Streather, John Jackson and John Sugden,
accompanied this time by his son, David, and I had also invited John
Disley to join the expedition. Dick had with him two new youth
leaders, David Giles and Adrian Baugh.

Dick particularly wanted the boys to be aware of the sacrifices for
the ideals of justice and peace which had twice been made on the
continent of Europe in the past fifty years; they were, I think, impressed as we drove along the battlefields in northern France, passing
cemetery after cemetery with their ranks of silent monuments,
thousands upon thousands of Frenchmen, Britons, Americans and
Indians. As we travelled along the East coast of Italy we came to
Castel di Sangro and I suggested that we should turn inland, following

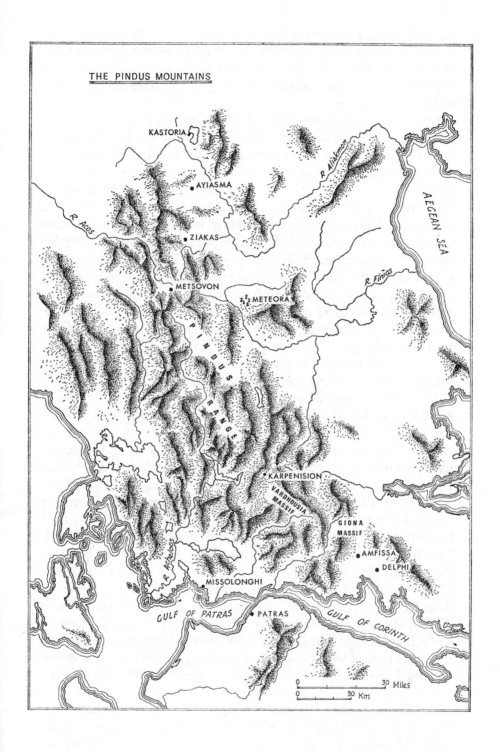

THE PINDUS MOUNTAINS

KASTORIA

AYIASMA

ZIAKAS

R Aoos

METSOVON

R Aliakmon

R Finios

AEGEAN SEA

METEORA

PINDUS RANGE

KARPENISION

VARDHOUSIA MASSIF

GIONA MASSIF

R Acheloos

AMFISSA

DELPHI

MISSOLONGHI

GULF OF PATRAS

PATRAS

GULF OF CORINTH

0   30 Miles
0   30 Km

the course of the river on which the Germans had based their Gustav Line and held our Eighth Army resolutely for seven months in 1943–44. We spent the night near the hilltop town of Casoli, which had been my headquarters when I was commanding 'D' Force in the springtime nineteen years before.

I stood in an olive grove, in that part of the front which had been held by my own battalion, beneath the shadow of the Maiella mountains, and tried to get my bearings. Half a mile ahead, at the edge of an escarpment and above a deep valley below the great mountain wall, there used to be a house we called 'Blue Shutters'. Most nights when we first arrived in the line, it had been used by German patrols; so I ordered the Sappers to blow it up. Below, in that valley, was a hamlet named Pissavini, which had been a base for aggressive patrolling by the enemy against our thinly held positions. One night during that month of April I had laid on a company-scale attack, with strong artillery support; it served its purpose of deterring the Germans, but I remembered the company returning in the darkness under their commander, Major 'Puggy' Powell, carrying their wounded and a dead officer. Joy and I walked some way up the slopes of the Maiella; we came to a farmhouse where we could look down on the village of Pennapiedemonte, where I recalled a solo stalk I had made, armed with a light-calibre American rifle slung on my back, to spy for enemy movement in the village below. It was strangely moving, this journey into the past.

Three days later, after crossing over to Greece at Igoumenitsa, we made another overnight stop at Missolonghi, the village which commemorates Byron, and where the 3rd/12th Frontier Force regiment of the Indian Army had suffered heavy casualties at the hands of a treacherous enemy in November 1944. Across the Gulf of Corinth was Patras, scene of so much frustration during the Greek Rebellion. Ghosts from the past beckoned me over the water; but now there was other, and more cheerful work to do. Next day, 28th March, we arrived at Delphi. It had been a tiring journey, especially those last two days over the rough roads in Epirus; but the sun was shining, the pear and almond trees were in full blossom, the Gulf of Corinth was indigo blue and the summits in the Peleponnese over the way were capped with snow. We were camping on a terrace looking out on all this loveliness, near a meadow carpeted with wild flowers. It was a good place to finish one journey and start off on another.

We received a great welcome from the friendly Greeks who were there to meet us. The Hellenic Alpine Club had come in some strength, twelve of them were going to join the long walk. So were four boys from the Anavrita School, imbued with the ideas of 'Outward Bound' from the regime of Jocelyn Young. And there were three officers of the Special Services Brigade attended, I noticed, by their batmen. We made the introductions over a gargantuan lunch in one of the hotels. John Sugden had gone ahead of our party to tie up details of the programme with Reginald Close, representative of the British Council in Athens. He had revised the tentative itinerary which we had sketched on our maps during the planning of the expedition in London. Like me, John was concerned that our hopes might prove too ambitious.

On the last day of March, divided now into three Anglo-Greek groups, we left Delphi in our transport for Amfissa, and along the road running westwards beneath the great massif of Ghiona and Vard-housia, which rises to over 7,000 feet above the road. At various intervals the parties stopped, to start their different ways towards the first staging place on the long journey north, Karpenesion. We had about seventy miles to travel before being replenished by Dick, who was to bring the vehicles round by the eastern flanks of the Pindus to meet us. From Karpenesion northwards there lay the highest and most demanding stretch of mountain country, some hundred miles of it, before we would arrive at Metsovon. Again, Dick was to bring us supplies to that point, before we set off on the last lap, another fifty miles to Kastoria; that town lay only twenty miles from the Albanian frontier and it behoved us to venture no further.

'Man proposes, but . . .' the weather did its evil worst to dispel these high hopes; it was, to put it mildly, as though the elements were out to demoralise and cripple the young adventurers, to say nothing of the seasoned and middle-aged veterans. It rained, it sleeted, it snowed as we sloshed our way up muddy tracks, plunged through soggy snow, knee-deep, for four days on our journey to Karpenesion. Villagers had heard news of our coming and we received generous welcomes: school-houses were cleared for our overnight stops; eggs and fruit were proffered; priests and chairmen of village councils offered us the traditional glasses of ouzo. It was heart-warming, but it did not cure blistered feet. On the last day of that journey, as we came down to the valley where Karpenesion could be seen in the distance, one of the boys in my group collapsed; his trouble was not serious and fortunately we had prepared for just such an emergency while training for the expedition in North Wales; the boys quickly constructed an improvised stretcher to carry him down. But it was a somewhat sorry party which was reunited in the little mountain town on 5th April.

We hastily modified our plans. The casualties under the leadership of John Jackson, unfortunately one of the halt and maim himself, were to travel in the transport fleet to the famous Meteora gorge, there to visit the monasteries on their pinnacle perches; hopefully they would recover in time to start ahead of the rest of the party along the final stretch of our route, from Metsovon to Kastoria. Re-grouped, the party would continue on foot by two different routes through the mountains to Metsovon, as previously planned. Thus, though not everyone would complete the whole 250-mile journey, we would be able to content ourselves with the fact that the party as a whole would have done so.

That central part of the journey took us through the finest stretch of the Pindus range; in places we climbed to over 6,000 feet, in others down to deep narrow limestone gorges; through tiny villages in which a handful of peasants remained throughout the winter. Occasionally we met elderly Greeks who surprised us by their words of greeting in American-accented English. We learned that they had made their small fortunes in one or other North American city in their youth; for them, our arrival was the first opportunity they had had to speak our language in thirty years or so. Most of the time we continued to wade through deep snow, arriving at the end of the day with soaking feet, to camp in the forest and dry ourselves out in front of a roaring fire. Sometimes we stayed in a school-house; occasionally in a dwelling-house which had been cleared specially for us at the insistence of these kindly folk, living as they were at the level of bare subsistence. We saw a number of golden eagles, griffon and Egyptian vultures. Several times we came upon fresh tracks of European brown bears; on one occasion a very big fellow had evidently slipped and slid down a snow slope and collided with a tree. We could imagine his ruffled feelings as he picked himself up and continued on his way. One night, camping beneath giant pine trees in a gorge which, even in summer, can rarely have been visited by human beings, we heard the call of a lynx.

On the tenth day of this superb stretch of country we came down off the snow into the town of Metsovon. Twelve years ago it was served only by a minor road from the east, and no motor road continued to the Adriatic coast. It was by no means the hub of tourism which it has become today. The 14th April was the Easter of the Orthodox church and the place was filled with village folk from far and wide, dressed in their traditional finery, the women according to their districts, the men in Evzone costumes with short black jackets and long white woollen hose, with pill-box hats and stout shoes adorned with woollen bobbles. But a touch of sadness was added, for the bishop had just died and we arrived to witness his funeral procession. On Easter Day the colourful proceedings were conducted by the senior priest, who headed the procession from church to church, a group of acolytes walking ahead of him dressed in saffron robes, followed by the mayor and councillors and a large crowd carrying candles.

Afterwards we were invited to join the happy parties sitting round their fires on which the paschal lambs were roasting on spits; we were given chunks of tender meat and cracked coloured eggs with them, as though we were members of the family. There was dancing on the square, men and women moving slowly in a half-circle, much as the Sherpas do, to the accompaniment of a string band.

In a land which first adopted the philosophy of stoicism, we particularly admired that quality in the women we met on our way: an ancient dame staggering all on her own through the snow up to a pass at 6,000 feet, bent under a large load; a group of young women travelling from their village, Karitsa, to a small town, Bezoula, in the plains two days' journey away. The track was not yet fit for mules, so they happily undertook the chore of being a pack train. Everywhere we met people, it seemed to us that the women were bearing the greater burden of work, sometimes with their babies, in bundles, papoose-fashion on their backs. We were also impressed by meeting a young teacher, and later a newly qualified physician, both doing their mandatory stint of two years' service in these remote mountain districts before looking for more congenial placements of their own choosing. It seemed to me that such a system, if it could be applied to teachers and doctors in the unpopular down-town areas of our big cities, would be no bad thing.

The men folk, sitting outside the primitive stores which also serve as drinking places, indulging in their favourite pastime of talking politics, seemed not yet to have reconciled themselves to a life of peace after long years of Balkan turbulence. They still appeared to be, at heart, fighters first, half-expecting some feud, ready to defend their village.

Four more days and fifty more miles to go. Jacko's party had gone ahead in good shape, so it no longer mattered so much that the rest of us complete the whole traverse. Dick and John Sugden, with Joy, George and Susan and some boys, went to the village of Ayiasma to make a study of village life and, at Dick's insistence, to offer themselves as a working party for any labouring job which might be needed. The offer was much appreciated, and they were put to work to re-construct a bridge over a stream which had been destroyed by the winter floods.

With Tony Streather and another group of boys, I continued the foot journey northwards over high and desolate country; we were now at 7,500 feet; and so, though we saw only their footprints, were the bears. On the fourth evening we came down to the village of Ziakas, named after a renowned fighter against the Bulgars in the war of 1912. The place had a reputation for strife; during the last war its menfolk had fought vigorously against the Germans, hiding in caves above the village while the German soldiers set fire to their homes. In the Rebellion of 1944–45 the inhabitants, most of them ardent supporters of EAM, had been a thorn in the flesh of the Government; the greater part of the small population had fled to Poland, Czechoslovakia or Romania after the collapse of the revolt, and from those countries they supplied their relatives with clothing and funds. We were touched by the kindness of these impoverished people, and surprised that the Greek government, to its discredit, had purposely neglected the rehabilitation of the village.

On 18th April a foot-weary but very happy band of travellers assembled once again, after our various activities, at the beautiful town of Kastoria. Once more the Hellenic Alpine Club was there to greet us and fête our achievement in making the first traverse of the Pindus mountains – 250 miles in nineteen days. Not all the Greeks had stayed the full course, but then, nor had all of us. What mattered was that the journey had been completed by the expedition and, even more, that some close friendships had been made.

At last we were on our way northwards towards the Yugoslav frontier, driving through villages gay with blossom. We travelled along the wide plains of the Struma river, where my Brigade had been deployed for the task of restoring order out of chaos at the end of the war. Two days later, disaster suddenly banished our happiness. John and David Sugden and one of the boys, Fen Thornton, had travelled ahead of us after leaving Belgrade on the long white ribbon of the Autoput, to find a camp site on the outskirts of Zagreb. They fell asleep and the vehicle left the road some ten miles south of the town and overturned. John and David both suffered severe head injuries, from which John died in Zagreb seventeen days later. Fen was more fortunate in escaping with a broken arm. John's death was a terrible blow. In Greenland he had been a tower of strength throughout our planning and during the expedition itself, a patient teacher who imparted his enthusiasm to his party of learner-geographers who helped him with the surveys he so greatly enjoyed. It was a sad note on which this second expedition came to an end.

In 1964 the British Council again asked me to undertake a lecture tour this time in Poland. Joy and I had a delightful visit during which we made a number of friends, while spending two days and nights trekking in the Tatras and sampling the splendid quality of the granite cliffs on the East Face of Mnich. By the end of our visit Paul Czartoriski, a Vice-President of the Tatra Mountain Club, and Andrej Kus, welcomed the idea Dick Allcock and I had been nurturing that we should bring one of our mixed expeditions to Poland the following

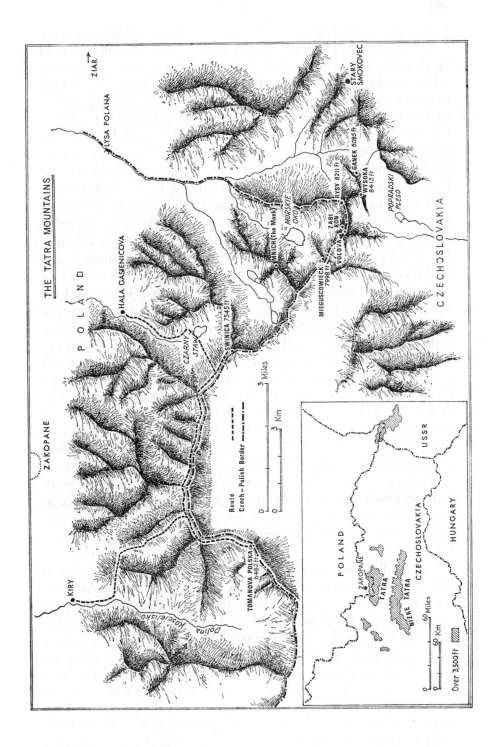

year. This time we hoped to add to the mixture by including as many
girls as boys in the junior group. We foresaw that this venture would
be different in emphasis, apart from the differences in programme
which would be called for by the small and restricted area of high
mountain terrain. It would be a more social affair, affording opportunities to share our experiences with people living with a different
idealogy beyond the Iron Curtain. It seemed a good idea, too, to
extend this tour to include Czechoslovakia, as I had kept in continuing friendly contact with Vilem Heckel, one of the climbers in the
Czech group we had met at the Spartak camp in the Caucasus in 1958.

Official machinery was set enthusiastically in motion by our friends
in both countries and our third 'youth and age' expedition set off at
the end of August 1965. Among the girls was our youngest daughter,
Jenny, who was already showing promise as a rock climber, and
twelve boys, all of them having graduated through the Award Scheme
or Endeavour Training. Because of the opportunities we would have
for rock climbing, we selected some of the young people because, in
addition to those qualifications, they had some experience on our home
cliffs. For the same reason the seniors were largely drawn from my
mountaineering friends. John Disley was once again in the party. Alf
Gregory, a member of the Everest expedition, agreed to join; Roger
Orgill came from the National Mountaineering Centre where, like
Disley, he had great experience of instructing young people in
mountain activities; Dr Hamish Nicol, Robin Prager and John Long-
land were all members of the Alpine and Climbers' Clubs. This time
we all travelled together by coach, passing through the Iron Curtain
at the frontier near Münich, where the young members of the party
were surprised and depressed to witness the grim reality of that
twenty-foot high, double wire barrier, heavily guarded by stern-
looking, alert armed men in watch towers, perched above the minefield.

Half a mile down the road towards Bratislava a lonely figure was
sitting by the roadside, which was as far as the authorities had permitted him to approach on his side of the border. It was Dr Ludwig
(Ludek) Koupil, with whom I had corresponded about the expedition
and who had travelled through the night to greet us. If we were a
very weary party 400 kilometres further along the road when we
reached our destination at Stary Smokovec, he must have been
utterly exhausted. Indeed, so tired were we that we were in no state to
do justice to the very warm welcome given us by the organisers of the
programme for our stay, Jindrich (Henry) Steindler, Vratislav Fibinger
and Jero Mazaryn; the latter was head of the Mountain Rescue Service.

The beginning of our five days on the Czech side of the Tatras was attended by the kind of weather which I had come to expect of those combined expeditions. As in Greenland and Greece, so in the Tatras it rained—indeed it poured; it enveloped us in damp, drizzly mist and, at best, it blew a gale which sometimes made for excitements while rock climbing on the frontier ridge. Our camp was on boggy ground in the dripping forest and we had a constant problem with wet clothes. None of this deterred the young adventurers, nor detracted from the enjoyment of the many contacts we made with Czech climbers and holidaymakers who arrived from all directions to meet us. There was a touching eagerness to shake us by the hand; it was as though people valued the chance to make physical contact with others who lived under freedom. Walking through the forest on the way back to our camp one afternoon I found myself in the company of a pleasant married couple, both of them well educated and intelligent people. He told me that he had held a professorial chair in a university: What was he doing now, I asked? 'I am a labourer,' he replied. He was evidently not in favour with the régime.

Each evening the social activities seemed to be given special flavour precisely because the weather was behaving so perversely; the big log fires around which we drank our cocoa and sang to the guitars of Roger Orgill, John Disley and the Fibingers, were all the more convivial. So were the gatherings at the Mountain House beside the lake at Popradski Pleso, where we joined with crowds of happy Czechs intent on forgetting for a while the restrictions in their daily lives, as we talked and sang and drank the excellent Pilsner beer. One of our hosts was a mountaineer, Gustav Ginsel, a German-speaking Czech who hailed from Sudetenland which Hitler invaded in 1938 to make his 'last territorial claim in Europe'. Gustav was an extraordinary character, irrepressibly gay and garrulous who, at the same time positively revelled in pursuing a spartan, almost ascetic existence. He laughed at everything and everyone, not excluding his own life-style. He also gave us some splendid illustrated talks about his expeditions in the Caucasus and elsewhere. Here was at least one person who had not been solemnised by the régime

Nor were we climbers unduly frustrated by the elements. Mist, rain and wind added up to typical Welsh weather; we were used to it. The integral traverse of the ridges of Wysoka was a superb mountain expedition; so were some of the climbs on mountains with strange names like Vólova, Zabi Kon and Ganek, which provided climbing at Grades IV and V, and on one of which: the Ganek Gallery, I was proud to learn that Jenny had performed with distinction at Standard VI. But I shall remember gratefully the one occasion when the weather did relent just long enough to enable the whole party, Czechs and

British, climbers and walkers, boys and girls alike, to stand on Rysi, the highest summit in our area, and admire the whole magnificent arena of the Tatra mountains. On both sides of the frontier the environment is carefully preserved as a National Park, in which stricter regulations are enforced than would be acceptable in our country. Henry Steindler and our other hosts were evidently under instructions to ensure that we adhered to the rules, and I'm afraid a few of our party gave him some anxious moments, tending to be impatient with the controlled nature of the programme and to go off on their own. We found that on the Czech side of the ridge a time limit is laid down for the use of the park; wardens were heard blowing loudly on their whistles at 4 p.m. as a signal for everyone to return to the valley. This also happens in Hyde Park, but it would be unlikely to evoke the desired response from our climbing fraternity in the Lake District.

For those who did not climb, there were some excellent walks to be enjoyed, even in the rain. Some members went to a village named Ziar where a wedding was in progress, with everyone wearing traditional costumes. They were made so welcome that they were persuaded to borrow costumes and join the merriment, one British boy and girl being cast, strictly for the period of the party, as an extra bridal pair. Apparently they were lucky to come back unscathed. After a Tatra wedding the hospitals for miles around are filled with wedding guests, if one is to believe the tall stories of my old friend Jan Czepanski. It was Jan who had translated *The Ascent of Everest* into Polish and he was among the group waiting for us across the frontier at Lysa Polana, after we had made our farewells to our Czech friends, and promised to invite them formally to Britain the following year.

Over the border we were aware of a different emotional climate, less anxious, more light-hearted. With Jan was another old friend of the previous summer, Andrej Kus, also Stanislav Kulinski and Lazek Laski. They had perfectly understood the hoped-for spirit of our enterprise and we were soon moving off to three different camp sites, widely separated along the range, each party accompanied by one or more Polish climbers. With ten days available for the mountain part of the programme, we arranged that each group would stay in one place for three or four days; then there would be a general post, so that everyone could get to know the whole area.

The Polish Tatras form a vast *cirque*, at the centre of which is the tourist resort of Zakopane. At the western end of the *cirque* the rock is limestone, the frontier ridge is wide and grassy, not unlike our Lakeland fells. Impressive crags and pinnacles soar above dark forests and the many caverns make it a great centre for spelaeologists. Deep ravines lead up to green pastures where the Taterniks live in summer with their cattle and their *liptoks*, huge white sheepdogs which are cousins to the Pyrenean breed. Further east the geological structure changes to granite. The ridge becomes rocky and serrated, huge rock buttresses support the summits and it is in this area that most of the real climbing is to be found. With so many varied interests, and so little time to pursue them, we were all kept extremely busy during those ten days; despite the most depressing weather. At one change-over period the group I was with traversed nearly the whole frontier ridge between the hamlet of Kiry and Morskie Oko, a mountain tarn nestling beneath the north face of Rysi; 'nearly', because we were driven off at the end of a long day by a great south wind, the *Halny*, which blew away our shelters and made it impossible to continue along the crest on the second day. Again, some excellent climbs were made. Joy and John Disley traversed the ridge along its most sporting section between Rysi and Micguscowiecki, and between us we recorded a number of fairly hard routes up to Standard V. Most of the party did some potholing in the Kiry area.

Amid all this physical activity there was also time for other things. Dick, anxious as ever to lend a hand to local people, found jobs for us all, from helping with the harvest to damming a stream. On our last evening Bigmir Khorosodovic, chairman of the Zakopane section of the Tatra Mountain Club, laid on a typical local entertainment in a meadow near Kiry: folk dancing around an enormous bonfire, the men in local costumes with black, brimmed hats trimmed with beads, short embroidered waistcoats and long white baggy trousers closed at the ankles; the girls with beautifully embroidered bodices and wide, flowered skirts at ankle length. They were led by a storyteller who related yarns of their forebears; mountain robbers, or freedom fighters who took refuge from persecution in Poland's years of tribulation under the Austro-Hungarian empire, and raided the baronial castles. There were also tales of their loves and misbehaviours. The dancing was vivid and vigorous, symbolic swords and wood-axes were swung as the dancers leaped around the flames. Sausages were thrust into the blaze on long stakes, good Polish Riesling drunk, and our own guitarists led us into a chorus, singing lustily with the song-sheets we had brought for just such an occasion.

We left the mountains on 17th September. A raft trip down the lazy Dunajec river, winding its tortuous way through the gorges of the Pienini hills, was just what was needed to recover from all our exertions.

A week later, after a pause on the way north to remember the horror of Auschwitz and pay tribute to its four million victims, we arrived in the Polish capital. Eight years before, when I had first been there, it was still partly in ruins. Now the old city had been restored, almost a replica of its pre-war antiquity and a monument, not only to those who suffered in its destruction, but to the devotion and faith of the new generation who had rebuilt it. Big new industries were sprawling out from the former bounds of the city. But there remained much clearance work to be done. Each September the citizens are expected to join in community action to remove the rubble; we, as visitors, volunteered to form a working party and arrangements were made for us to do our stint. On two afternoons we tidied up a park overgrown with twenty years of weeds and overlaid with débris. We also lifted four lorryloads of rubble from a cobbled street. In one of my shovel-fuls I picked up a rusted key. Whose hand, I wondered, used to place it in the lock of a warm and loving home, all those years ago?

There was a follow-up to our Tatra journey. In 1966 and 1967 we received groups of Czechs and Poles who came to spend three weeks visiting our mountain areas and making friends with our climbing folk, Dick's Endeavour Training organisation was also involved in the programme. Dick himself went back to Czechoslovakia with another party of young people to stay with some of our friends in Brno, where they extended the circle of friendships. Alf Gregory went to stay with friends we had made in Krakow.

In 1971 another expedition, composed on lines similar to our Tatra journey, went further afield under the leadership of Lieut-Colonel Tony Streather, to the Semien Mountains of Ethiopia; George and Sue and Joe Brown were among the seniors. As on the previous occasions, a number of their young Ethiopian hosts joined them in their programme of walks and climbs, and in their search for the rare Abyssinian ibex. Although I was unable to accompany that party, I was able to enjoy it, for the idea was sown when I spent the night in Addis Ababa during the Prime Minister's return from his visit to Nigeria in 1969.

One theme was common to all those ventures. Sharing experience just about sums it up.

I have mentioned the interest which had been aroused in the Award Scheme in a number of countries and Commonwealth territories. It was exciting, therefore, to be asked, after retiring as Director of the Scheme, to make a tour of several Commonwealth countries in the summer of 1967.

The first part of our itinerary was in Canada, which was celebrating its centenary of Dominion status and independence. One of the items in the programme of centennial events was a major mountaineering jamboree, organised by the Alpine Club of Canada in the Saint Elias

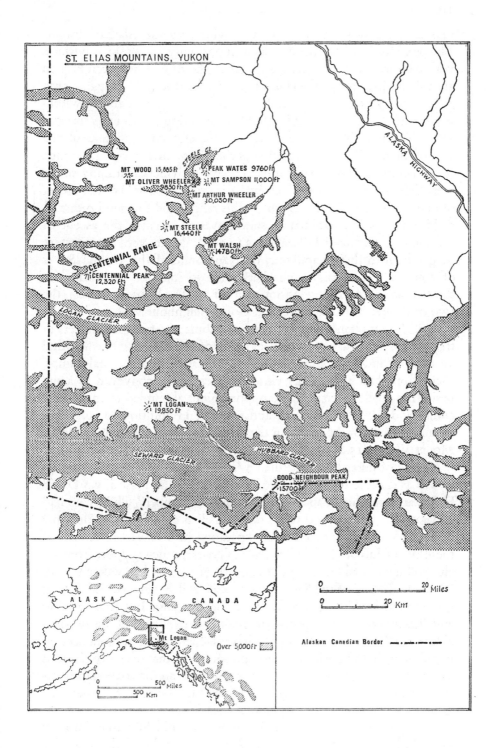

ST. ELIAS MOUNTAINS, YUKON

STEELE GL.

MT WOOD 15,885 ft   PEAK WATES 9760 ft
MT OLIVER WHEELER   MT SAMPSON 11,000 ft
9850 ft   MT ARTHUR WHEELER
10,050 ft

MT STEELE
16,440 ft

MT WALSH
14780 ft

CENTENNIAL RANGE
CENTENNIAL PEAK
12,320 ft

LOGAN GLACIER

MT LOGAN
19,850 ft

SEWARD GLACIER   HUBBARD GLACIER

GOOD NEIGHBOUR PEAK
15700 ft

ALASKA HIGHWAY

ALASKA   CANADA

Mt Logan

Over 5,000 ft

Alaskan Canadian Border — · — · — · —

0   20 Miles
0   20 Km

0   500 Miles
0   500 Km

massif, in the west of the Yukon Province, on the Alaskan border.
This was, for Joy and me, a golden opportunity to combine business
with pleasure; as an honorary member of the ACC I had been invited
annually to join one of the club's meets in the Rocky Mountains; now
at last I had a chance to accept. Of all the climbing expeditions within
my knowledge, this was by far the most ambitious, both in its size and
scope. To mark the national centenary, the club chose an unexplored
part of the massif, which it named as the Centennial range. The range
sported thirteen worthy summits. Twelve provincial climbing teams
were designated, each of which was directed towards the first ascent
of one of the splendid mountains in this range; and for good measure,
a thirteenth party, national in status, was to attempt the ascent of
the highest, Centennial Peak (12,320 feet). Moreover, as a gesture
of goodwill to their neighbour, the 52nd State of the United States
of America, six Canadian climbers were to join six Americans for
the first ascent of a 15,700-foot summit on the border between the
two countries; it was to be named Good Neighbour Peak.

As if the simultaneous deployment of some ninety mountaineers in
that remote area was not a sufficient token of Canada's first one hundred
years as an independent nation, two successive international camps,
each of one hundred further climbers, were to be conveyed to a site
beside the Steele glacier, where opportunities abounded to make new
climbs and name other peaks and glaciers, in addition to repeating
ascents of some of the giants in the range: Mount Steele (16,440 feet),
Mount Wood (15,885 feet), Mount Walsh (14,780 feet).

No one of lesser brilliance than a 'Master-mind' could conceive of,
as well as execute such a grandiose campaign. That person was David
Fisher, an Englishman and a member of our Climbers' Club, who had
emigrated to Canada and taken out Canadian citizenship; at the time
of the Yukon Alpine Centennial expedition he was Vice-President of
the Alpine Club of Canada. He had, of course, much support from his
club colleagues and members of the Arctic Survey under Walter Wood,
'Grand Old Man' of the Saint Elias massif; full provincial and federal
government backing and funds were forthcoming. But the planning
and direction of the enterprise were mainly in the hands of this remarkable man. Whatever reservations I have had about big mountaineering
expeditions, both in principle and on grounds of the social problems to
which they can give rise, especially those with an international membership, this was a unique project in which I was delighted to take part,
with no management responsibilities whatever.

So it was that we flew from Edmonton in mid-July 1967 into the
Gold Rush country of 1897. From Whitehorse on the Alaska Highway
we continued by coach to Kluane Lake, where the expedition had its

rear base; thence by truck another fifty miles up the highway and into the bush to the west, to reach a small clearing from which two small Bell helicopters were working a twenty-four-hour schedule, moving the first group of one hundred climbers and baggage, two people at a time, to the base camp. As Joy and I flew westwards, over dense forests inhabited by moose and bear, we crossed the wide Donjek river and continued up a tributary up the Steele valley. Beyond, stretching as far as the eye could see, even at an elevation of about 2,000 feet, and further still beyond our horizon to the Pacific seaboard, was a vast area of sub-Arctic glaciation, with some impressive-looking peaks, including the highest, Mount Logan, rising to over 19,800 feet. Indeed, they seemed to be Himalayan in scale. But this winged approach was too sudden to take it all in, and we were glad to be put down some miles downstream from the Base Camp, in order to speed up the helicopter journeys. Gradually, as we walked beside the glacier, we were able to absorb our new surroundings and feel less as if we had descended on to the surface of some other planet. The most striking feature of the foreground was the glacier itself. The Steele was in a state known as 'surge', which is still not fully understood by glaciologists. In its lower regions, this enormous glacier was moving at a quite exceptional speed of some two feet a day. Higher up, the ice was receding from the containing flanks of the mountains, leaving vertical walls. At its snout, the ice was arrested, perhaps by some obstacle on the surface of the valley. The result, in the general area of the Base Camp, was dramatic. The ice rose as much as a hundred feet above the lateral moraine in a chaotic turmoil of tottering turrets and pinnacles, themselves in a constant state of disequilibrium; they collapsed only to be replaced by others thrown up by the pressures from higher up the glacier. The whole vast mass literally groaned with the action of the ice.

We were greeted by many friendly faces: Bob Hind, former President of the ACC, Roger Neave who had recently succeeded him, and David Fisher, whom I had last met years before in North Wales. There were also three professional guides, expatriot Swiss and representatives of a number of countries were beginning to arrive. The camp had, perforce, an ordered, almost military appearance, its tents in neat ranks. Married quarters were set apart from the other accommodation; there was a huge mess tent, kitchens, stores tents and offices. With so many people gathered there for a fortnight, before being replaced by a second contingent, a programme had to be drawn up. The many unclimbed peaks were of unknown difficulty; some might call for strong and experienced mountaineers. Yet the occasion was that of an international 'meet' where it was desirable that we should mix and climb together, the more expert helping the less experienced. Dave and his 'Climbing Committee', which I was later invited to join, solved the problem with admirable logic; members were invited to put their names down on lists posted each evening on a notice board, under the headings of the various known, but still unnamed, peaks in the area. The names were then sorted out, respecting individual preferences as far as possible, but endeavouring to compose climbing parties which would be adequate to the chosen peak; leaders were nominated and the lists re-posted. It was quite a novel experience to consult a notice board in order to discover what mountain one was expected to attempt during the next day or so, and who were to be one's companions. Yet it seemed to be accepted by everyone in the spirit of the enterprise.

On my first expedition I found myself in charge of a group of seven, including, in addition to Joy, nationals from Scotland, Canada, the United States and Poland. In deplorable weather we made the second ascent of a nice little peak, later named Peak Wates (9,760 feet), which included a few good ice pitches. The whole area provides ice climbing *par excellence*, but such rock as appears through the glacial sheet is quite appallingly loose and dangerous. A subsequent and longer expedition took us successively up two glaciers, known later as the north and east branches of the Wheeler glacier, in attempts to solve a much more difficult ice mountain, subsequently known as Samson (11,000 feet). During those two separate sorties, I led parties up both these approaches in attempts to discern chinks in the intricate armour of ice defending this fine double-headed mountain. On the first occasion we climbed up a couloir some 2,500 feet in height and angled at a moderate 45 degrees, scoured board-hard by descending avalanches. At its upper end, and just beneath the final stretch of summit ridge, I stepped out to the left on to unstable rock, and found myself on much steeper ground. The snow had a thin crust, beneath which was deep, incoherent powder into which I sank to my waist—it evoked memories of Karakoram and Himalayan experiences. Forty feet higher, facing into a fierce wind blowing down from the crest, I reckoned that this was no place for most of my companions, two of whom had never climbed with crampons before. There remained only 100 feet to reach the ridge and there were no problems from there to the top; but I turned back. It was as well that I decided not to press the matter, for we had quite an adventurous descent of the couloir, with our inexperienced companions, one of whom slipped no less than four times. But the company and the pleasure of the climbing far outweighed the disappointment. In my diary that night I noted, 'A good little expedition.' And so it was.

A few days later, with another party, I turned my attention first to the East and then to the North Faces of the mountain. In the first attempt we were faced by a labyrinth of seemingly impregnable crevasses, wide, deep and interlocking: far more formidable than the Khumbu, or any other icefall I have seen. With much time available, it may well have been possible to penetrate those defences, but we turned away and addressed ourselves to the North Face, climbing for 800 feet up a slope suspiciously ripe to peel away in a windslab avalanche. It held us, but the mountain produced its trump card only 200 feet below the top: a vast crevasse, 50 feet wide, running right across the length of the face, and wide open throughout that distance. It was firm and final defeat, but not, I like to think, without honour.

On yet another of those little expeditions, determined to record success on a particularly attractive peak which rose above the junction of the Steele and Foster glaciers, and numbered as Peak 3 (later Mount Oliver Wheeler, 10,050 feet), we combined with a veteran climber of great repute to compose a fairly strong climbing party, regardless of the notice board. Fritz Wiessner had left his native Germany and was naturalised as an American citizen before the war; he had taken part in the ill-fated American expedition to K2, second highest mountain in the world, in 1939; his reputation had suffered from the tragic events on that climb, for it was there that a sick climber, Wolfe, had been left at the highest camp and two Sherpas, our own friends Pasang Kikuli and Ang Kitar, who had volunteered to climb up to fetch him down, had perished with him. Now, at the age of seventy-five, the incident was forgotten and Fritz had been readmitted to the American Alpine Club. Still full of energy and enthusiasm, he was there with his son Andy, longing for a climb which would match his mettlesome spirit.

With a Harvard undergraduate and Bostonian, Colin Godfrey, and an Edmonton Professor, Ernst Reichold, we made the first ascent of this fine summit on 19th July, by a fairly difficult route up its East Face and along its elegant, mile-long North Ridge; it was a wholly delightful experience, in very pleasant company. With typical courtesy Fritz, who had done the lion's share of the leading, stepped aside just below the final steep little snow cone, and invited Joy to pass through first on to the summit. It was well deserved; throughout that day she climbed magnificently. As we returned down the ablation valley beside the moraine of the Steele glacier I was dragging my feet with exhaustion, and I'm sure the other men were too, for we had been on the move for eighteen hours. Yet Joy was still going strongly, and when my thoughts were concentrated only on the moment when we would be sitting down to a hot meal in camp, Joy was sufficiently alert to spot the fresh prints of a grizzly bear, for which we had been on the look-out since someone reported a sighting a few days earlier.

Reflecting on our adventures in the past fortnight, as we flew back across the swamps and forests towards the Alaska Highway, I could say that after half a lifetime of mountain travel, this had been something entirely new. We had seen some wonderful country, and made many new friends, we had sighted flocks of Dal sheep, made intimate acquaintance with ground squirrels, weasels and lemmings, even seen the claw-marks of a grizzly. But there was more to it than that. While some climbers had been committed to the serious business of making first ascents for the honour of Canada and its ten Provinces, and two Territories, we had shared our less ambitious experiences with a cosmopolitan group of people whose ages ranged from the twenties to the seventies; some of them were famous mountaineers, others hill walkers with no aspirations to reach the high summits. Whether despite, or because of our large numbers and other differences among us, it had been a uniquely shared experience.

14

Crime and Circumstance

1967–73

THERE WAS GREAT DIFFICULTY IN FLYING US OUT OF THE SAINT Elias mountains in one of the two small Bell helicopters which were the only means of communication with the outside world for some 150 mountaineers. The weather had been appalling. For several days not only were the various climbing groups cut off, scattered as they were in a vast area of glaciated desert, but even the main base beside the Steele glacier was isolated from its rear link on the Alaskan Highway. At last a helicopter was able to slip in below the lowering cloud base and we were on our way: first flying across the forest and tundra to the great road, severed at intervals by swollen rivers; then travelling at high speed in a truck towards Whitehorse, in the slight hope that, despite the delay, we might yet make our connection with the daily flight to Edmonton. It was not to be. Just as we approached the shanty town the aircraft rose from the runway on its way south. Feeling somewhat disgruntled at the inconvenience and the delay before we were scheduled to join the first Duke of Edinburgh Award Commonwealth expedition, we found quarters in the town and resigned ourselves to our uninspiring surroundings.

The desk clerk called me over: there was a transatlantic telephone call. At the other end of the line was a familiar voice. 'This is Roy Jenkins. I've had some difficulty tracking you down. I was told you were somewhere up a mountain. I would like you to be Chairman of the Parole Board which I'm setting up in pursuance of the Criminal Justice Bill which has just received Royal Assent. Will you think it over and let Philip Allen have your answer as soon as possible?' The Canadian sub-arctic regions were an unlikely place to have one's thoughts turned to crime. I was still attuned to an environment whose only inhabitants were the white Dal sheep and the brown grizzly bears. I needed a little more time to settle back into the world of men and the laws they make—and break. I had not followed closely the debates on the Criminal Justice Bill which had become law in June of that year, I knew little about the meaning of Parole and I scarcely appreciated the compliment which the Home Secretary was paying me. It was obvious that this appointment would mark another turning point into uncharted territory, which I was not sure I wanted to explore. I said yes with little enthusiasm.

Reluctant though I was at the beginning, acutely aware of my lack of qualifications for the job, I soon began to find the task of pioneering the Parole Scheme quite an enthralling experience. Today, eleven years on since the Act which gave it the force of law was placed on the Statute Book, the meaning of the word 'parole' — conditional early release, under supervision, of offenders sentenced to substantial terms of imprisonment, so that, subject to good behaviour, they may serve the remaining part of their sentences in the community — is widely known and generally accepted by most people. At the risk of over-generalising, it was seen in 1967 by politicians and penologists as the most important advance in penal reform for many years; by the police it was viewed with varying degrees of suspicion and some hostility; by many probation officers, worried about the extra work and responsibility for supervising difficult clients who would other-wise have remained in prison, with considerable misgivings. Inside the prisons, Parole was received with approval and, by many of the inmates who would become eligible for consideration under the new scheme, with great expectations, encouraged by certain sections of the press. The management and staff of the prisons were, I think, generally glad about this measure, which would have the effect of shortening considerably the length of prison sentences, and thus reducing over-crowding and the pressures to which this gave rise; they knew, too, better than anyone else, the deleterious effects of long periods spent inside their walls. As was only to be expected, Parole was not acclaimed by all members of the judiciary; but I can speak in gratitude and admiration of the enlightened and helpful judges of the High Court and of the Crown Courts, who were my colleagues and counsellors on the Parole Board. Like most people, I had always had a healthy respect for the law in all its majesty. I think I was not excep-tional among the majority of people who have had no personal contacts with senior judges, in regarding the holders of that high office with a certain amount of awe and even a little trepidation. Both sentiments were corrected as we sat down together at Board meetings and on our smaller and more intimate panels to consider general matters of policy and to examine and discuss the cases of prisoners which, to the tune of some 5,000 annually, were placed before us. The Board members are drawn from widely different areas of national life: probation officers, teachers, social workers, policemen, prison governors, criminologists, psychologists and psychiatrists; but also people in industry or commerce or, like myself, with no obvious qualifications, but who, as citizens, are concerned both about crime and about the problems of those who break the laws of the land.

Another group of people with whom I had no previous acquaintance and about whom I had entertained misconceptions and shared commonly held myths, was the prison population itself. I had never been inside a prison. I shared with a great many people the simplistic notion that the majority of offenders were criminals by inclination rather than by force of circumstances. I recall having felt distinctly nervous and tense before my first two visits as Chairman of the Board, to the local prison in Bristol and the training prison on Dartmoor. The latter name had always haunted me from boyhood; Conan Doyle had something to do with it; the image of 'drab uniforms plastered with broad arrows, heads closely shaven' dies hard. I came out of its ancient, crumbling walls disabused of those over-generalised concepts about men under sentence.

Frank Mitchell had only recently made a spectacular escape, as a result of which he was to die at the hands of his accomplices who conspired to set him free. Following a report of a committee chaired by Lord Mountbatten of Burma, there had been a tightening up of security arising from this incident and the more dramatic escape of George Blake from Wormwood Scrubs. Despite this, I found the atmosphere in the prison relaxed, the relationships between staff and inmates by no means as stiff and severe as I had expected. This was the more remarkable for the fact that, only a few weeks previously, some prisoners had staged a demonstration in one of the workshops and temporarily overpowered the officers on duty. It was apparent that a certain 'esprit de corps' existed among the men; it seemed that a term on the Moor still retained a *cachet* from earlier years when more hardened and dangerous types, labelled as convicts, were confined there. It is a measure of my naïvety that I was surprised to find no embarrassment while chatting in the quarry with a man armed with a sledge hammer; it would, of course, hardly have advanced his prospects of parole to have clobbered me on the head. A colleague, herself accustomed to dealing with disturbed and delinquent children and their equally delinquent parents as headmistress of a comprehensive school in one of our big cities with a high incidence of crime, was even more apprehensive than I was. She came out hugging a large teddy bear, which had been made by the prisoner who, perhaps hopefully, presented it to her; the incident was not without a touch of pathos. And as we left the prison, I was unable to restrain my climbing instincts from demonstrating to the Governor how the wall could be scaled.

Admittedly, it would never be a popular route, for I made use of a crack on the outside. Later I learned that the wall had been raised a foot, which must have raised the standard of that climb.

If I have introduced a note of flippancy into a difficult and serious subject, I have done so deliberately as a way of dispelling certain myths. In the following years I visited most of our prisons, some of them on a number of occasions. I have watched the programmes of training inside and without the walls: I have seen inmates on recreation, in the classrooms, relaxing in the libraries and at mealtimes. I have witnessed the degrading routine of 'slopping out' the nocturnal chamber pots and the ignoble labour of stitching mail bags. I have spent time talking to men in solitary confinement under Prison Rule 43, whether they were there for punishment or at their own request and for their protection; and I have spoken to occupants of top security wings in which, until a few years ago, people rated as the nation's most notorious and dangerous criminals were confined. Inevitably, I have formed some firm opinions about the punishment of prison, both in its humanitarian aspects and as a deterrent to the commission of crime.

Familiarity with life inside prison walls has not, in this context, bred in me a contempt for the system, nor for most of those who live and work there. To admit that I came to look forward to visits by the Parole Board to penal establishments does not imply that I have created for myself another myth: that all geese are swans; nor that I came to enjoy the spectacle of men and women denied their liberty. Prisons are necessary evils, some of whose occupants are, like some others living in freedom, enemies of society. But the institution of imprisonment, and the spirit in which it is now administered in Britain is, in general, a humane response to anti-social and illegal acts by members of the community, some of whom have committed serious offences and may continue to endanger the lives or property of innocent and law-abiding citizens. Far too little is known about life within prisons by the average man in the street. My own initial misconceptions are still harboured by some people, of a harsh regime enforced by stern-faced 'turn-keys'; the 'warders' of press terminology helps to perpetuate a misleading image of prison officers. Some would wish it that way, entertaining as they do, another fantasy that all prisoners are villains, living at the expense of the tax-payer in idle luxury; for them, the longer they stay out of circulation the better. Their complaint is that offenders are treated too leniently. Whatever our prejudices and fears, nothing but good can come from the belated concession by the Home Office to lift the curtain a little, through the broadcasting media, on the mystery which has lain too long behind those grim walls.

There are, of course, exceptions to every generality, but the truth is that the great majority of prisoners are not evil men and women. Certainly there are professional criminals, some of whom deliberately have resort to violence, others to more subtle means of suborning, or extorting cash and goods from simple and trusting citizens, in pursuit of criminal ends. Some are dangerous despite themselves, and cannot be released until they have responded sufficiently to medical treatment or isolation from the community to be adjudged no longer to constitute a threat. But there are many more people inside prisons whose offences, usually against property, are less serious and whose background of social deprivation has placed them at a grave disadvantage. They are to be counted among the 'failures' of a competitive society rather than its enemies. They are inefficient even as burglars or petty thieves and they are caught time and time again. After each fresh spell inside their capacity for standing on their own feet when released, and to keep within the accepted norms of behaviour, is weakened. Sooner or later, prison becomes the only place they can find security, food and warmth without giving offence. Some, indeed, purposely commit offences in order to get back; prison has become their home. These are some of the people whom the Courts send to prison for want of appropriate alternative forms of punishment or treatment, and who should not be locked away; they include the prostitutes, the drunks, the drug addicts, the fine defaulters, and some mentally abnormal offenders.

Britain has the dubious distinction of being second only to West Germany in the number of people committed to prison in relation to the size of the population; if Scotland were separately assessed, they would be top of this inglorious competition. But I cannot draw from this shameful statistic the conclusion that we breed the largest number of criminals in Europe. Our laws and their interpretation by the Courts have something to do with it, and behind both the legislators and the judiciary there are prevailing public attitudes both to crime and social injustice. I am far from excusing criminal behaviour; for every misdeed there is a measure of individual responsibility. But after reading many thousands of prisoners' dossiers and visiting parts of our inner cities, I began to wonder that so many people, particularly the younger ones, succeed in keeping their noses clean under those disgraceful conditions.

In the grossly overcrowded state of our prisons, prison officers do a difficult, sometimes dangerous and little appreciated job with firmness, moderation and humanity. It is worth remembering that the system, difficult as it is to administer in these conditions, would be unworkable but for the fact that—with the exception of a few rare and much publicised occasions—the prison population puts up with its lot remarkably well, and encouraged by prospects of remission of part of the sentence, settles for co-operation with the regime. A sense of humour is often a saving grace on both sides, 'screws' and inmates alike. The BBC programme 'Porridge' caught the spirit of it. 'Aren't you the bloke who did some climbing?' asked an inmate of Wakefield prison, as I walked along one of the landings. I confessed to this and he went on: 'I did some climbing, Guv'. That's why I'm here.' In the early years of the Parole Scheme the covers of two magazines produced by prisoners featured cartoons of an impossible-looking mountain, with myself standing triumphantly on top, up which numerous prisoners, using unorthodox techniques and curiously equipped, were in a variety of difficulties on their way up. Whatever some prisoners may say and many others, in the depressing, frustrating and un-natural environment of their cells and exercise yards certainly feel, there is a good deal of *bonhomie* between staff and prisoners. Welfare work is done for inmates, not only by probation officers serving inside as part of their job, but by prison officers on the landings on behalf of their men. Many officers have brought the skills of man management and attitudes of caring from the armed forces. Recently I had supper with the residents of a hostel for ex-prisoners in London, which is run by a prison officer in his spare time.

Prison is an unsatisfactory and largely ineffective method of combat-ing crime; but some useful therapeutic work is done in some of our prisons which helps in the rehabilitation of men and women who need special treatment. The psychiatric prison at Grendon Underwood, the industrial prison at Coldingley and the prison for young offenders under the age of twenty-one at Aylesbury have especially impressed me; so did the 'open' prison at Leyhill in Gloucestershire. The fact that the worst aspects of the system are to be seen in the local prisons in our cities is no reflection on the staff. It is due to a combination of anti-quated mid-nineteenth-century buildings, the large number of prisoners being held on remand from the Courts, the demands on officers in acting as escorts during Court hearings and, above all, the gross overcrowding which often requires, to an increasing extent, that three men occupy a cell designed over a hundred years ago for one person. In these circumstances, training and recreation are reduced to a bare minimum and men may spend more than twenty in every twenty-four hours locked up in their cells.

One aspect of prison which I found most chilling was the policy of establishing areas of maximum security—top security wings—within prisons which were themselves designed to reduce to a minimum the chances of escaping. In those electronically sealed, clinical quarters lived eight or nine men totally insulated from the other inmates, watched over day and night by a high ratio of officers to inmates, and by closed-circuit television, which denied them any privacy. In such isolation life ceased to have purpose or meaning. I found myself moved to pity even for the dangerous people I met there and despite the heinous nature of their crimes. That policy has now been changed for one of dispersal among a wider population in the high security prisons; this has, alas, created further difficulties, for the influence and status which these men command in the minds of other prisoners has greatly added to the problems of control.

It has not been my purpose to write a treatise about the prison system, simply to correct perspectives from personal observations, and to impart my own impressions and beliefs. I have pointed out that prisons are a necessary evil; they are a consequence of misdeeds which are themselves products of our urbanised living conditions; to point to an obvious contrast, there are neither criminals nor prisons in the rural areas of Nepal. None of us is justified in washing his hands of this consequence and pretending that it is no business of his. I have no hesitation in saying that there are many prisoners who would be able to rejoin the community and pick up the threads of their lives and livelihoods sooner than is the case at present, were it not for the fact that rightful condemnation and deprivation of liberty is so often accompanied by a refusal to forgive. This is true even of a few people who have perpetrated some fearful crime which will long be remembered.

There are, of course, some who have been persuaded that their crimes, no matter how dastardly, are justified by their political objectives. However visionary and idealistic their aims may seem to some, that kind of offender neither seeks nor needs sympathy. But for others, when they come to terms with the damage they have caused to the lives of other people, there should be room for sympathy. I have experienced this sentiment while sitting in a cell with men and women whose crimes I abominate; there is a certain pathos in walls plastered with titillating nudes, for an emotional outlet, as there is in making soft toys for a small relative. It is a remarkable fact that there has often been a spontaneous response among inmates of our prisons to subscribe, from their token earnings, to appeals for funds when a major disaster occurs in the world outside. Prisoners find delight in helping with Christmas parties for children in the neighbourhood. I recall attending a Christmas carol service in Lewes prison in which not only a large number of inmates, but also local citizens and the Home Secretary, Jim Callaghan and his wife, took part. It seems to me that we could do with more of this kind of link between prisoners and staff serving inside prison walls, and members of the community at large, some of whom, but for the grace of God and social advantage, might be inside too.

The parole system has already given rise to a spate of literature by qualified penologists and others. I will avoid a battery of statistics, which are for ever shifting. Suffice it to say that the Scheme has made progress—I use the word advisedly, being aware that not everyone would agree with it—to the point where rather more than half the prisoners who qualify to be considered for it are released early; that is, at some point before the time when, having earned remission for good conduct, they would have completed their sentences in prison. Under the parole system, the sentence continues to be served, but in the community instead of inside prison. During the parole period a prisoner and his family receive advice and support from a probation officer, to whom he must report regularly, and to whom he is responsible for complying with other conditions imposed by the Parole Board. About 26,000 prisoners have been released on Parole since the scheme started in 1968 and failures due to the commission of further offences during the period while they are under supervision, are few: only about 8 per cent have been recalled to prison. Serious crimes during the Parole licence have been rare. Whether the granting of Parole has contributed to a reduction in the incidence of crime is not clear from statistics so far available. But it is certain that many offenders have been helped by their probation officers to earn a living and settle in their neighbourhoods, or in some new environment. At any one time there are about 2,750 offenders among us who would otherwise have been detained for longer in suspended animation in prison, at a cost to the taxpayer of £80 each per week. There is also a saving in terms of the social services, for a release plan which includes arrangements for employment is usually a condition of early release. Most parolees are trying to make good at work, many are helping to bring up families. But for this fact, our prisons would be even more over-crowded; indeed, at the present time it amounts to a saving of the population of six large prisons.

Some opinions which were entertained about parole at the beginning have been reversed. Most people, I believe, have come to accept it as a normal part of the penal process. But there are those who, as the crime rate rises, are even more entrenched in their conviction that offenders should receive harsher treatment and serve for even longer periods; for them, parole is perceived as a weak and woolly-minded response to law-breakers; a folly of 'do-gooders'. This line of thinking is unsupported by any evidence that long sentences are a more effective deterrent than relatively shorter ones; its logical conclusion could be the creation of a police state. Others have been reassured. But among those who welcomed the Scheme in 1967, penal reformers and prisoners have been among its harshest critics. They contend that parole is not widely enough granted; that it gives rise to severe tensions, anxiety and disappointment; that since reasons for refusal of parole are not given, justice is not seen to be done. Some maintain that parole should become a right, an integral part of every substantial prison sentence, rather than a privilege granted at the discretion of the Home Secretary. Others aver that parole has proved that sentences are needlessly long and that the criminal law should be amended accordingly. There is truth, or substance in all these criticisms and contentions.

The scheme has proved to be a challenging task for those of us who were called on to advise the Secretary of State, and to make decisions. Our approach was pragmatic; we have been primarily concerned with the public interest. There is often a difficult balance to be struck, whether in a matter of public policy or in a particular case. It is sometimes not easy to determine where the balance does lie in the all-important matter of protecting society and stemming the tide of crime. It is always important to take into account the effects, in human and economic terms, of separating men and women from each other, from their families and the community, for long periods. It is essential to bear in mind the debilitating effects of long imprisonment on human personality and the difficulties of recovering from the experience. Of all the problems created by imprisonment the one which has caused me most concern is the distress and loneliness suffered by wives and children of men serving sentences. As Chairman of the Board I received numerous heart-rending letters from wives and close relatives; I have often visited prisoners' wives to see and hear about their difficulties at first hand. The Christian convention is 'for better or for worse, for richer or for poorer', but whether or not one subscribes to it, this seems to me to be an area of acute social hardship.

Certainly chairing the Parole Board was a rewarding experience in itself. In addition to achieving a very close relationship among members of the Board, the work brought us in continuing contact with other people involved in the prevention of crime, the administration of justice and the treatment of offenders, whether inside prisons or in the community.

We made a point of building up our contacts with the review committees in the prisons, with Governors and their staffs, with Home Office officials, with probation officers, with the police forces; we visited hostels and on one occasion even arranged a meeting with landladies who provide lodgings for ex-prisoners. It was quite an eye-opener to me to find among these motherly people a degree of caring which I had not been aware of. In the course of our tours we made a practice of discussing the parole scheme with prisoners and with offenders serving on parole license.

The debate about the penal system will continue and the future of the Scheme within the general policy and pattern of reform, will be reassessed. My own reflection upon the system, from a position of relative detachment four years after retiring from the chairmanship of the Board, but with a continuing link with the Probation Service as President of its professional association, is that parole is serving the public interest well. I now believe that, without any significant increase in risk, it would be a social advantage to grant it even more liberally. But if so many offenders can be released into the statutory supervision and after-care of the Probation Service when they have completed less than two-thirds of their sentences—many of them after one third—are not many sentences too long? Shorter sentences would mean fewer people in prison; with fewer inmates the regimes would be less tense, more relaxed; it would be possible to improve the amenities and to give more time to education, training, recreation and useful industrial production. It would reduce the problems created by long periods of isolation from the community and dependence on the system. This is a line of argument with which I have long been in sympathy. Evidence in support of it is available in a number of European countries which members of the Board visited during the early years, where fewer people are committed to closed penal establishments, sentences are much shorter and crimes rates are lower than ours.

But changes in our penal system, desirable and overdue though I believe them to be, can only become politically acceptable to the extent that there are corresponding changes in public attitudes; this will come about only if there is a more wide-spread understanding of the underlying causes of a good deal of crime: sufficient to moderate our natural indignation and fears about the misdeeds of others, especially when one or other of us is the victim. Today there is a strong reaction against those in the van of penal reform, on the part of those who claim, with some justice, that too much concern is being expressed about criminals, too little about those who suffer at their hands. I am no different from anyone else in my own reactions when I read of some odious act of violence or a diabolical fraud which is a gross abuse of personal trust; but how to make the punishment fit the crime as well as fit the offender and reform him is a question, the answer to which still continues to elude us. In some situations a choice has to be made between inappropriate punishment and some prospect of reform, often very slight. But if there is any hope at all of reducing crime within the ambit of our democratic system, it should be sought by more efforts to bring offenders back into society, on terms which are tolerable to society. Community Service Orders are a step in the right direction. Penal treatment must be a dynamic, not a static, let alone a retrogressive process.

One serious difficulty in the way of moving forward in penal matters is the growing evidence of lawlessness. Such challenges to authority increase anxiety and anger among law-abiding people, whose demands for sterner measures are becoming more insistent. This is a natural human reaction prompted by the need of society to protect itself in times of danger. But a danger of a different order is that of generalising about crime and punishment; this is a time for steady nerves, for if we apply stronger sanctions without careful discrimination between the really evil people and those whose offences are, in large part, a product of social circumstances, we will make our troubles worse rather than better.

It is impossible to write of making the punishment fit the crime without raising the question of capital punishment. It was temporarily suspended thirteen years ago; by abolishing it five years later, we find ourselves in good company with every other country in Western Europe except Spain and France, with the countries of the old Commonwealth and with most of the States of North America. Yet in the face of armed gangsterism, kidnapping and increasing acts of violence, of political terrorism by bombings, shootings and hijacking, public opinion now bears heavily upon Parliament to change its mind, at least for certain degrees of murder and other heinous deeds which constitute attacks against society. The question has been debated in both Houses on a number of occasions, and each time capital punishment, in any circumstances, has been firmly rejected. But public opinion polls have shown that feeling outside Westminster is running strongly in favour of the ultimate sanction for acts of terrorism and it is likely that, in a referendum, a majority would call for its extension to other murders. In this matter, Parliament must consider what is just and expedient, not only what is popular. But if humanity cries loudly and insistently enough against acts of inhumanity, that voice of anguish and indignation cannot for ever be ignored.

So emotive and complex a subject requires either to be discussed in depth, or it should be limited to a simple statement of belief. In the context of this book I will simply record my view that, having abandoned the grim and grizzly process of what has been described as judicial murder, which has been occasionally committed by a miscarriage of justice, we should not resort to it again unless and until law

15

and order, and the safety of individual citizens were to become so seriously and widely endangered as to reach the dimensions of a national crisis. There is quite insufficient evidence that an increase in murders for personal revenge, financial gain, reasons of emotional stress or pure sadism in the past ten years can be attributed to the abolition of the death penalty; nor, even if that step could be held partly accountable, has it reached crisis proportions. As for acts of political terrorism, history has shown that executions create martyrs and myths, strengthen and prolong political campaigns, and too often strike at front men and symptoms rather than the leaders and the causes for which they are fighting. There is also the pragmatic point that, in these days of kidnaps and hijacks, judicial executions can be countered in triplicate and more by the murder of hostages. That terrorists should be shot *en flagrant délit* at the time of their crimes, if it is possible without endangering their hostages, is a different proposition with which I wholly agree. But capital punishment by due process of law may serve the cause of the enemy instead of destroying or remedying the trouble. What is more, it degrades and de-civilises society. Should the time come when we are forced to resume its use, I fear that we would be on the road to authoritarian rule.

In my work with the Duke of Edinburgh Award Scheme I had come to see the spirit of enterprise and adventure among young people as a feature of the British scene holding out some hope for the future of our country. But it is not a panacea for all our troubles. Nor can such a programme as the Award Scheme insulate individual people against the pressures and temptations of their daily lives. On one of my prison visits, I was passing a personable young man at his lathe in the workshop. He turned to me and said: 'I remember you, sir. You presented me with my Silver Award.' He was serving five years for a very serious offence. Regrettably, the growing trend towards lawlessness among the young is a cause for concern, bordering on alarm. In his last Report as Commissioner of Police for the Metropolis, Sir Robert Mark stated that 56 per cent of crime in London is committed by children and teenagers between the ages of ten and sixteen. The Chief Constable of Merseyside has said that some children in Liverpool are not merely delinquent; they are skilful and daring criminals. What a horrifying state of affairs! The boys and girls from disturbed or broken homes who regularly play truant from school in our large towns, or who are excluded from school because of their disruptive influence, the seriousness of which is the greater for being out of all proportion to their numbers, create problems for the education, the social and probation services. There has been a sharp rise in the numbers of young people committed to Borstals and Detention Centres; relations between youths and the police and between groups of youngsters of different ethnic origins have worsened, despite the efforts of community relations officers and of the police themselves to defuse such potentially explosive situations as the Notting Hill Carnival. A disturbing sign in this dismal corner of the social landscape is the evidence of increasing resort to hard liquor, as well as drugs, among the young. So is the opportunism by extremist political groups to exploit youthful idealism or the aggression of unemployed and rootless young people. No one can afford to ignore the significance of the rate at which delinquency has been growing in this country in recent years.

No penal system can be expected to reform society itself. The more obvious causes of delinquency, whether they lie in the home or the schools, in television or in housing policies, or in the insidious influence of liquor and drugs and the sex industry, are themselves symptoms of something very much more complex in the nature of our democracy and in human nature itself, the cures for which are more problematical. Local authorities have made commendable efforts, within the limits imposed by political and taxation policies, to clean up some of our most sleazy slums, to make provision for the sick and elderly; to ensure more equal opportunity for the young generation to develop their talents through the education system and to make provision for their opportunities in leisure time.

But political priorities are subject to the public will. There is more pressure for bigger wage-packets than for a thorough-going attack on the deprivation and poverty in which criminality is bred. Such are the fears and prejudices of many people about offenders who are sent to gaol that it takes years to negotiate the use of a dwelling house to accommodate homeless men when they leave prison. So wide are our social and economic divisions that few people living in middle-class suburbia have any notion of the ghettoes in which many of their fellow citizens live: in Birmingham's Sparkbrook, for instance, or Manchester's Moss-side, and especially in some of the housing estates in Liverpool and in some London boroughs. In such areas as these family relationships are strained to breaking point, boredom and frustration are rife, and racial tensions explode in the ghetto conditions in which many coloured immigrants are forced to live. Ten years ago I spent a year observing and reporting to the Department of Education and Science on the problems of young immigrants from countries in the new Commonwealth. My colleagues and I pointed out that their difficulties stemmed in large part from general social conditions from which they had no escape. Today, while visiting those areas again to discuss the work of probation officers, I find no discernable improvement; indeed high-rise building policies have in some respects made matters worse. I question whether the political will is strong enough; whether, under the freedom of choice which our kind of democracy confers upon us, the electorate would endorse the cost to themselves of the sweeping changes which are necessary. I can sympathise with social workers who, face to face in their daily work with people and their problems in some parts of our urban areas, are prone to feel that the Welfare State only serves to prolong, or even perpetuate disadvantage for their clients; that their own services so condition them to hand-outs from the State that they lack the will to change their standards and their life-style. I agree with their diagnosis of the causes of some criminality which stems from this state of affairs. But I am quite unpersuaded that the destruction of capitalism, which is the policy pursued so assiduously and skilfully by the Marxists, would of itself do other than sacrifice freedom at the cost of great unhappiness, without changing human attitudes. Whatever our political beliefs, and much though we might wish it to be otherwise, freedom does not equate with universal and permanent equality; justice will always be a relative term. The word we so frequently overlook in our strivings after all these ideals is the fraternity acclaimed by the triumphant French revolutionaries of 1789. Only within the spirit of caring implicit in this word is to be found the removal of these social evils in our cities.

To pursue this line of thinking would carry me beyond the limits of this chapter. I have touched upon it only in order to make a single point which I believe to be true. If we can regenerate that quality of caring, especially among the young generation, it will have a direct influence on the problem of delinquency, and consequently on the chain of more serious criminal behaviour which frequently follows from those beginnings. That this quality is to be found among our youth, and can be helped to manifest itself, I have no doubt whatever. While I was working in the Youth Service I met many young people who were in trouble with the law, or with their parents, or both. In the former Approved Schools, in Borstals and Detention Centres I watched inmates experiencing a disciplined life under the orders of courts of law not dissimilar from that experienced by those who, like myself, had attended residential schools as they were run in the 1920s, at the behest of their parents. In such structured and supportive settings most boys and girls respond well to firmness, hard work and exercise; they enjoy the challenges set for them through games and other forms of competition in an environment detached from their normal lives. Some of them have the opportunity to do some service in the neighbourhood, and they enjoy that, too. Our young soldiers in Northern Ireland whose backgrounds are in many cases identical to those others who are in trouble with the law display extraordinary patience, restraint and courage while performing a distasteful and dangerous job. There is ample evidence of the latent good in the young generation which, in the circumstances of their daily lives, has no opportunity for useful and rewarding expression. Very many young people enjoy giving a helpful hand to the elderly and sick, and in projects for improving the environment. It is to be seen in extra-mural activities in and from our secondary schools and our youth organisations. There are also many bodies whose whole ethos is to render community service whether in this country or further afield: Voluntary Service Overseas and International Voluntary Service, Task Force, Community Service Volunteers come to mind at the national level. There are numerous examples of community action in our towns which brings together people from several generations.

All these enterprises attract mainly those young people who respond readily to calls on their sense of concern for other people, or for the conservation of nature, or other aspects of community welfare. But there are many others who, from force of social circumstances, do not come forward of their own accord. The introduction of Community Service Orders as a method of penal treatment available to Courts of Law under the Criminal Justice Act of 1972, as an alternative to imprisonment, has brought some of these unmotivated and aimless young people, as well as some older offenders, into the field of community service. It is a measure which many penologists perceive as being at least as significant as was the introduction of parole ten years ago. Under its terms an offender who has embarked on the dreary road through the former Approved Schools, Community Homes, Detention Centres, Borstals, fines, probation orders and suspended sentences, and would at that stage otherwise have been sent to prison, may be required to undertake some suitable and agreed work, for a stipulated number of hours in his own neighbourhood. The timetable is arranged to suit his working and home circumstances, and placements are arranged at the request of, and by arrangement with hospitals, old people's homes, children's playgrounds, hostels, the Parks Departments of local authorities and environmental bodies; in fact, wherever there is a need for jobs to be done which can be done without detriment to someone else's paid employment, and which would not otherwise have been done. Much of this work is in the same range of jobs as those undertaken by voluntary bodies; but experience has shown that the volunteers and the offenders can work together and, if only because of the enormous amount of useful work available in many neighbourhoods, in some places requests for CSO workers are growing faster than the availability of clients on whom these orders have been served. So far, the evidence is that more than 80 per cent of offenders complete their orders successfully. Perhaps more telling than this figure is the testimony which I have received from many sources, that those who have been granted this penal treatment have enjoyed the experience. For many of them, the needs of other people and the suffering they have seen, have come as a revelation. 'I never knew there were other people who had troubles,' was a remark made by one young man. Some have even volunteered to continue lending a hand in the neighbourhood and in one area of high juvenile unemployment I was told of friends of offenders serving CSOs who have come to take part in some of the projects. A report from the Durham Probation and After-care Service sums up the situation: 'The Community Service Order has shown that there is a social vacuum in the field of leisure activities for the young adult. Accidentally, the punishment of community service has filled this vacuum for many and the word is spreading. Probationers and ex-probationers and, dare we say, ex-offenders, are coming forward without an order from the court to work with and for others.' There is no doubt that, when more money is made available, more use will be made of this option available to the courts, and not exclusively as an alternative to a prison sentence.

The effect on the crime rate of such measures as parole and Community Service Orders is not very encouraging, on the evidence available so far; but both cost the taxpayer far less than imprisonment. More important than this fact is that these non-custodial forms of punishment are positive and constructive; they involve members of the community in helping offenders to cope with their problems, if only by living in the same street with them. For most law-breakers, isolation from the community behind walls and bars has been, and will continue to be no answer; for some of them it makes a continuing life of crime even more difficult to avoid. The only hope for such people is to be encouraged to feel that they belong to the rest of us, not to be relegated to the bitterness and despair of pariah status.

I am among those members of an older generation who regret the end of national military service. I believe that if it had been continued on a wider basis, to include various kinds of community work, we would have less lawlessness today. However that may be, there is little likelihood of a universal obligation to national defence being reintroduced in peace-time. Nor was military service in its original form an ideal arrangement of young people's lives. The gap between school leaving and call-up, which was creating difficulties for boys at the time we introduced the Duke of Edinburgh's Award Scheme, would still be a problem today, even though the interval would be shorter with the raising of the school-leaving age. But a sense of responsibility towards other people in the community is of such vital importance to young people and for democracy that, with the voting age now reduced to eighteen, I believe that some obligation should be placed on all young citizens to involve themselves helpfully in their neighbourhood (or if they wish, elsewhere) after they leave school. The impact of Community Service Orders, the response of youth to purposeful work in structured situations, and the great need for more help in urban areas which remains unfulfilled – all this leads me to the conclusion that it might become a politically acceptable proposition to prolong the obligation on young people beyond the statutory age of school-leaving. A general acceptance of community obligations would be a big stride forward towards a new concept of a society which has a greater resolve to tackle its own problems, instead of for ever looking to the State.

15

One Nigeria

1968–70

THE BRITISH INTERVENTION IN GREECE AT THE END OF 1944 had, at its outset, no other expectation than that of enabling the Greek people to re-establish a government of their own choosing, and of assisting them to restore their ravaged country. The civil rebellion which followed swiftly on the heels of our arrival was not, despite the warnings of British officers who had been working with the Partisans, foreseen by the High Command; nor, I believe, were its far-reaching implications for the Western powers. Had we not repelled the EAM bid for power when we did, Greece would have entered the post-war period in 1945 as a communist state and, if the history of Hungary and Czechoslavakia is any guide, would still be a satellite of the Soviet Union today. The Iron Curtain would have been drawn along the eastern coastline of the Adriatic sea and the Russian Navy would probably have been established in the Mediterranean thirty years ago. The balance of power on the continent of Europe in the following years might have been significantly affected; it is even questionable whether Tito could have sustained the independent stance of his country against the pressures of the rest of the Soviet bloc.

Twenty-four years later I was again involved, in a minor rôle, with another rebellion whose causes were totally different, but whose consequences for the stability of a continent were also profound. On 2nd July 1968 I was invited by Harold Wilson to head a mission to Nigeria, for the purpose of advising HMG on appropriate forms of relief aid to be supplied by Britain for people who were suffering from the consequences of the civil war in that country. The war had been in progress for just over one year, but there was no sign of its ending. Besieged for the past eight months by three divisions of the Nigerian army, the secessionist territory called Biafra was virtually cut off from essential supplies to feed several million people. The sight of starving children presented nightly to world audiences on their television screens, and the huge numbers which the media were claiming to be in dire distress, were having a profound effect on public feeling; most of this was in strong sympathy for Biafra, the little 'David' making, as it seemed, a courageous stand against the 'Goliath' of the Federal Military Government. The British Government, former colonial power in Nigeria, which was responding to the call of its Commonwealth partner for support with the supply of arms to quell the secessionists, was taking the brunt of the odium, not only from most other countries, but also from its own countrymen. Anxious to acquit itself of the charge of callousness towards innocent people dying of hunger in the Biafran enclave, the Government had decided to take a major initiative by attempting to send relief supplies into the war zone, on both sides of the military front line.

Much water has flowed under the great new bridge over the Niger at Onitsha since 1970; but the memories of that tragic war are too fresh in the minds of many, the positions taken up during the conflict are still too entrenched for a true and dispassionate judgment to be made. A country of about 360,000 square miles, with stark contrasts in climate and terrain as between the north and the south of its territory, comprising some fifty million people of several different ethnic origins and over a hundred tribes, Nigeria under British rule had been administered in three regions. The Northern part of the country is an arid plateau inhabited by the Hausa-Fulani who are Muslims; the former Western Region inhabited by the Yorubas contained a mixture of Christians, Muslims and Animists; the Eastern Region was mainly an Ibo area—they were mostly Catholics; the small Midwest Region was the relic of the old Benin empire, the stronghold of the Animists, though it had many Christians in it. In the southern areas the rainfall is heavy and the forest belt is infested with the tsetse fly, which prevents cattle farming; this has an important bearing on diet and health.

Five years after the grant of independence in 1960 a *coup d'état*, on 15th January 1966, had toppled the government under its highly respected Prime Minister Sir Abubakar Tafawa Balewa. The mainspring of this revolt had been young Army officers of the Ibo tribe, whose homeland is in the former Eastern Region. Their motive was certainly to check wide-spread corruption and, to this extent, was generally welcomed; but there may also have been some intention to end the predominance of northern influence in the government; the murder of the Prime Minister and a number of other leading northerners lends colour to this belief. However that may be, the fragile unity superimposed by the British on hundreds of years of tribalism was broken and the stability of the fledgling State severely shaken. A fearful revenge was wreaked in due course by the Northern soldiers on the

Ibos. Sir Abubakar's successor, the Ibo General Aguji Ironsi, who unwisely attempted to abolish federalism and create a strong, centrally administered republic, was himself murdered six months later. A period of civil disorder ensued, acts of revenge were committed against Ibos living in the Northern Region, which developed into large-scale massacres. Some Ibos struck back with acts of sabotage. Another army officer, Lieut-Colonel Yakubu Gowon stepped into the political vacuum left by Ironsi's brutal death. On 27th May Gowon, a Christian and a member of a minority tribe, made a strong plea for unity. His theme was 'One Nigeria'. He decreed that the country would be divided into twelve states with devolved powers, within a federal structure, thus reversing the centralised control imposed by his predecessor; for the time being the nation would be under military control. The Ibos would be in an East Central State.

But Lieut-Colonel Ojukwu, an Ibo officer who had been appointed by Ironsi as military governor of the Eastern Province, had meanwhile emerged as leader of the Ibos. To protect his people against the murderous attacks to which they were being subjected he had called on all Ibos to return to the safety of their homeland. Instead of responding to Gowon's plea, Ojukwu raised the standard of revolt against the Federal Government. During the following twelve months of efforts, both by the Federal Government and the Organisation of African Unity, to resolve the crisis on a constitutional basis, Ojukwu's attitude hardened; his secessionist ambition widened to include not only the Ibo tribal area on the east of the River Niger, but the whole of the former Eastern Region, adding a further five million people of four different tribes to his own seven million Ibos. It was made abundantly clear that there was little support for this move in the newly formed minorities States of the South-East and Rivers, but the Ibos kept a tight hold on them. The Ijaws, Akois, Efiks and Ibibios had not suffered persecution at the hands of the Northerners. In the homelands of these tribes were the sea ports of Calabar and Port Harcourt and both inland and offshore were the rich oil fields being developed by a joint company formed by Shell and BP. This was expansionist politics. There are grounds for believing that Ojukwu, in making a later call for 'Southern Nigerian Solidarity', by marching west to occupy the Mid-West State and bombing Lagos, was entertaining even greater aspirations. Be that as it may, his hopes were short-lived. Defeated at the decisive battle of Ore in September 1967, he was driven back across the Niger into a shrinking enclave in the East-Central State, whose capital Enugu was captured by the Federal troops. Biafra was, by mid-1968, a beleagured fortress. From then on the Biafran position was militarily untenable. A territory only the size of a large English county, she was, within a hostile country almost the size of South Africa, cut off from all outside supplies by land, sea, and – in daylight – even by air.

There was, in fact, a political and military stale-mate which might have been swiftly resolved had the Federal Military Government been sufficiently ruthless to deploy the power of its air force and its superior army strength to storm the Biafran citadel, without regard for the lives of civilians and soldiers. But quite aside from a genuine reluctance to cause such suffering, Gowon was obsessed with the political ideal of 'One Nigeria'. Although the Ibos inside Biafra saw it otherwise – their resistance was the stronger for being fed on fears of reprisals – Gowon wanted reconciliation, not bloodshed; he was also aware that many others beside Ibos were trapped in the enclave. But Gowon's policy of containment gave the Biafrans time to rally world opinion to their side. Gowon wanted to localise the struggle. The Biafrans wanted to internationalise it. The plight of little Biafra, skilfully presented by an American public relations agency in Geneva, aroused the sympathy of public opinion in most Western countries, and there was strong pressure among governments in Britain and elsewhere to support the secessionist regime. World opinion was more divided, but the pictures on the television screens of Western Europe and North America of starving children produced a shocked reaction among many good people. The malnutrition diseases of Kwashiorkor and Marasmus have been endemic in many parts of Africa, but this was the first time most people in the affluent West had seen starvation face to face.

Quantities of arms, as well as food supplies and other forms of relief aid from countries which supported or had formally recognised Biafra, were being flown in covertly by night, at considerable risk, mainly from Lisbon to an airstrip near Uli, close to its western border. But the scale of supply brought in along the narrow air corridor leading from bases on the Bay of Biafra, or directly from Europe during the night, was quite inadequate to feed the millions of trapped people. An interesting feature of this situation was the fact that General Gowon tacitly permitted the mercy night flights. It is true that his fighters were handicapped by lack of night-flying aids at their bases, but he was concerned not to tarnish his image further before the accusing eyes of the world by a deliberate policy of sealing off Ojukwu's meagre supply of food.

At the time of the arrival of my mission, relief on the scale needed to avert catastrophe had barely begun. The International Committee of the Red Cross had not been long established in Lagos and there was little co-ordination of their efforts with those of the Nigerian Red Cross and the various national and international voluntary bodies. The concern voiced by governments had not been matched by action to alleviate the suffering. The initiative of the British Government was being watched with great interest and the arrival of Sir Colin Thornley, Director-General of Save the Children Fund, Dr Maelor Evans of the Overseas Development Ministry and myself was the focus of much attention by the press. I had insisted that the task we had undertaken must be seen to be independent. Our terms of reference, in order to ensure the most effective use of £250,000 made available by HMG for relief aid, were 'to assess the forms in which this humanitarian aid should take'. The fourth member of my team, Brian Hodgson, Deputy Director-General of the British Red Cross, was to follow three days later.

Accepting the good offices of Sir David Hunt and the UK High Commission to facilitate our programme, we lost no time in making the necessary contacts and getting down to our job; the following fortnight was the most intensive period of activity in my experience. It was the more demanding in that, unlike my colleagues, I had no previous knowledge of Africa. We had to determine first what kinds and quantities of aid were needed, then how they should be administered and, in particular, how to channel the required supplies into the war zone territory held by Ojukwu, in accordance with the strict impartiality desired by the British people. I made the last of these tasks my first priority. In London I had sent a message to Colonel Ojukwu via his representative Mr Kogbara, but had received a negative reply to my request to enter his territory. Just before we left, however, there were hints that there might be a change of mind on the part of the Biafran leader. When I met General Gowon, he confirmed his willingness to allow me to send Brian Hodgson as an emissary to his enemy and, depending on the outcome of the meeting, to let me go myself, at our own risk. On 12th July he had offered to make it possible to open a land corridor into Biafra via Enugu, which had been captured from the Ibos in the fighting in October 1967, to Awgu, by which supplies could be carried in lorries under the auspices of the ICRC. As a result of a meeting which I had arranged with British firms based in Lagos I was able to tell General Gowon that, in addition to transport which would be forthcoming from the British Government's aid fund, some fifty trucks would be made available by these firms. I stressed the urgency of having the transport columns ready to move quickly, if the Biafrans agreed to open the corridor at their end. One of my main reasons for wishing to see Ojukwu was to negotiate the opening of this corridor, which could greatly increase the flow of supplies. Moreover, General Gowon was willing to allow a daylight airlift into Biafra, under certain conditions.

In military terms these concessions made no sense; they would help to sustain morale, as well as improve health in the secessionist territory and thus to prolong the resistance. That Gowon should be ready to make them was typical of the man. I came away from that first interview charmed by his shining personality and impressed by his statesmanship. Essentially, here was a good and honest man, as well as an able politician. While he inveighed heavily and at length against Ojukwu personally, he remarked half in jest that the real trouble with him was that, unlike himself who had received his military education at the Royal Military Academy, Sandhurst, Ojukwu had been trained at the Officer Cadet School at Mons Barracks, Aldershot; the inference was that he was, therefore, not an 'officer and a gentleman'. Being aware of Ojukwu's distinguished parentage and his public school and Oxford education, I refrained from comment on the second part of this proposition; but as a former Senior Under Officer at Sandhurst myself, I relished the Head of State's distinction. Indeed, Gowon evidently took immense pride in his training at Sandhurst and all it stood for.

Colin Thornley and I held meetings with the ICRC, the Nigerian Red Cross and the various Nigerian and foreign voluntary bodies involved with relief aid. There emerged a very clear need for a much greater sense of urgency and for effective co-ordination; I sent a telegram to the Prime Minister recommending that British aid should be channelled through the ICRC and urged that the latter body should be encouraged to appoint a high-level representative for the oversight of the entire relief operation in Nigeria. In the first few days following our arrival it was very apparent that our mission would have a rôle far wider than was envisaged in our terms of reference.

Having received from these and other meetings in Lagos, some preliminary ideas of the scale of the problem and the general nature of the supplies which were required, Colin Thornley and I left separately to reconnoitre the situation along the perimeter of Biafra: with Dr Evans, Colin travelled by air to Enugu to inspect the northern part of the front, in the area of operations of the 1st Division, then commanded by Colonel Shuwa. Accompanied by Mike Newington of the High Commission Staff, I left for the central area, passing through Benin in the Mid-West State to reach the Niger at the shattered village of Asaba, whence the bridge over the river leads to Onitsha on the east bank; the bridge lay in twisted ruins, blown up by the Biafran Army during their retreat the previous winter. Colonel Haruna, commanding the 2nd Division, was at pains to persuade me of the absence of hatred towards the Ibos; he pointed out that the officers of the opposing forces had been his comrades in arms before the war.

Indeed, both Colin and I received the impression that so little were the officers in either of these formations disposed to take the offensive that this might have some bearing on the prolonged state of siege. I was also impressed by the care taken by his Division for displaced people, many Ibos, in a camp at Onitsha. Here were some 3,500 women, children and old people being well cared for by an efficient government administrator and a small staff, but mainly managing their own affairs. I could, however, easily believe the information that it also served as a flourishing brothel for the troops.

Returning to the State capital that night. I was again favourably impressed by the trouble which had been taken to keep records of properties and their contents which had belonged to Ibos who had fled to the east. The State government had even assessed the rentals of these buildings for later repayment by the present occupants; I was assured that a number of Ibo owners had claimed and been paid their dues. These may have been slender pieces of evidence, but they tallied with other indications in the Enugu area that the Federal Military Government was in no way guilty of conducting a campaign whose object was genocide, a dread word so loudly broadcast in Britain.

When Colin's party and mine were reunited in Lagos a few days later, Brian Hodgson had arrived and set off with Mr de Heller of the ICRC for Fernando Po. It would be several days before he could expect to have fulfilled his difficult and dangerous mission and I was anxious to have his report before making my own journey into Biafra. Colin and I with Maelor Evans and the Government Commissioner for Rehabilitation and Relief, Chief Omo Bare, and Mr Bulle of the ICRC flew to Calabar with speed and comfort in the Chief of State's personal HS 125. This was the area where, unlike the other parts of the front we had visited, active fighting had been in progress for some time, and conditions were said to be most chaotic. We spent a hectic and harrowing three days, travelling by steamer up-river to Oron and from there by military transport northwards towards Ikot Ekpene, where a battle was in progress. Whereas there were believed to be some 20,000 hungry and homeless people along the Niger line held by the 2nd Federal Division, the plight of some 200,000 refugees in the southern area of the fighting zone was desperate. Some were being fed from camps run by Red Cross workers and Roman Catholic priests; there were three hospitals in which nuns were working day and night; most of the displaced people came out of hiding once or twice a week to have a single meal before they again disappeared; the death rate was high. I went to the bedside of the Mother Superior of a convent where she lay, sick from under-nourishment and overwork. 'It is

getting worse every day,' she said. 'I don't know how it will end.' But
the notion of abandoning her patients was never in her mind.

Human misery on a scale such as this was difficult to grasp; to me,
stunned by what little I was able to see and hear from the brave and
selfless people who stayed to do what they could, the reality was
brought home by a single incident, in the person of a diminutive
Ibibio boy. He was tottering along the verandah of a Catholic hospital
at Use, just away from the fighting front; we could hear the guns
firing at the time. He said nothing, he was not even whimpering. He
was just a little bundle of skin and bones and he held out his arms, thin
as match sticks, to Colin. As we walked round the fetid wards, staring
at starvation and sensing death by every cot, the child trotted at Colin's
side. He was dying too. Since that moment I have often been haunted
by the memory of that child. He did not know the meaning of 'Biafra',
or 'One Nigeria'. He only wanted his mother and he wanted to live.
This is how it was with hundreds of thousands of other starving
children. Our best estimate of the extent of suffering in the area
occupied by Federal troops around the whole circumference of Biafra
in July 1968 was half a million destitute people; at that time there were
probably more than three million refugees inside the besieged area.

We called on the Commander of the 3rd (Marine Commando)
Division at his headquarters in the offices of the oil company near Port
Harcourt. The Division had made assault landings from the sea at
Calabar and Port Harcourt the previous autumn. Benji Adekunle,
another product of Sandhurst, had made a reputation for himself as a
dashing, ruthless and skilful officer. We made our call at a most
inappropriate moment while he was personally conducting a battle,
his radio earphones clamped on his head, in animated dialogue with
his forward troops. Having waited respectfully for some twenty
minutes, we were then treated to a vigorous dressing down by this
extraordinary little man; we were no more than tiresome do-gooders
interfering with the vital business of winning a war. As a former
professional soldier myself, I had some sympathy with the Colonel.
Tim Omo Bare did his best to make us sound respectable, to little
apparent effect. We withdrew abashed. Hardly had we reached the
verandah than Adekunle came out, all smiles and bonhomie. 'You
must be tired after your journey?' he said. 'What about a beer?' His
mood had changed completely and he was at pains to assure me that
his soldiers did what they could to feed refugees and limit the hardships of innocent civilians.

Later I received a charming letter from Benji Adekunle. Expressing
his 'deep appreciation in respect of your maiden visit to Port Harcourt'.
He went on. 'Even though you made your visit at a time like this, I

must confess that it was no burden at all to receive you . . . it added to our pleasure to welcome you as an indication of your interest in the Nigerian crisis . . . the end is in view and the next problem is the resettlement and integrating of the misguided lot.' He had disarmed me with his social charm. But my diary note about him on the evening of our encounter was, 'His bite is about as bad as his bark.' The press had given him the nickname of the Scorpion, mistaking the Octopus insignia of his Division which he wore on his battle dress. He was certainly a curious character. Some months later, when I accompanied Harold Wilson on his visit to Lagos, Adekunle was at his most swaggering and swashbuckling worst at a public reception for the Prime Minister at Port Harcourt. His knee-length cavalry boots polished to mirror perfection, he smacked his thighs with the horse switch which he was prone to use to smarten up his soldiers. No wonder the men of the 3rd Commando Division were, unlike the other formations, a tough and aggressive lot; they were also the least well disciplined in their behaviour towards the civilian population.

Brian Hodgson had still not returned from his mission to Biafra when we came back to Lagos. During the following days I concentrated my attention on this part of my task. Messages came from Umuahia, the Biafran capital, in confusing contradiction. Ojukwu had declined to see Hodgson, expecting me to make the visit, as emissary of the British Government. On 17th July I was about to depart in a specially chartered plane, when word came that permission had been granted for de Heller and Hodgson to go in on the earliest available air lift. They were reported to have left for the island of Sao Tome, where supplies for Biafra were stockpiled. I then made arrangements to fly to Sao Tome myself on 18th July, so as to save time in reaching Biafra by meeting Hodgson there on his return; it was doubly disappointing to learn shortly afterwards that there had been another hold-up. It was now becoming urgent for me to return to London, in order to follow up my many signals about relief supplies, with a personal report. After consulting the Commonwealth Secretary I left Hodgson with full discretion to continue his efforts, or to follow the rest of our party back to Britain. Then, at a press conference on 18th July, General Ojukwu (as he then was) stated that a visit by my mission would not be welcome; that was the end of the matter.

So I failed in my priority objective of a meeting with Ojukwu, as a result of which I hoped to negotiate a 'mercy' land corridor into this territory to relieve the misery of his overcrowded and under-nourished subjects. Despite my self-styled independent mission, I was inevitably seen by him as the representative of the British Government, which regarded him as a rebel and which backed the Federal Military Government. Certainly Ojukwu was deeply distrustful of Gowon, suspecting that he would take advantage of a mercy corridor. But it is possible that it suited him better to play on the sympathies of the peoples of the world for the plight of the Biafrans, which strengthened support for his political objective. This confusion of humanitarian caring with the cause of Biafra as a fledgling State struggling to achieve its freedom, was skilfully manipulated by Ojukwu's public relations organisation throughout the war. The following year Harold Wilson failed too. He offered a choice of eleven alternative rendezvous outside Biafra, and delayed his departure for a meeting with the Emperor Haile Selassie while awaiting a reply from Ojukwu. None was forthcoming.

Before leaving Lagos I spoke to Sir Adetakunbo Ademola, Chief Justice and President of the Nigerian Red Cross, about the desirability of appointing a new and dynamic person to administer the relief operations in Nigeria. I impressed the same point, in regard to the international aspects of relief supplies, on the British Government; the whole effort had been in too low a key and the ICRC, though efficient, was, represented at too low a level and did not command enough respect in the eyes of the government. On the Nigerian side, someone younger and more dynamic was needed than Omo Bare to direct the relief effort. More high-powered people were needed at the head of both organisations to cope with the tremendous task ahead. These suggestions were to bear fruit. Before leaving Lagos I paid calls on a number of foreign ambassadors, telling them what I had seen and how I assessed the needs in the light of the British Government's initiative. I expressed the hope that there would now be a wider response to the call for help.

The response on all hands was most heart-warming. When I accompanied the Prime Minister on his visit in March of the following year, the relief situation had been transformed. I had been kept in touch with developments by the Commonwealth Office, and had a number of meetings in Geneva and London with the newly-appointed head of ICRC operations in Nigeria, August (Guss) Lindt, who had been seconded from his post as Swiss Ambassador in Moscow. From then on we worked together and struck up a close friendship. Lindt was a tough and indefatiguable worker, who supplied the drive and quickly brought about the co-ordination which had been so lacking on my first visit. The ICRC relief effort had several abjectives; first to deal with distress in the areas occupied by the Federal Government; secondly to organise supplies to be moved into Biafra, either at once by mutual agreement of both sides; or at the end of hostilities; thirdly to move supplies by air at night directly into Biafra from Fernando Po.

Large stockpiles had been built up in neighbouring Cotonou, in

16

Lagos and Enugu; food, clothing, tents and blankets were available in the forward areas. Road transport was operating efficiently from Enugu and Calabar and aircraft chartered by the ICRC were operating jointly with the Lisbon-based Caritas planes from Fernando Po in the Gulf of Guinea. Most important of all, many relief teams were in position along the front, supplied by Eire, Sweden, Austria, Germany, Italy, the United States and, most numerous of all, our own country. Indeed, my diary noted wryly, 'Relief is continuing beyond the margin of actual need, in order to conform with the ICRC plan, which is based on maintaining stocks in five depôts at a level of 40,000 tons (enough for 4½ million people for a month); any reduction of demand from the sources of supply would cause a slow-down in the tempo and a cooling of the philanthropy which motivates it'. It was unfortunate that Lindt, whose insistent pressure on the Federal Government to get the supplies thus stockpiled allowed into Biafra, thereby became increasingly *persona non grata* to the Nigerians. In July 1969 there was a crisis. A Federal fighter shot down a Swedish Red Cross plane flying at dusk into Biafra, when it disobeyed orders to land; the Government claimed it had been carrying arms. It was the only freight aircraft shot down in the air in the war. This incident aroused world criticism, to which the Government reacted angrily. They banned all unauthorised night flying through Nigerian airspace; they cancelled the ICRC's mandate to co-ordinate relief; and they declared Lindt unacceptable as the ICRC representative. Gowon had to contend with the fact that the subject of relief aid was unpopular in his own government. Depressed by the way the war was dragging on, many Federal leaders reacted increasingly against outside interference, which they thought was prolonging the war; they were sensitive to any tendency to ignore their sovereign rights.

None the less, it is my firm opinion that had Ojukwu been as concerned for humanity as Gowon, rather than determined to pursue his policy of secession and his obsession for power, much of the misery to his own people and to the many other refugees held against their will in camps within Biafra, would have been avoided.

The final act followed the flight of Ojukwu and the collapse of his dreams as an independent Biafra, on 10th January 1970. Four days later Colin Thornley, Brian Hodgson and I, accompanied by Roger Dawe, one of the Prime Minister's Private Secretaries, and Nick Huijsman of the Ministry of Overseas Development returned to Nigeria for the last time to draw up another shopping list of urgently needed aid. Maurice Foley, Minister of State in the Commonwealth Office, was also in Lagos when we arrived, but he was engaged on other government business. While the others in my party went to Enugu, this time travelling by road through Benin and across the Niger, I flew south again, accompanied by Ahmed Joda, Permanent Under-Secretary in the Ministry of Information, Said Mohammed, the energetic and capable Administrator of the Nigerian Red Cross, Henrik Beer, Secretary General of the League of Red Cross Societies and Tony Ingledew of our High Commission, entering the former rebel territory by road through Aba.

It was a strange experience to continue into the final stronghold of General Ojukwu at Owerri. There I met the new Commander of the 3rd Division, Colonel Olusegun Obasanjo (now Head of State of Nigeria). He and his Brigade Commanders were conferring with their opposite numbers in the Biafran Army, Brigadier Kalu and a number of other officers. The matter under discussion was that of persuading troops in hiding to come out of the bush, under assurances from the Nigerian commanders that they had nothing to fear. I congratulated Obasanjo on the remarkable job his Sappers had made in constructing and repairing bridges over the road by which I had travelled. As former Chief Engineer of the Army, he was pleased. I went on to ask if I might have transport and a guide to visit Uli air strip. The Colonel obligingly provided me with the services of a Biafran Colonel Benjamin Nwajei. Now that the war was over, it was vitally important to bring in the supplies which had waited so long in the depôts; we were still not sure of the numbers to be succoured, but shortly before the end of hostilities some alarming figures – amounting to ten million – had been bandied about. It was strange indeed to be speeding down that runway which, in spite of some heavy bombing in the latter part of the fighting, had only minor potholes. The wrecks of seven aircraft and the graves of their crews added a grim reminder of the sacrifices made in running the gauntlet of darkness, storms, low cloud and enemy fighters. We saw and heard much else, of which the following diary note conveys some sense of only one among many other horrors:

> They took us to an adjacent hospital for war wounded which they had first visited today. We found 30 to 40 men, and a few women war casualties, abandoned since the advance into Biafra a week ago, in a frightful state. Four or five of them dead and all of them starving. Awful stench of gangrene, and more dying. The doctors and helpers had cleared one ward and placed some men and had fed them from their store. It was a really shocking sight. There had been about 1,200 casualties here during the war, but most of them had fled into the bush and most must have died. All the Biafran doctors had fled.

But we also saw much else to give us hope for the future. There was a massive movement of families along the roads leading out of the former enclave, to make new lives for themselves in their own tribal areas in the South-East and the Rivers States, and in the Mid-West; an estimate made by a US team was 6,000 a day along one road alone. Some half a million probably left the secessionist territory in the first ten days. Allowing for the inevitable instances of rape and plunder which are the finale of every conflict, the general conduct of the soldiers was reasonably good and in the case of the 1st Division, under Colonel Bisalla, notably so. There were many reports of troops feeding and sheltering refugees, thus belying the largely imaginary fears built up by Ojukwu's propaganda. The tragedy of the war, as I wrote in my report to the Government, was not on account of the alleged numbers of its victims, but the fact that the suffering was so great.

The tension and pathos of that long day were marvellously lifted from us on the night of 17th January, when my group returned to Owerri to spend the night in the headquarters of the rebel commander. A party had been arranged by the commanders of both sides, to which a wide range of officials, both Nigerian and 'Biafran', had been invited. Friend and foe were united in the spirit of instant reconciliation. The scene was almost unbelievable. Beautiful Ibo girls, dressed in fashionable gowns, danced with partners from both armies in their bush battle dress, to the accompaniment of a band which would have done credit to any London ballroom; both band and beauties had apparently emerged, miraculously unharmed, from the bush. Speeches were made, beer flowed. Everyone seemed to be on first name terms. They were a band of long lost brothers and sisters.

But I had to record another failure at the end, to add to that of failing to make contact with Ojukwu at the beginning of my mission. On returning to Lagos I pressed very hard, directly with members of the Government and senior officials and with our own Government in London, to get the ban on flights into Uli lifted. My efforts were not helped by well-intentioned attempts from outside the country. That great samaritan, Group-Captain Leonard Cheshire VC, announced his intention of flying to Fernando Po in order to organise the resumption of the cargo flights by the mercy planes which had supplied Biafra during the civil war. Indeed, it was thought that he intended to land at Uli himself, despite warnings that this would not be allowed. Cheshire and his wife Sue actually set off, only to be again refused permission to land on any Nigerian airfield; they had to fly on to Libreville. When I saw Gowon to say goodbye, he gave me a firm 'no' to my final plea about Uli. He spoke scathingly about Leonard Cheshire: 'He wants to earn a second VC,' he said, very unfairly.

Nigerian feeling about Uli ran deep. It had become the symbol of the rebel resistance and of Nigeria's critics around the world. It was the place to which guns and ammunition were run, along with the food and other relief supplies. As international pressure was built up to get the food into Biafra, so Nigerian resentment grew. Moreover, Gowon did not favour direct airlifts from outside the territory because he wished to demonstrate to the Ibos that Federal Nigerians were their brothers; he wanted all relief to come through Nigerian channels. In the first ten days or so after the collapse of the rebellion, when the former rebel territory was still crowded with refugees, bridges destroyed, roads chaotic with troop and civilian movement, and lorries to move the stockpiles still insufficient, the use of Uli would have been invaluable. But with every day which passed the situation was improving; the need for direct airlifts into the heartland of the Ibos became less.

Just before we left Lagos to hasten the despatch of the transport and supplies which we had identified, my third daughter, Prue, arrived with a Save the Children team of doctors and nurses on her way into Biafra. Prue had qualified as a nurse and had spent two years nursing in Nepal and India. Now she had come to another country in which, like those others, I had worked and which was in greater need of medical care. It was an emotional moment for us both as we met on the terrace in front of the High Commissioner's Residence beside the river.

Independent of the British Government though our enquiries and advice had been, we could scarcely have carried out our programme, or made our numerous contacts, without the splendid help of the staff at our High Commission. What is more, Sir David Hunt and his wife Iro and, when he left for his new post in Rio de Janeiro, Sir Leslie and Betty Glass were generous and charming hosts. Their residence was a haven to which we returned, hot, dirty and exhausted and from which we set forth again refreshed. I recall the many earnest discussions in the drawing room with high Nigerian officials, with Guss Lindt and his staff, and others; these talks were the more fruitful for the hospitality of the High Commissioner's *ménage*. It was during a discussion with Leslie Glass, standing chest-deep in his swimming pool, that I was persuaded not to overplay my hand over the use of Uli air strip.

In an episode so charged with the emotions of countless caring people, the responsibility of everyone directly involved in the problem of bringing relief to innocent and suffering civilians and helping to end the conflict was especially heavy. In situations like this it is a great consolation that friendships are quickly made and that they tend to run deep. I remember with affection many Nigerians with whom I worked briefly, but intensively in that period. There was the highly respected Chief Justice Sir Adetakunbo Ademola, who was a kindly host, a wise counsellor and whose influence as an elder statesman was considerable. Tim Omo Bare, Commissioner for Rehabilitation and Relief in 1968 was nearing retirement after a distinguished career in the Nigerian Police. He was a delightful companion who provided me with much useful background as we travelled together to the forward areas. Ahmed Joda, Permanent Under-Secretary in the Ministry of Information with whom I entered the former rebel territory at the end of the war, quiet and thoughtful and totally devoid of the spirit of revenge; he carried into the centre of recent resistance to his Government, the message of instant reconciliation which the Head of State preached to the nation and the world. These, and others, made a difficult job easier and more memorable.

We flew into London on the night of 21st January to meet a barrage of critical questioning by the news media. Reporters who had travelled into Biafra the day after my party had been there had seen and heard, as I had, the evidence and the stories of starvation, rape and plunder. They must also have witnessed the great exodus of refugees, now liberated, leaving the enclave, but they chose to ignore this highly significant fact. While acknowledging the truth of some of the stories, I had struck an optimistic note in my report; I felt indignant about the treatment which continued to be meted out to General Gowon and his Government, especially by the BBC. Only the *Financial Times* and Gerald Priestland of the BBC gave a fair and a hopeful picture. At a press conference I accused Fleet Street of telling half-truths and, of course, they did not like it; I was treated to some large and unfriendly headlines; it was a sobering experience. The Prime Minister had to deploy his customary skill in dealing with some awkward questions in the Commons. In fact, I could understand the difficulty for editors who for the past eighteen months had taken a pro-Biafran line, some of them using grossly inflated statistics about the extent of the suffering (and a few of them bandying about accusations of genocide) in coming to terms with their misconceptions. But I was determined that the truth should now be told.

I sympathised with reporters during the civil war; they were given the minimum help from the Federal Military Government. I remembered the resentment expressed by a group of wet, tired and dispirited journalists for whom I had arranged an airlift back to Lagos in the plane taking my party back from Port Harcourt in 1968. The Federal Military Government, who deeply resented the bad press they were receiving, failed to appreciate the fact that if a better image were to be projected to the rest of the world, it was essential to cultivate the press rather than cold-shoulder its representatives.

By contrast, Ojukwu was extremely skilful in the matter of his public relations; an agency in Geneva played an important rôle in cultivating sympathy for the Biafran cause throughout the civil war. In losing his bid to create a new state in Africa he will rightly be remembered for his tenacity, his courage and political skill. He was a man who commanded deep loyalty among his soldiers as well as among a number of highly respected and able Ibo leaders. And he inspired his people to great sacrifices. But there is no doubt that much of the desperate stubbornness of the Ibo resistance was due to fear, assiduously fostered by Ojukwo, who even told his people that any relief supplies which came through Nigerian channels would be poisoned.

When the Western European and North American press wrote about the threat of genocide, Gowon accepted a team of international observers to check on the behaviour of the Federal troops in the battle zone and dispel those rumours. The reassuring reports of these observers received little publicity and when the war ended, events provided a dramatic refutation to the forecasts. No civil war in world history has ended with less revenge and retribution.

What Price Democracy?

I TOOK SOME TIME TO BECOME ACCLIMATISED TO THE RAREFIED atmosphere of the House of Lords; its ancient traditions, its titles and their rankings, its occasional pageantry, its quaint proceedings and its curious modes of address. When you have been so unmistakably singled out as a member of this venerable establishment, you are liable to be set apart in the public mind, under the well-disposed misconception that you have been exalted on to a pedestal as a minor monument of society—and that can be insidiously flattering. It is nearer the mark, if less agreeable, to be perceived as an outmoded anachronism. But among my friends there were, for a while, some who seemed to think that I had undergone a mild form of transfiguration. The identity of some peers disappears without trace upon entering that political stratosphere; they return, as if in a new incarnation, under an entirely different name.

Yet gradually, as I came to understand the workings of the House, I began to appreciate its value as part of the apparatus of our constitution. In its rôle of providing a forum for discussing the important national issues, whether the theme be social, political, economic, constitutional, or philosophical, I believe that the House of Lords makes a valuable contribution to the life of the nation. Tedious though they often are, I have even come to enjoy some of the sittings. There are times, during a big debate in a full and attentive Chamber, when I have had a sense of being involved, in a very humble capacity, not only in an historical procedure, but even in the making of history. There is an absence of explosiveness, of cut and thrust and extrovert behaviour and the not infrequent uproar which are characteristic of the Commons. But the Upper House does not lack some sharply contrasting personalities, some brilliant debaters, people with deeply held convictions born of a life-time of experience, all of whom combine to make the Lords a very human and sometimes exciting place. I have a painful memory of one occasion when, carried away with enthusiasm by a speech I was listening to, I started to clap. Fortunately this outrageous departure from the traditions of the House appeared to pass unnoticed.

It may seem invidious to single out a few stars among a galaxy of oratorical talent, but few would deny the nonagenarian elder statesmen, Lords Brockway and Shinwell, a special mention: Fenner Brockway, whose deep humanity spans the globe; Manny Shinwell, delighting the House from a fund of home truths delivered impartially across the Party lines with good humour and without rancour. On the front bench of the Conservative Party, Lord Hailsham can still rouse his audience with his fervour and make us join him laughing at his quips. Nor is Lord Barnby, another nonagenarian, without the power to make an impact in defending the White policies in Southern Africa, with a pungent turn of phrase administered with endearing courtesy and charm. And the Liberals, for all their paucity in numbers, possess some potent performers in the pugnacious Frank Byers and the measured legal mind of Basil Wigoder. The prelates, too, have speakers to be reckoned with, particularly those with the Socialist convictions of the Bishop of Southwark and the Methodist, Lord Soper. Donald Soper, with a lifetime of experience at Marble Arch and Tower Hill, is probably the most polished orator in the House of Lords. On the Cross-Benches we have the easy, persuasive fluency of Lord Redcliffe-Maud, the monosyllabic and booming interventions of Lord Boothby, and rapid fire advocacy of Lord Goodman, who presents a severe challenge even to the speed and skill of the Hansard stenographers. But more important than the oratory are the knowledge and experience which the Upper House possesses in its membership. It is, incidentally, a pleasantly informal and friendly place, for all its curious customs. For those who enjoy club life, the House is an excellent club.

Of course, the big occasions are fairly rare. Of the various debates in which, on fifty-odd occasions, I have spoken in the last ten years, I, an infrequent speaker and an irregular attender, can think of only a dozen or so which stand out. These include the first debate on the Southern Rhodesia Order, imposing sanctions on that country, when I found myself placed to speak immediately after the late Marquess of Salisbury, an eminent supporter of the White regime; the Second Reading of the 1968 Immigration Bill; a Debate on capital punishment in 1975, on a motion in my name; and a number of others on such matters as the Nigerian civil war, Northern Ireland, penal measures, and questions relating to education, youth service, the environment and sport. On some such occasions the House has been well filled; more often, especially after the opening speeches, the Chamber is thinly attended and, of those who are present, not all are awake. At such times I have wondered what it is all in aid of, and whether peers' expenses for attendance are fully justified. From a strictly personal point of view, attendance in the Chamber has helped me to acquire some patience as an attentive listener and I have even found the enforced physical immobility oddly satisfying.

But in amending legislation during the Committee and Report stages of Bills before Parliament, it is a different matter; the important point then is, not so much that there should be large numbers constantly in the Upper House, which, no matter how it votes, must eventually defer to the Commons, as that a high degree of expert knowledge should be brought to bear on points of detail as well of principle. For this work there is an enormous amount of talent in the House. Improving draft legislation, often hastily processed through the House of Commons, is a most valuable function of the second Chamber, as is the work of its Select Committees; for instance, in scrutinising the legislation of the EEC before it receives approval of our Parliament.

But the powers of the House of Lords should be reconsidered, and its present composition is overdue for reform. The perpetuation of hereditary titles is harmless enough; similar links with ancient history have survived revolutions in other countries and there is no reason why they should not be retained in Britain. The right of their holders and their successors to vote in Parliament carries the incidental benefit of bringing in some brilliant young man on succeeding to their titles, while highlighting the perpetuation of a hereditary disadvantage for women. But this does not compensate for an undemocratic system. When the Chamber fills up with Peers who are seldom seen in the House at any other time, as it occasionally does during the closing stages of a debate on the Second Reading of an important Bill which has been passed by a Labour majority in the Commons, I feel some sympathy with the abolitionists. It is true that the Lords can only delay measures which have been passed by the elected Chamber, but the latter having expressed its explicit intention, a reversal by a built-in Conservative majority in the Lords is unwarrantable. Moreover, time and again the same range of political arguments is deployed for a second time, and sometimes a third time, in both Houses as a result of such reversals, in the course of shuttling legislation to and fro between the two.

Reform of the Lords has been in the air at intervals since before the First World War. In 1968 broad agreement was reached between the front benches of all three political parties on the main lines for change. But this accord was reached without the back-benches of the Parties. When the House of Lords Reform Bill was debated in the Commons it was thrown out, largely thanks to the powerful advocacy of such improbable allies as Michael Foot and Enoch Powell. More recently, various new proposals have been discussed and given a public hearing through the media. Among them has been the suggestion that members of the Upper House should be elected from regionally-drawn constituencies; alternatively, that the principle of appointment by patronage should be retained, but that the rights of hereditary Peers should be limited, only some of them being nominated by their Parties to vote.

My general view about the reform of the House of Lords is that it should not be undertaken until the electoral system of membership of the Commons has been changed so as to make it more representative of the political persuasions of the electorate and thus more fair to the various political Parties. Until this has been done, there is a strong case for reserving to the Upper House the powers which it has at present. Indeed, a committee under the chairmanship of Lord Home of the Hirsel which reported to the leadership of the Conservative Party early in 1978, has proposed that those powers should be strengthened, justifying the case by a system of election for a proportion of its membership. If this were done without, or in advance of a reform of the Commons it would, in my opinion, be putting the cart before the horse; indeed, it might have the effect of constructing a vehicle inappropriate for the new horse. There is a growing gap between Parliament and the people, and one essential step towards bridging it is to make the elected representatives correspond more closely in their numbers to the actual votes cast by the electors. There is a strong tide of opinion in and outside Parliament for electoral reform, on some formula for proportional representation. It is true that this might have the effect of increasing the numbers of Parties, and the formation of coalitions might be a condition of government. To ensure stability, there would be a premium on the quality of political leadership. But this combination of leadership and a greater feeling among the people of involvement in parliamentary government is of crucial importance to democracy.

On the assumption that the composition of the Commons has first been changed, my suggestions for the reform of the second Chamber would be based on the premise that power should rest in only one place, not in two assemblies elected by different processes and different constituents, which could produce a different balance of power in each assembly. Nor do I believe that there would be much public enthusiasm about being expected to go to the polls for two separate parliamentary elections. Given that the House of Commons were more truly representative which would, I believe, induce more people to cast their votes than is the case of present, I would like to see the present powers of the second Chamber removed.

Thus far, my argument might appear to favour those who would abolish the House of Lords. But there remains the value – indeed, given the pressure of work upon MPs – the necessity of having draft legislation carefully scrutinised, and improvements suggested, preferably by another body than the Commons, which the Lords do at present on a Party-political basis. Today it is more important than ever for MPs to spend more time in their constituencies, as one means of strengthening the link between Parliament and the people. So there is something to be said for having this second, or Committee Stage, in the processing of Bills undertaken by another body, and from an independent stand-point, rather than by Committees of the Commons. There is great value, too, in parliamentary debates, out of context from particular Bills at their Second Reading, on broad general issues affecting society, as well as on local and particular matters. Because such debates may, in certain instances, be the harbingers of legislation, they will continue to take place in the Commons. But there are other matters which individual members of a Second House may wish to raise from time to time. It seems to be accepted that debating is of better quality in the calm and relaxed *ambiance* of the present House of Lords, which does not have pressing work both in and outside Parliament.

So I believe we need a Second House – which I will call a Senate – without powers of decision or delay, whose function would be to apply its wisdom and knowledge to throwing light upon important issues, and whose committees would advise the elected Chamber on how to improve, and make practicable, the laws it intends to enact, from a position – or rather positions – detached from the committed and entrenched postures of Party politicians. Such a body would be chosen from those who have particular and exceptional qualifications, rather than experience in Party politics. The Senate would be considerably smaller than the present House of Lords can be if most peers of the realm are present. It could consist of people appointed as individuals, on their own merits as fairly senior citizens, so as to provide a sufficiency of knowledge required to deal adequately with the business referred to it by the Commons. I would expect to see trade union leaders included, as well as religious leaders from all denominations, and people eminent in medicine, in commerce and industry, in the law, the arts, social work and so on; each according to the knowledge required in the House from every area of our national life. On the other hand, I would not see the Senate as a repository for politicians after retirement from the House of Commons, inclined as some of them are to carry on the old battles in the same old way.

Holders of titles would not, of course, be excluded, provided that they had something of value to contribute to the work of the Senate. Indeed, the wealth of talent in the present House of Lords would be a fruitful, if not a main source for the selectors in the first instance. But the tradition of conferring baronial titles, if it continues, would give no right to a seat in Parliament.

The main business of the Senate would be to undertake the Committee stage in the scrutiny of draft legislation, both from Europe and the Commons; the legislators would thus be relieved of this task. But they would receive the amended Bills at the Report stage, when they would be able to give the proposals of the Senate a 'political' scrutiny. So the Senate would set up expert committees to draft amendments to Bills before they returned to the Commons. What is more, having served on a Royal Commission and on several other government-appointed bodies, I believe there would be merit in charging the Senate with the responsibility for forming these select bodies as well, following a Government decision to set up some enquiry. The composition of such committees would thus be decided independently of Ministers and civil servants. There would, of course, be nothing to prevent the Senate from initiating reports itself for consideration by the Commons. Eminent lawyers in the Senate would provide a final Court of Appeal, as they do at present in the House of Lords.

There would be a prescribed term of service for senators and, notwithstanding the exceptional abilities of some of the existing octo- and nonagenarians in the Lords, there would be an upper age limit of, at most, seventy-five. The job would be remunerated, either on the basis of fees for particular assignments on committees, or by payment of a part-time salary, or both.

A Senate whose function was to be on the lines I have suggested would not be expected to meet regularly as a whole assembly, as the Lords are expected to, although there would doubtless be continuous work for some of its members. How should nominations be made to the Senate? Given that it has no powers, but has a statutory right to be consulted in the matter of legislation, it would present no threat to any political Party; the spirit of its work would be that of co-operation with the Commons; its duty would be to serve Parliament, not the Government. I therefore see no reason why selection of Senators should not be made by an all-Party committee of the Commons, or of Privy Councillors. The committee would presumably be chaired by the Prime Minister who would, however, have no powers of personal patronage in making appointments.

The advantages of a bi-cameral system along these lines would be that the redundant and repetitive work at present undertaken by the

Lords would be eliminated and replaced by some of the work at present done, at the Committee stage, in the Commons, whose members would thus be relieved of some of their present burdens, but without prejudicing or duplicating their political prerogative. In order to play its part in the parliamentary process the Senate would be composed of people who, by virtue of age and experience, would bring their knowledge to bear on the affairs of State, unhampered by the dogmas and disciplines of the political parties. A number of such people are already to be found sitting on the Cross-Benches as Independents and there are certainly many more around the country, with other special expertise, to complete the requisite range of knowledge available in the Senate. Not least important would be the fact that, without sacrifice of thorough scrutiny, there would be a considerable saving in time in the passage of legislation.

But this question of reforming Parliament, important though it is, is only one of the measures needed to give a new look to democracy in Britain. That it is as much endangered in peace today as it has been during two world wars is plain for all to see; with the difference that the dangers are both within our body politic and from outside our islands. Not all the problems which face us are of our own making, nor are they all within our capacity to cure. Obsessed with the notion of unending growth, humanity at large is in heady competition to exploit and develop the natural resources still at its disposal, speeded by the pace of man's restless energy and inventive genius. The countries of the Third World see the gap widening between themselves and the richer, more developed countries and are beginning to use their power, as possessors of some of the vital resources, to redress the imbalance. Our economic recession in Britain is only one example of similar experiences in other countries. As elsewhere, it has been accompanied by a dangerous spiral of rising prices and wages and a serious epidemic of unemployment; for this there is also a more intractable cause in advancing technology, which helps to improve the economic wealth of the nation, but exacts the price of many people's livelihoods. A most worrying aspect of the shrinkage of labour-intense industries is the lack of jobs for young people coming into the labour market from various levels of full-time education. And the worst to suffer from this situation in Britain are the young citizens from those under-developed countries whose poverty and insecurity attracted them to seek a better life in our country, whose colonial heritage has imposed upon us obligations towards the immigrants, but whose citizens have been reluctant to accept them as permanent residents. In a situation where immigrants from the new Commonwealth countries are competing with the native British for jobs, this reluctance easily turns to fear, resentment and prejudice. Now we see the beginnings of an immigrant backlash, as the new citizens, and others who have been settled here for more than a generation but whose colour makes them objects of the same prejudice, band together to defend and fight for themselves.

In our industries, the balance of power between management and the work force is changing and human relationships are often un-satisfactory. Economies of scale operate to the disadvantage of small enterprises, in which a few people can work happily together. Mam-moth undertakings emerge from the competitive struggle, in which contacts between top management and the shop floor are infrequent, where they exist at all. Power lies at the level of the shop floor units of the trade unions, whose spokesmen use it, not only to push up wages and improve working conditions for their members, but often to demand a greater say in the policies and management of the firms in which they are employed, and in pursuit of political objectives which are extraneous to the business of the firm in particular, or industry in general.

Unemployment, industrial unrest, racial tension, deprivation and squalor in some of our urban areas; the contrasting advantages which others continue to enjoy, a few of them in great opulence, with the power which it wields; crime and delinquency with a strong under-current of violence which arises from some of these situations, to say nothing of international terrorism: these are conditions which are ripe for exploitation by people dedicated to the overthrow of capitalism, who seeing the evident need for all humanity to move towards an ordered world community, believe that human beings can only be effectively marshalled under the banner of Marxism. In Britain they are few in numbers, but they are strongly motivated by their beliefs and highly skilled in their methods. But there are many others who, while deploring some of the conditions which call for change in Britain, are no less opposed to revolutionary change. Indeed, they are so opposed to the prospect of the chaos which would ensue that they could be persuaded into the need for harsh measures, such as those advocated by another small minority, whose extremists stand for action reminiscent of the early days of Adolf Hitler's intervention when he stepped in to check the chaotic conditions in Germany during the 1930s.

Complex and important as they are in themselves, I see all the troubles as symptoms of a more deep-seated malady in the free world. In our own nation, it may be perceived in the apparent weakness of a political will among us to bestir ourselves, not so much to defend as to deserve the freedoms which we so much take for granted by building them on durable foundations. There is still a great majority of moderate, decent and reasonable people; but we do not hear sufficiently that voice of reason, moderation and concern for others to outmatch the arguments of the humourless zealots of the extreme Left and to halt the measured tread of the hard-faced hatchet men of the extreme Right. In part, there is still a degree of complacency, a vague feeling that our troubles will somehow go away; that what is happening elsewhere as other democracies disappear, could not possibly happen here; that we have a genius for muddling through. In part, there is apathy, a loss of self-respect and of national pride, a rejection of traditional standards and of the moral values on which they are based. Apathy about the common weal, together with an obsession with self-interest, is a cancer in our midst. Freedom is seen as sacred, but its price in caring and responsibility seems too much to pay.

If this is seen as the language of despair, I have indulged in a jeremiad in order to profess my conviction that human beings get the government they deserve, and that if we wish to preserve our freedoms, we must be prepared to pay a price. The older generation owes it to the nation's youth, whose future is at stake, to create a credible alternative to the ideals and objectives of communism; to mouth the word freedom as holy writ, out of the context of accountability to the community is simply not good enough. The answer must be the improvement of our educational system. As a convinced comprehensivist who believes that equality of opportunity means starting at the earliest stages of schooling, and should, on principle, exclude selective segregation in grammar schools and an option for some parents to perpetuate advantage to their offspring by buying them a flying start in private schools, I none the less criticise our State schools for a failure to cultivate sufficiently the qualities of leadership which are to be found and can be developed in most young people; for sending out too many of them, only two years before they will have the right to exercise their votes, inadequately literate or numerate, insufficiently informed or interested in the community in which they will live and work, ignorant of institutions and affairs of their country and its leaders; without even – and in alarming numbers – the ability, let alone the desire to read. And how many junior citizens could define democracy and freedom in terms which would make for confidence that democracy in Britain is a living and virile force? Democracy, however it is defined, implies in simple parlance helping to make a go of the life of a family, a neighbourhood and a whole community, just as much as it does the casting of votes or the show of hands when it comes to making decisions. For democracy to survive, especially at a time when it is under economic strain and the subtle attack from its enemies, our young citizens need to understand, not only what

Basil Goodfellow on the East Ridge of the Weisshorn, with the Dom and the Täschhorn beyond.

With Joy, looking across to the Pelvoux–Ailefroide Ridge.

With Paul Jouffrey, below, and right, with Albert Eggler.

its bonuses and benefits are, but also the obligations it involves for them, and how its loss would affect their lives. They need to learn to care. Only through such an understanding can they acquire the will to resist the siren voices of Marxism and National Socialism.

I believe that democracy may not survive unless it is built up from the grass roots of youth. It does not follow that the new plant, when grown to maturity, will resemble our mixed economy. But I share with some others a faith that, while removing the chronic poverty and controlling the abuses of liberty which are still tolerated in our society, it would preserve the essential freedoms: to speak one's mind, to worship if one wishes, to move about at will and without fear. I see no reason why it should not be possible, under socialism, to continue to provide free outlet and encouragement to the voluntary spirit; indeed, this would be an essential condition of building socialism with a caring and human face.

The final year of all compulsory schooling should be designed as a transition from school to adult citizenship. The academic curriculum should be about general knowledge and current affairs; activities should include involvement between the pupils and their neighbourhood, its industries, its institutions and its community activities; commitment and involvement in the society they are preparing to enter as citizens, should be the key-notes. Of course, some of this happens already in many schools throughout the country. But the jealously guarded responsibilities of local authorities and the correspondingly weak authority of central government, to say nothing of the wide discretion traditionally left with school heads, makes a patchy picture of progress towards the realisation of a universal principle that education is the life blood of a whole people; it is not only for the benefit of its individual members.

I would like to see the principle of training for citizenship extended beyond school-leaving, into a further commitment to day-release education for everyone up to voting age, in which some involvement with voluntary community work would be included. Universal further education is one of those ideas put forward by distinguished educationists in reports which have been pigeon-holed by past governments; the cost, in working time and in the teaching establishments, has been deemed too great. So has the cost of developing adequately provision for leisure, despite the fact that earlier retirement may soon become inevitable as one means of making room for more young people at work; despite, too, the prospect of a permanent condition of less jobs with the advance of new technologies. The trend is towards a shorter working week and fewer working hours, with a corresponding increase in leisure. The opportunities to use leisure more

17

fully and profitably, both for individual happiness and to provide for the needs of others, is going to loom large in the future pattern of living; large enough, perhaps, to justify a department of State to promote its possibilities, not by generating bureaucracy, but by promoting private initiative independently of commercial exploitation. We need to work in these directions to bring about a quiet revolution in defence of democracy: a revolution in attitudes at work and to leisure; above all, in concern for other people: a determination to build a kind of society which is better than the suppressive régimes which now rule about one third of the world.

Utopian? Perhaps. We are constantly reminded that politics is the art of the possible. But too often this hackneyed phrase is used as an excuse for not doing enough in the direction of desirable change. Politics is also a creative art; pursued with skill and conviction, it can achieve goals which may seem impossible. It is, perhaps, not too much to suggest that we in Britain are suffering a crisis of conviction about what we do stand for, as distinct from what we are against. There are, of course, many people with strong convictions about what is fair and right and with the courage to stand up for them; people whose faith is founded on love rather than hate, or on abstract ideologies. But their caring and courage need to be more widely shared and more strongly buttressed if our freedoms are to be assured for the future generations.

Rudyard Kipling's poem 'If' is a personal challenge which may be perceived by many people as old hat today, but it enshrines some unchanging truths. It is on this premise that I will presume to add a few more 'ifs' which I see as a challenge to us all and which, I believe, are not beyond the bounds of creative politics and a change of heart within our nation.

If our youth were better provided with an education which would enable more of them to understand the nature of the problems confronting the society which they are about to join as adult citizens; at least to the extent of appreciating how complex these problems are for any government to solve, under whatever system; *if* young people were able to see that many of the problems have to be dealt with at the grass roots level, as well as in the corridors of Parliament; that there are opportunities for them to play their parts, no less important for the fact that their efforts may be limited to their own neighbourhood; *if* more were expected of young people by adults and more outlets were available to more of them both for their spirit of adventure and for their idealism, then the young generation, which will inherit the earth and all that's in it, challenged to show its mettle and called upon to serve society, could be the saviours of democracy.

17

Playground of Europe

1920 Onwards

IN GIVING THE TITLE *PLAYGROUND OF EUROPE* TO A COLLECTION OF essays on his climbs in the Alps in the early years of mountaineering, Sir Leslie Stephen, man of letters and one-time clergyman, gave a touch of levity to the subject. This was typical of him, but in those days of primitive maps, poor communications and absence of high shelters in the mountains, the title scarcely does justice to the achievement of those intrepid pioneers, which savoured more of exploration than of sport. Not everyone would agree that, even today, mountaineering should be equated with sport in its more familiar connotation of an organised pastime. But a century after Stephen's day, when guidebooks furnish the climber with detailed descriptions of numerous routes up all the Alpine peaks, graded according to technical difficulty; when numerous mountain huts are filled to overflowing with people from many nations, in many instances assisted on their way up from the valleys by aerial ropeways, after leaving their cars in crowded parks, mountaineering in Europe has indeed assumed more the character of 'the games that climbers play' as one of our foremost exponents, Doug Scott, has described it. A dangerous and arduous game withall.

Mountaineering in the Western Alps in the nineteenth and early twentieth centuries was an indulgence of a fortunate minority from the leisured classes, mainly from Britain, whose position in life enabled them to travel in Europe and who were possessed of more enterprise than the majority of those among their countrymen who undertook the 'Grand Tour'. In the circumstances, it was no chance that the Alpine Club was founded in London in 1857, the first of many clubs which were to follow suit later in other countries. The Alps, not the crags and cliffs of their homeland, were the playground of those pioneers. It was twenty or thirty years after Alfred Wills climbed the Wetterhorn in 1854 that the opportunities in Britain to practise rock climbing and, mainly in Scotland, to use the skills acquired on steep snow and ice in Europe, were exploited; even then, these were not regarded by many alpinists as serious mountaineering. That was the view of George Finch, a leading British climber in the years shortly before and after the First World War and one of the early exponents of amateur climbing without professional mountain guides. His book, *The Making of a Mountaineer*, given me for Christmas when I was fourteen, inspired me to start climbing myself. I had first seen a mountain with snow on it at the age of ten, while my mother, Hugh and I were staying in the village of La Chieza, above Lake Geneva. The Dents du Midi, which provide the picture postcard background to the famous Château de Chillon beside the lake, was our daily scene during that August in 1920. Of course, we children lived mainly in a foreground of chalets, meadows, flowers and butterflies; we were more aware of these things, and the music of cowbells, than of the distant scene; but the Dents du Midi was all a part of it. For me the Alps began at that point in time and my association with them will not, I trust, end with the completion of this book; so I have placed this chapter at the end, hoping that the story will continue.

I was twelve when I was first tied on to a climbing rope by a tall, bronzed and heavily moustached Swiss with the Guide's badge of the Swiss Alpine Club pinned to his grey suit. With my mother and brother and a schoolfriend I was making what seemed to me an adventurous sortie on to the ice of the Grindelwald glacier, a favourite tourist attraction in the 1920s. There was, of course, no difficulty, and no danger whatsoever; we children just felt heroic. Now, the glacier has retreated far up the mountain; where we dared to tread is bare limestone, smoothed and scoured by the ice which once moved upon it. Above us, dominating our scene almost daily during those blissful, sun-filled summers, as we swam and fished for perch in the Thunersee, took the paddle steamer to Beatushöhlen or Interlaken, climbed the Niesen, visited the cheese-makers in the Justustal, caught swallow-tail butterflies on the Schynnige-Platte, were the famous trinity of the Eiger ('The Ogre'), the Mönch (The Monk)' and the Jungfrau ('The Young Lady'). I knew them as things apart from my little world, yet as part of a childhood landscape; I was aware of them, but only in a vague sort of way.

After those early summers in the Bernese Oberland my mother took us on long walking tours across parts of the Alps, when we would stay in inns, hospices and mountain huts; with hindsight I see it now as all part of a progress towards the real thing. In 1924 we began to spend summer holidays in the Engadine; that was the year when the disappearance of Mallory and Irvine on Everest made headlines in the British press; instead of putting me off, it made me want to climb. We

already knew the two guides in the village of Campfér, where we used
to stay: August Klucker, a short, wiry man with dark-tanned, aquiline
features and a glass eye; I was never sure which one was looking at me.
He had been our ski teacher for the past three seasons and my brother
and I were a little afraid of him; he was somewhat uncouth, had a
great liking for schnapps, was apt to wax impatient with his pupils
and, mumbling Swiss German with a cheroot between his teeth, his
instructions were difficult to understand.

Yet it was to Klucker that, after much badgering on my part, my
mother at last agreed to entrust me, to take me up an easy peak,
the Piz Palü (12,811 feet); it was, in fact, our favourite mountain,
which was a part of our scene during ski tours on the Boval and Pers
glaciers. She insisted that a second guide should accompany me and
Karl Kaufmann, a quiet, courteous man with a red face and tooth-
brush moustache, was engaged; he was a much more congenial
companion than Klucker, and I liked him on sight.

I walked up to the Diavolezza hut ahead of my guides, armed with
a walking stick on which were carved numerous rings, each marking
some walking 'expedition' in the mountains. But this was different. I
was elated, but also a little afraid, unsure of myself. I felt lonely, too,
without my mother and brother. In those days the Diavolezza was an
old-style mountain hut and that night I lay awake under the rough
blankets on the communal straw mattress, every nerve tensed with the
strangeness of it all. I listened, anxious and decidedly shocked, as the
guides indulged in horse-play with the girl who worked in the hut
kitchen; chivalry prompted me to intervene. I little realised that she
was probably enjoying the experience. I was embarrassed, stretching
out my hand in the darkness, when I made contact with a woman
lying on the mattress beside me.

A match was struck. August Klucker's bearded face peered, squint-
eyed, at his large pocket watch. It was 2 a.m. and time to get up. It
scarcely needed his hoarse whisper to stir me to action. Fearful and
excited at the same time, I dressed. We drank a bowl of coffee, dipping
into it a slice of bread and honey. The climbing lantern was lit and we
were on our way.

All that day I followed my guides in a kind of dream. There were
few difficulties and the situations were not really alarming; for but an
impressionable beginner it was all thrilling and awesome enough, as
we plodded up the glacier in the growing light, negotiated an easy
bergschrund and eventually reached the snow ridge which led us to
the summit. Then down we went, along an easy rock ridge to the
Bellavista Saddle and off the mountain to the Boval hut. There was
only one other party on the Piz Palü that day; when forty-four years

later, I climbed it again by the East Spur on its North Face, literally hordes of cheerful, noisy tourists were pouring along its summit ridge.

Later that first day, we came down to Morteratsch; I was in a bad way. I was exhausted, badly blistered by the sun and suffering the first discomfort of snow blindness; for no one had thought to provide me with snow goggles or glacier cream. It was an uncomfortable initiation to the high mountain scene, but for some reason it made me even more keen than before to climb, and go on climbing. In the following years Klucker, Kaufmann and I climbed many peaks in the Engadine and Bergell, some of them in winter with the help of skis. I grew to like the gruff, bearded little man as we shared these experiences; it was quite a test of our relationship that we once, to spare my mother's purse, even shared a bed in a sleezy *pension* on one ski tour.

For my first six alpine climbing seasons I climbed only in the Alps, knowing little or nothing about the possibilities in Wales and the Lake District. This had the great advantage of enabling me to climb a considerable number of peaks, including a few of the great classic routes, and to have the experience of a relationship between an amateur and professional mountaineer which had been enjoyed by all the earlier generations. But something was lacking. It was the chance to learn the craft of mountain-climbing, for my guides were not instructors. It was the chance to lead, the chance to share the excitement and the problems of a climb fully with like-minded companions.

It was not until 1933 that I first climbed at home and, from the discovery of those experiences, went to Chamonix with friends to test those special pleasures on the bigger peaks. It was a moment of transition which, by passing from the one state to the other, has given me a feeling for the pioneers of more than fifty years before my time.

It would scarcely be possible to write about the Alps without making some mention of Chamonix. For most British climbers, nurtured on their native crags and gritstone edges, Chamonix has for many years been an alpine honeypot; the famous aiguilles, the precipices of the North Face of the Grandes Jorasses, the southern buttresses of Mont Blanc, have been in Sir Leslie Stephen's phraseology, their favourite playground. There is good historical cause for Chamonix' claim to fame, for it was from there that Dr Michel Paccard with Jacques Balmat set forth in 1786, burdened with clumsy instruments and curious aids to climbing, seeking to prove, for the honour of Chamonix, by his scientific observations that the mountain was indeed the highest point in Western Europe. Mont Blanc is the magnet which today still draws the tourists in their tens of thousands every year from all over the world.

For me, the Chamonix valley is a kind of second home. It was on the Grépon, the Blaitière and the peaks around the Argentière glacier that I began climbing without guides in 1933. It was there that Joy and I used to climb and ski during our holidays with our French friends, while I was serving on the Allied staff at Fontainebleau. It was from the Chamonix valley that I climbed with Wilfrid Noyce, David Cox and Mike Ward for three seasons after Everest, in which our encounters with Mont Blanc stand out in memory.

But, aside from those occasions and the climbing to which they have given rise, I think of Chamonix mainly in terms of people; for this Mecca for mountaineers draws climbers as it does the tourists, not only from Britain, but from every nation. You meet old friends and you make new ones, wherever you go in and above the valley; in the restaurants and bars, on the camp sites, in the mountain huts, on some rock face or summit ridge. It was while traversing the Drus that Joy and I first met the Austrian Hermann Buhl, who first reached the summit of Nanga Parbat and survived a night out alone, in 1953; he was racing down ahead of us with his companion Kuno Rainer after they had climbed the North Face. It was on the terrace of the Montanvers, while Wilf and I with the others in our quartet were about to leave for the Refuge du Couvercle to traverse the Moine by its SW and North Ridges, that I came across Walter Bonatti, fresh from the triumphant Italian first ascent of K2. He was pacing up and down, waiting impatiently for the weather to improve. He told me that the route he had in mind was the North Face of the Drus, alone. It was only ten days later that the climbing world was astonished to learn that Walter had made the first ascent, on his own, of the SW Face of that mountain, spending six days during which he had to haul great quantities of pegs and other heavy climbing gear, in addition to his food and survival kit, up pitch after vertical pitch, day after day, in fair weather and foul. And it was here that we met British climbers relaxing among the fleshpots after making history for our own mountaineering annals: Tom Bourdillon and George Fraser after the first British ascent of the Drus' North Face, and Joe Brown and Don Whillans after they had added the West Face of the same mountain to British laurels.

Most frequently we enjoyed the friendship of French friends: Paul Payot, then Mayor of Chamonix, a living encyclopaedia of knowledge about the history of the valley, and the owner of a priceless collection of pictures and books; Maurice Herzog, a Deputy in the French parliament who became Minister for Youth and Sport in the Government of M. Pompidou and later succeeded as Mayor of the town; he was better known to the world at large as the gallant leader of the

French expedition which first reached the top of Annapurna in 1950, breaking a symbolic climbing altitude barrier of 8,000 metres. Jean Franco, leader of the expeditions which made the first ascents of Makalu and Jannu, was Director of the Ecole Nationale de Ski et d'Alpinisme. But best of all were our special friends with whom we used to climb, whether from the valley or, more modestly and less seriously, on the sandstone rocks in the Forest of Fontainebleau: the famous guide Gaston Rébuffat, a Parisian banker Bernard Pierre, a businessman Jean Deudon, and a physician Jean Carle. More occasionally Pierre Allain, who was with the first party to conquer the North Face of the Drus, joined us. He it was who, while staying at our home near Henley was frankly bored when we took him on a tour of Windsor Castle, but evinced a professional interest in climbing its walls.

I can forgive Chamonix its modern garishness and growth on all of these accounts, but most of all because of those friendships. I am proud of the privilege of honorary citizenship of the town, which was conferred upon me by the President of the French Republic, Vincent Auriol. As a soldier, an honour which I value no less than that distinction was my promotion to the rank of corporal in the Chasseurs Alpins, at a ceremony at the Ecole de Haute Montage.

In 1956, David Cox and I had started our holiday in the Bernese Oberland. For the sake of tradition we climbed the Wetterhorn, one of the first of the big alpine peaks to be climbed in the dawn of mountaineering; we followed this with an excellent route on the West Face of the Klein Schreckhorn; a few days later, now in the company of Robin Hodgkin, who had been one of Jimmy Waller's companions on the Masherbrum in 1937, we were up at the Guggi hut under the North-East Face of the Jungfrau. The weather was awful, but next day we explored a long way out across the face, to the summit of the Schnee-horn, before truly terrible conditions forced us back to the hut, where still besieged by the elements, we whiled away the time, half in fun, practising from a beam the *prussik* technique for climbing out of a crevasse, just in case we were ourselves victims of an accident in the ill-famed Kühlauenen icefall and the Giessen glacier. It was almost as though we had a premonition of what was in store for us.

On the third day, the weather was still poor, and much fresh snow now covered the rocks and glacier surface; but we were determined to force the Guggi route rather than give in. Again we climbed up past the Schneehorn on hard frozen snow and crossed the Giessen glacier. and continued to the foot of the steep slope below the Silberlücke, a col on the main ridge leading to the summit. Here a cold blast warned us that the Lady was in no mood to entertain us; she had covered her face with a veil of cloud and once on the ridge we received a chilling welcome. Our fingers were numb with cold and it became very difficult to climb the snowed-up *verglas*-covered rocks; it was soon obvious that we were in a difficult situation. To continue to the top would have been a very slow business, and we would have reached the summit in a white-out; to reverse the climb would soon become no less hazardous as the falling snow covered our up-tracks. Yet prudence demanded that we take that alternative and without delay; we could console ourselves with the knowledge that we had climbed the Guggi route, and reached the normal way up the Jungfrau by the Silver Saddle.

We were halfway down the icefall, searching vainly for the faintest traces of our footsteps of only an hour or so earlier, when events happened with a startling suddenness. David was leading, followed by Robin with myself bringing up the rear. Without any warning, not even a shout, David disappeared into a crevasse. One moment he was there, the next there was a large hole in the snow, with the rope snaking into it with gathering speed. Robin, taken unawares and standing on hard snow, was immediately pulled over and shot down the slope to the hole. I managed to throw my weight on to my axe, plunged it in deep and hitched Robin's rope round it; for it seemed certain that he would be dragged into the abyss after David. But Robin showed commendable resource. He twisted his body athwart the crevasse and lay there, with some sixty feet of rope now taut between him and David, somewhere in the depths below him. Somehow, he managed to roll over to the lower edge and, once secured there, I was able to skirt round the gap and join him. Faintly, seemingly from an infinite distance, we heard David's voice; he assured us that he was unhurt. It was incredible luck.

The rescue operations, which we had rehearsed the previous day, were now put to good effect. David's axe had remained stuck at the lip of the crevasse and we sent it down to him, together with two looped ends of our spare rope; it took us only about a quarter of an hour to bring him to the surface, suffering from shock but with no worse physical injuries than a gash on his nose and a loose tooth. The mountain had hardly behaved with lady-like decorum towards her three respectful suitors, but we came off lightly. About a week afterwards, two climbers were reported missing at about the same place where our accident had occurred; they were never found.

It was a most fortunate circumstance for me that I chanced to be President of the Alpine Club in 1957, the year of its centenary. As Switzerland had been the scene of many of the early conquests of alpine peaks, epitomised by Whymper's first ascent of the Matterhorn, with its dramatic and tragic sequel, in 1865, the Alpine Club proposed Zermatt as our venue for part of the celebrations. It was typical of the Swiss Alpine Club that they responded enthusiastically to our suggestion. The Meet, which brought together mountaineers from many nations, was a most happy and memorable affair. There were many social activities at which much excellent Wallis wine was drunk, but which did not prevent some good climbs also being recorded.

The Zermatt peaks were a happy hunting ground for me. In 1949 I had helped to run a course, under the auspices of the Alpine Club, based on Täsch, during which a number of the classic climbs were done; in 1950 and 1951 Joy and I with friends had added a number of other routes. But there remained several other climbs which I had long wanted to do, and 1957 provided the opportunity: one of them, the South Face of the Obergabelhorn, provided a dramatic climax, in which disaster appeared inescapable, but — some would say — for the intervention of Providence. With two friends, John Tyson, a schoolmaster, an intense and burning enthusiast, and John Hobhouse, a barrister, quiet, cool and deliberate in his manner and speech, I had bivouacked beneath the cliffs in company with a trio of Royal Marine Commandos led by Mike Banks. After a bitter and cloudy night the day dawned brilliantly and we climbed quickly and easily up the slabs which defend the steep upper cliff; but not so quickly as a Zermatt guide, a member of a famous family, who arrived with a French client and soon passed on ahead. After climbing a big rock pillar, a kind of rocky rake slants up to the right, towards the nick in the summit ridge known as the Gabel which gives the mountain its characteristic name. Here the guide advised us to follow him directly upwards rather than continue along the slanting shelf, which was filled with *verglas*. We found a break in the vertical cliff above the shelf which made it possible to traverse back left-handed; we were now on very steep ground. John Tyson, who was leading our rope, had just made a difficult move round an awkward bulge, when he reported that the guide was in difficulties above him.

The guide had tried unsuccessfully to lead up to the finishing chimney which gave access to the ridge. He made a second attempt but, this time, was pulled up short because the rope between himself and his client had jammed in a crack, owing to the inattention of the client. Then, according to John, who shouted a running commentary to the rest of us as we waited, awkwardly perched on small ledges, the Frenchman had left the stance, where he was supposed to be supporting the guide, and was climbing up in an effort to dislodge the jammed rope. Events occurred with sickening inevitability. The French climber slipped and fell; the guide, spread-eagled higher up on very small holds could do nothing to help and would, in a second or so, be dragged down in his turn. But the Frenchman snatched desperately at the rope, jammed in the crack and, now taut, it held and he was dangling on the rock face. But it was still only a matter of time before the guide's strength gave out, for he had been clinging to his precarious position for over twenty minutes and was audibly tiring; we could now hear his laboured breathing, and his hoarse shouts. I almost prayed for a swift end to the suspense. As a last resort, we started shouting too, hoping that there might be a party on the summit. Yes, indeed! there were answering shouts. John reported that a rope was being lowered from the ridge above; the guide had tied on and was being helped up the last, very severe forty feet. It was over and we could start to enjoy the finish of the climb.

The Alphubel was the scene of a different kind of rescue operation, a few days later. Joy and I had gone up to the Täsch hut with John Hobhouse and our daughter Susan, who was keen to make her second alpine climb during the Meet; after her début on the Pointe de Zinal we had chosen the Rotgrat as a suitable route for a promising beginner. But at the hut we learned that a party of two Alpine Club members and an eighteen-year-old schoolboy were missing on the mountain; they had last been seen on the summit the previous evening; the weather was now deteriorating and there was serious cause for concern. The pleasant family climb we had planned was re-vamped into a rescue operation, with Sue remaining at the hut to administer later to the benighted climbers — always supposing we found them, and alive. Two of our parties went towards the Alphubeljoch, while John Hobhouse, Joy and I climbed the Rotgrat, as planned. In normal conditions this is an enjoyable route, but there was now a high wind, mists were swirling round to obscure our view as we searched the glacier below for the bodies of our friends; the rocks were glazed with ice and it was desperately cold; so cold that the water froze in our water bottles.

We reached the long summit snow ridge, with visibility so short that I had to steer by compass as we began to traverse it. Indeed, it seemed scarcely necessary to deviate before descending to the Joch, for there was no sign of our missing friends. At the end of the ridge we turned to go back and, suddenly, there was a rent in the mists; framed within it we could see two figures, standing motionless by a snow hole. We shouted excitedly, but they continued to stand there, as though unable to comprehend rescue was at hand. Somehow they had survived through that bitter night, their stamina gradually ebbing.

As we nursed them down the ice slope towards the Joch, we heard shouts from the summit behind us: a rescue party of guides from

Saas-Fee had arrived and we had just beaten them to it. Geiger, too, the famous air rescue pilot, was somewhere in the clouds overhead. Back in the Täsch hut, Susan was able to play her part as the ministering angel to the rescued trio. We felt quite inordinately pleased with ourselves, for we knew that a few hours later one or more of them would have succumbed. And, incidentally, a tragedy would not have been a happy ending of a centenary Meet.

If this episode demonstrated Anglo-Swiss collaboration there were other opportunities for joint climbs, less traumatic than the Alphubel affair. The Swiss had climbed Everest and Lhotse the previous year and two of their team, the leader, Albert Eggler and Fritz Luchsinger, came to our Meet. I had skied with Albert at Mürren a few months beforehand, where he created a sensation with his two Tibetan Apso terriers, a gift from Tenzing; they struggled up the ski tows behind him and enjoyed the runs, riding in his rucksack with their heads peeping out of the back. The three of us were together on the Young ridge of the Breithorn and in later years Albert and I often skied and climbed together. With Ernst Reiss, another member of the Swiss Everest team, we made one of the early ascents of a particularly fine rock climb, the South-West Face of the Wellhorn, above Rosenlaui, which Ernst had himself pioneered in 1950 with a fellow Everester, Dölft Reist. Whether it was a climb of that high grading of difficulty, or on a mountain walk, Ernst was an engaging companion, with an endless fund of stories and *Lebensfreude*. We once spent a night in a hay loft, sharing the accommodation with some cows, after Ernst, to his embarrassment, had succeeded in losing his way in mist while conducting David Cox and myself to climb a favourite route on the Gespaltenhorn, in his own home territory of Mürren. I have ever since enjoyed pulling his leg for brushing aside my suggestion, as the weather worsened, that he might need a map and a compass.

In August 1970, Joy and I were in the Dauphiné. We were walking down the track from the Refuge des Ecrins to our car, which we had left in the crowded park on the Pré de Madame Carle. I was indulging in a spell of self-pity, having entertained high hopes of making my third ascent of the Ecrins. Forty years earlier I had traversed the mountain from the Refuge du Temple with the La Bérarde guides Henri Rodier and Elie Richard; and twenty years later, in 1950, I had climbed it again from the Glacier Blanc with John Hartog. But this time I was not fit and we had given up just below the final ice slope; if there were ever to be another time, I said gloomily, I would have to do some lesser climbs before tackling a 4,000-metre peak. We stopped for a moment to admire the view; the magnificent sky-line of the

Pelvoux-Ailefroide ridge across the glacier made me forget the present and replace it with the past. 'Do you remember?' I asked.

John Hartog, Joy and I had left our tent near the Refuge Cézanne in July 1950, bound for the traverse of Mont Pelvoux by the Arête de là Momie. It promised to be a long climb and we had decided to bivouac some way up the ridge; to lighten our loads we had reduced our climbing gear to the minimum: two axes, one pair of crampons, a piton hammer and a few pegs, 120 feet of nylon rope. It was almost dark when we found a site, uncomfortably tilted, beside the couloir in which we had been climbing and in which a trickle of water was still running; the rocks were horribly loose. Joy struggled with our small primus stove while John Hartog and I scraped out a narrow platform just large enough for the three of us to sit, prising out rocks with our axes and the piton hammer. It was quite dark when we had finished and fetched water from the fast freezing trickle, but by then soup was ready and we crawled into our sleeping bags, after fixing a safety rope across the platform and tying ourselves on with slings. This was just as well, for later in the night our unstable seat partly collapsed. The water was silent; in the distance thunder rumbled; in the nearby couloir stones crashed down from time to time; a bad sign, for it meant that the temperature was too high for safe climbing next day on this awful rock.

In the early hours of the morning, with thunder still growling and occasional flashes of lightning, the weather seemed so unpromising that I was in two minds whether to go on or retreat; but Joy had brewed tea and, our morale slightly restored after much discomfort and little sleep, one by one we crawled gingerly out of our bags; for we were on very steep ground. In the growing light we climbed up towards our arête, which itself led to a junction with a converging ridge, the Arête des Violettes; most of the going was not specially difficult, but there was a good deal of ice on the rocks, and these were so loose that we advanced slowly, sometimes one at a time; the weather, which had seemed to cheer up before we had left the bivouac site, was getting rapidly worse. At the meeting place of the two ridges we had to make a long horizontal traverse across a steep rib of rock; Hartog was leading and had continued beyond the end of the level part to the main ridge, fifty feet higher. Joy followed him, stopping at a ledge before reaching the leader, because of the shortage of rope; it was my turn. I asked jestingly whether there was any difficulty in making the next move, round a bulge of rock, and started across. Suddenly, the ledge on which I was standing broke away and I was falling down the appalling steepness between the Momie and Violettes ridges. There were about forty feet of rope between Joy and myself, most of it in coils in my left hand; I remember anticipating anxiously the moment when all the slack rope would have run out, and doubting whether Joy was secure enough to withstand the violence of the tug when the rope tightened; indeed, I fully expected her to join me in a long and rapid descent to the glacier. Thinking thus, it was a considerable relief when, a moment later, I found myself sprawling in the steep snow of the couloir, unharmed except for rope burns on my fingers. My axe which had been slung to my wrist, had broken free, but by a miracle I found it, only twelve feet below me, held by the pick in the snow. On climbing up to Joy I found to my astonishment that she was not belayed at the time of the fall, but had been hugging a solid block of rock for dear life. It was a magnificent effort on her part.

After that incident, it mattered not at all that we were now surrounded in dense mist, through which the great iron cross on the summit loomed into view only when we were a few yards away.

Six days after the drama on the Pelvoux, we were at the Sélé hut on the opposite side of that mountain from our climb, after traversing the Râteau from the Brèche de la Meije, the Aiguille Dibona by the Voie Boëll, the Écrins and, for good measure on our way to the hut, the easy Pic Coolidge; in military terms, it had been a highly successful campaign. Now, we were bound for a traverse of the Ailefroide. Next morning we reached the summit at midday by a sporting and difficult route, and looked along the ridge: it was most inviting. We also consulted the sky, which had been a source of worry ever since leaving the hut. I reckoned we would require two and a half hours for the traverse and a further two hours to the Brèche des Frères Chamois on the far side — five and a half hours before we would have completed the climb and have only the descent of the glacier to end the day. I gave the weather three hours to work itself up to a storm. In retrospect, I had to admit that mountaineering sense pointed to retreat down one of the easier routes to the Ailefroide glacier.

The climbing was exhilarating and for two hours we made good progress, untroubled by the merest breath of wind. There is nothing to compare with the joy of moving along a great alpine ridge, often concentrating on the problems to be negotiated, but all the time conscious of the depths below and the wide panorama of mountains on all sides. Then, alas! We were slowed up; it took us an hour to descend by a *rappel* into the Brèche de Coste Rouge and climb out on the far side. The storm broke, exactly as I had forecast, at 3.30 p.m., but while we were as yet still engaged in the passage leading to the final summit tower. Its advent was sudden and dramatic. So heavy was the initial fall of hail that, when my turn came to cross a slab and climb the final chimney, all the holds were masked and the rocks were streaming with sleet. At the top, visibility was so poor that we had to steer by compass down the South-West Ridge. We had hardly started when a violent electrical storm struck the mountain. Only a few days previously we had experienced electrical side-effects during our traverse of the Râteau, but this was of quite a different order. Three times in twice as many seconds, we each experienced a terrific blow on the head or shoulder; in my case I was knocked down by the force of the impact. With one accord we stopped and crouched down in such meagre shelter as we could find on the south side of the ridge, laying our axes, which were humming as they conducted electricity, some distance away. For half an hour we remained thus, soaked and cold. In an apparent lull we resumed the descent, but within a few minutes we all had the same sensation of being struck, followed immediately by a blinding flash of lightning. There was no alternative but to take shelter once more; it was only an hour later, in the rapidly diminishing daylight, that we could continue on our way, visibility was down to a few yards and the rocks plastered with fresh snow. I think we chose about the right place to leave the ridge and descend its left flank towards the glacier, but in those conditions any way off would have been as difficult and treacherous; we had to admit ourselves virtually lost. Indeed, as the light failed we stood for a few minutes, debating whether to make the best of a bad night in the couloir we were climbing in, tired, dispirited and sodden though we were. But the prospect was so unpleasant that I decided to have one more attempt to get on to the easier ground; it could not be far below. For no special reason I was just beginning to feel hopeful as I slid down an awkward groove, when a thinning of the mists showed snow slopes below. I found myself at the foot of the slabs, and miraculously, almost trod on to a cairn. We had arrived at the exact spot where the normal route up the South-West Ridge begins. As we plunged on down in darkness towards the hut, the valleys were filled with a strange and fascinating light – electric blue – such as I had never seen before.

Twenty years before there had been no one in the Pré de Madame Carle, apart from ourselves. In Leslie Stephen's day this valley had been so cut off from civilisation that cretinism was common among the peasants in the village of Ailefroide. Now, it was a huge car park and camp site, all garish colour, noisy transistors and seething humanity in holiday mood.

Some days later on I stepped back even further into the past. We had moved our camp to La Grave, through which Edward Whymper had passed in 1860 and crossed the seemingly formidable Brèche de la Meije, on his way to assault the Barre des Ecrins, highest summit in Dauphiné. I called at the Bureau des Guides. A plump, grizzled veteran looked up from his desk. 'Pourriez-vous me donner des nouvelles de M. Paul Jouffray? Si, même, il existe toujours?' The effect of this overture was extraordinary. The old man's eyes filled with tears. He heaved his portly figure to his feet with more alacrity than I would have believed possible; he held out his arms. 'C'est John Hunt,' he exclaimed. We embraced and I confess that my own eyes were not quite dry. Next evening Joy and I sat on the terrace of the Hôtel de la Meije, where my mother, brother and I had stayed in 1927 and 1928. With us were Paul Jouffray and Georges Dode, who in 1927 had been a licensed mountain porter – they have long since been styled 'guides-aspirants'.

Even in those days Paul had been stocky and short, his face round, traversed by a wide, waxed and needle-sharp moustache. I looked across the table and the years dropped away. The moustache had gone, so had most of his hair; but the twinkle was still in his eye. It was the same Paul. Georges Dode had changed more; I found it difficult to pare away the heavy, thick-set figure and the wrinkles, crown the baldness and reconstruct the lithe, good-looking twenty-year-old who had followed, tweed cap on his head, at the end of the rope, a merry smile breaking on his face as he appeared from the steep chimney on to the summit of the Tour Carrée. Did we remember . . .?

We looked up at the Brèche, which we had first crossed in 1927 in a round trip past the Refuge du Promontoire and over the Col des Chamois to the chalets de l'Alpe; from there up the Pic de Neige Cordier and then to the Refuge Adèle-Planchard to climb the Grande Ruine; it was a sort of proving run for myself. Apparently Jouffray was satisfied, for the following year he guided me over the Meije and the Tour Carrée de Roche-Méane, and other summits.

I had read about the Meije during the previous term at my school. I knew it was the last great alpine peak to be climbed; the names of De Castelnau and his guides, Gaspard *père et fils*, were part of my climbing repertoire, as were the rock pitches on the climb whose names I rehearsed during a short and sleepless night in the old wooden hut on the Promontoire: the 'Dalle des Autrichiens', the 'Pas du Chat', the 'Dos d' Âne', the 'Cheval Rouge', especially the 'Brèche Zsigmondy'. I can recall today the exhilaration of achievement when, at midday, I sat drying my socks outside the Refuge de l'Aigle below the Pic Central.

The past had become so much a part of the present that I almost forgot the immediate future; one of the reasons for calling at the Bureau des Guides. I asked Paul for advice about the Aiguille Meri-dionale d'Arve which I had wanted to climb in my youth and which Joe Kretschmer, Derek Bull and I had planned for the following day.

Joy contemplating the Dru.

On the West Ridge of the Schallihorn, with Mont Blanc in the background. In the middle distance are Dent Blanche, Pointe de Zinal and, behind it, Grand Combin.

He pulled out an envelope and drew me a sketch of the 'Mauvais Pas', a fifteen-foot step which is the only serious obstacle. Those three pinnacles used to be rarely visited, but we were made aware of the altered circumstances next day when we were held up for more than an hour while a group of seventeen French students, some of them most inappropriately clad, struggled, shouted and occasionally screamed their way up the crucial pitch—not all of them successfully. Worse was to follow in the couloir below, during our descent. A storm had broken and demoralisation set in among the youthful group; there were feminine tears to mop up and spare garments to lend. The climb had degenerated into a mini-rescue operation.

In 1968 I was on the way up to Val d'Isère with our parliamentary ski team. The reservoir below the gorge through which the road passes on the last lap before reaching the famous ski resort had been emptied for repair work on the *barrage*; and I looked down on the mud-coated skeleton of the former village of Tignes. It evoked ancient memories. I remembered the bitter opposition of the villagers to the building of the dam, which became a major political issue in France in the early 1950s. And there were earlier recollections still. As children, my brother and I had stayed in the little old-world mountain village of Val d'Isère, which it was in the nineteen-twenties when it boasted two simple inns and one all-purpose shop. In 1926 and the following year a girl who was on holiday with us, Winifred Young and I engaged the services of the local shoemaker, M. Gunié, to guide us up the easy mountains around the valley: Tsantaleina, Grande Aiguille Rousse, Aiguille de la Grande Sassière, Pointe de Méan-Martin, for the princely sum of £1.00. Where nowadays a wide road from the new village of Tignes brings skiers and other tourists to the foot of the Grande Motte, and a *téléférique* then lifts him nearly to its summit at 12,500 feet, we had plodded for hours along a rough track and then for more hours up the snow slopes to reach that point. Now Val d'Isère is one of Europe's leading and smartest ski stations, in which hotels like palaces abound, and all around the mountains are festooned with a cat's cradle of lifts and ski tows to provide numerous ski runs leading from all directions towards the valley. But Tignes had gone beneath the waters; all that remained were its bones beneath the wall of the dam: a mud-coated bridge over the former course of the Isère, the outline of a few streets and the foundations of razed buildings.

Gunié, however, had not passed away. There had been a touch of pathos about our meeting in 1953, for I came across him shovelling snow on to the track of one of the ski tows during our training for a race against the Chambre des Députés; it seemed to be a demeaning occupation for a mountain guide. But there was mutual delight at the moment of recognition, and in remembering those two summers in the nineteen-twenties.

Much else has changed, and much gained. More power is generated to drive the wheels of industry which, in turn, has created prosperity and thus there is more leisure for the many, rather than the few. The way to enjoy it in the mountains is now wide open for all; the approach to the heights is made easy. But there is no gain without some loss. As the Alps become more of a playground, less of a mystery, less of a challenge, something of value to the human spirit is sacrificed in the name of progress.

Just in case the alarms and excursions which I have chosen from among other Alpine occasions, make the Alps seem more of a battleground than a playground, I will try to place them in a truer perspective; such dramas, inasfar as they may sound exciting, are the exception, not the rule. More often than not, my own climbs having been a mixture, or sometimes a contrast of experiences. There have been breath-taking moments, not only when I have been afraid, but also for the sheer joy of movement in rhythm up steep and sensational places; of balancing warily along some blade-like crest of snow, of dangling airily down some rock wall at the end of an abseil rope. Nor are difficulties and sensations the only mountain memories. To step upon the summit of the Matterhorn, when the crowds have been deterred by the mist and wind and falling snow, and find it bathed in sunshine under a blue sky above the surrounding sea of cloud; to reach the top of the Grand Combin in a tearing gale, when the weather has done its utmost to deter you—these are experiences on easy climbs which I would not exchange for many a much more difficult one. Even the easy Haute Cîme of the Dents du Midi, my childhood mountain, in mid-winter and in good company, is a fine experience. Each was a moment of emancipation, when I was nearly bursting for the sheer joy of it.

A different kind of delight is that of simply walking from day to day and hut to hut at high level, along broader ridges and across easier passes, as from Chamonix to Zermatt, or in the Austrian Tyrol. At such times the mind is less focused on the problem of preserving the equilibrium and working out the next move for hand or foot; more poised between the beauty of the mountain scene and the pleasure of companionship. There are other times when it is good to be alone, to be still and allow the mountains to work their spell upon the mind. These experiences are not the stuff of newspaper headlines; they are not identified with any particular mountain occasion. I have found them everywhere: in Snowdonia and Glencoe as much as in the

Pyrenees, the Tatras and the Himalayas. Nor are they peculiar to steep places such as these, for they are a part of the climate of feeling I experience whenever I stand on Offa's Dyke above our cottage in Llanfair Waterdine, and look southwards over the whale-back ridge of Radnor Forest to the Black Mountains and the Brecon Beacons. If I associate them especially with the Western Alps, this is because it was there that I first experienced that kind of euphoria as a boy. They are part of the mood of a man on a mountain; a mood which Claude Elliott, one-time President of the Alpine Club, gently chided me for attempting to interpret to an audience at the Alpine Club; he called it 'Alpine Uplift'. His reproach was justified, particularly in that côterie; I have ever since shied away from an attempt to describe it again. But the fact remains that the mood, or climate of feeling during times which I have shared with friends, or spent alone, among the hills and mountains anywhere in the world, has meant more to me than the moments of high drama and near-disaster. I would guess that it is part and parcel of the emotional make-up of most mountaineers, though they might be reluctant to admit to it. If explains – if it can be explained – the main reason why we climb.

Index